BY A MASTER GUIDE

This is the first book about the Alaskan bush pilot by a bush pilot.

AND WINNER OF THE AWARD OF MERIT

FOR "SPECIAL SERVICE IN THE ARCTIC REGIONS"

Someday these rugged professionals will find their place in American folklore alongside the pony express rider and the stagecoach driver.

"Helmericks writes out of personal experience with this vanishing breed. He tells of the early trading posts, the trappers who later became guides for hunters and fishermen, and relates some pretty exciting tales of adventures and close-calls in a cozy fireside style. His book is a delightful document of a part of Alaska's history, and a labor of love by the author."

—*Publishers Weekly*

THE LAST
OF THE
BUSH PILOTS

HARMON HELMERICKS

BALLANTINE BOOKS • NEW YORK

Library of Congress Catalog Card Number: 68-23939

SBN 345-24005-7-150

This edition published by arrangement with
Alfred A. Knopf, Inc.

First Printing: June, 1974

Cover photo by Harmon Helmericks

Printed in the United States of America

BALLANTINE BOOKS
A Division of Random House, Inc.
201 East 50th Street, New York, N.Y. 10022

TO MARTHA

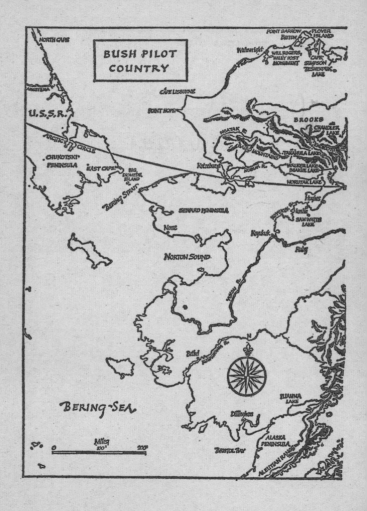

CONTENTS

ix

ILLUSTRATIONS

Jim Helmericks

Bud Helmericks, the pilot

Kisik and Oineak

A Brooks Range fishing camp

A bull caribou

A Sinclair oil well on the Arctic coast

Diesel oil-transporting truck

A map is found on pages vi and vii of the front matter.

PREFACE

Without overdramatizing my own profession, I think it is safe to say that the bush pilot of Alaska must take his place eventually alongside the stagecoach driver, the dispatch rider, riverboatman, voyageur, and the Pony Express man as a communications pioneer in the country's history. Because the last frontier in our country has been and still is Alaska, this has been the scene of his most famous activities and exploits. As the carrier of news, passengers, mail, and freight, he has been for four decades the swiftest and often the only carrier in this wilderness.

There have been journalistic accounts of the bush pilot's activities in newspapers, magazines, and books. Someday those activities may attract the attention of scholars who will do a formal history of the activity. This book makes no pretense of being such a record, although I would hope that it may be good enough to serve eventually as part of the data for such future studies. Rather, I shall attempt two things here: first, to add to the record a more formal account of one bush pilot's activities—in this respect this book will complement the other books by the Helmerickses and by myself; second, I shall include here as much of the record of my contemporaries (and predecessors) as I can document from my own contacts, experiences, and knowledge of other men who have flown the bush on wheels, skis, and pontoons. Insofar as these men constitute a type, I shall try to limn in what characterizes their common traits. But they are too individualistic to be typed. Indeed an intense individualism is their only common character trait. As to their skills, these are subject to more generalization, though even here many of these men became known for special kinds of activities and accomplishments.

It is my wish that the reader will get some notion not only of bush pilots and bush piloting from this book, but of even greater importance, a sense of what it is like to participate in the development of a frontier land. I hope I have conveyed some sense of this, and, more, some sense of "this wonderful country before it was touched by the hand of man," if I may use for *this* frontier a phrase Captain Gillette of the Texas Rangers used to characterize another, earlier one.

I would like to thank all of those who have helped with this book. The ways they have helped will be clear from the text itself, but elsewhere I have made acknowledgment to particular pilots, trappers, trading-post owners, bush men of all kinds, sportsmen, oilmen, and entrepreneurs, service personnel and last but not least friends among Alaska's Indians and Eskimos whose advice to this pilot was often the most valuable of all.

1

A DAY'S WORK

The bush pilot's days are coming to an end, or rather I should say have come to an end, for the bush pilot already has faded from the scene just as did the Pony Express rider and the stagecoach driver before him. The Civil Air Authority, now the Federal Air Authority, made this passing official and ended an era by changing the bush pilot certificate to that of air-taxi operator, and this describes the job today of those who still fly the "bush," as the land beyond the roads is affectionately called. The outposts still exist; the cold and the vastness and the beauty of the land are there but all in smaller measures. The bush pilot's task was one that couldn't last. Like the trail herder and the mountain man who opened the way for the railroad, the bush pilot took an untried machine into an unknown land and broke the trail. It was a one-way road; and so it is today that intercontinental jet contrails span the Arctic skies that just yesterday belonged solely to the bush pilot. Oil wells rise on the Arctic plains where not long ago I had a hard time just hauling in enough fuel for my little plane. I know that almost every bush pilot was torn between two desires as he did his job: the first was to help the people and know "this wonderful country before it was touched by the hand of man"; the second was to gain a knowledge of the land as it was and to keep the mob away—as Sam White so clearly put it, to "hold back the killin' and the burnin'."

I know how I felt when I saw the last wilderness area disappear as the "killin' and burnin'" began, and I helped start it. I would have prevented it if I could, but I couldn't, any more than the Pony Express riders could have halted the spread of paved roads and highways. But I knew real sadness when I saw the first needless mud-ripped trails of tractors and Nodwells across the Arctic plains, the big piles of trash and empty gasoline drums strewn in their wake. The hand of man had come to the land and the faithful propellers of the Bellanca, Norseman, Stinson, Fairchild, and Cessna Air Masters no longer rule the wilderness skies but are fit only for souvenirs or ashtray stands.

This is a book of real experiences. It is all true. There are parts I wish with all my heart were not true, but they are. The episodes are not dramatized, for I would like you to know the people and the land as it was and is. Thus I will tell the complete story a small part at a time, until all the pieces of the jigsaw fit into place, and perhaps you will be able to feel the coming of spring, hear the awful silence of a dead engine, see across a thousand miles of untouched prairie, and share in the life of the free. Then if it had been your lot to have shared in this era you too would, as Ed Badten once put it, "feel good to have been counted among the men."

Fortunately I kept a written day-by-day logbook right from the start and today it covers several feet of shelf space. Because of this complete diary I can turn to any date and find facts as I recorded them then not as memory may have colored them. The temperature, winds, happenings, the feel of the land, they are all there, and at times I will quote directly from this record.

The night was black. Darkness pressed about me and I turned the instrument lights down as low as I possibly could and still be able to see the turn and bank indicator, altimeter, and air speed. I let the airplane down slowly until I could see the snow drifts in the landing lights just a few feet below. Snow crawled and twisted around them like white smoke, which indicated that a wind of some twenty knots was blowing from the northeast. A glance at the ice between the drifts confirmed it to be salt ice. In that area glare spots would have shown between the drifts if it had been freshwater ice. My altimeter read ten feet, so everything was as it should be; according to my calculations, I was near home. Home was a snow-walled tent drifted under by many Arctic storms and indistinguishable from the rest of the land except for a stovepipe protruding from the snow. My wife, Martha, and our nine-year-old son, Jim, would be listening and waiting with kerosene lanterns, ready to come out and mark my landing spot the moment they heard the engine. A lantern unprotected would be blown out by the storm and cold, and, anyway, on such a night they could hear me from farther away than I could see a kerosene lantern.

I snapped off the landing light so my eyes would become adjusted to the darkness, climbed to two hundred feet, and began to work out a grid pattern. I would work out an area about ten miles square, and if I didn't find home I would just have to camp on the prairie until it was light enough to see. On the second bar of my grid a lantern light popped up right off my left wing tip, followed by a second, and wedgelike shadows twinkled as the lantern carrier's legs took him across the snow.

I had "lucked through again," as Bill Lavery used to say. I could see the steady pinpoints of light marking out the best place to land, each light shielded by a fur-clad figure. No need to worry about wind direction, for if you can see the lights you are coming into the wind. I shook the seat of my pants loose and centered down for the landing so I could feel the ship's every whim and move. The first lantern was coming up fast. Landing lights picked out the drifts, the skis caught one, ricocheted to another drift, and the plane came to a bouncing stop.

"It is a good landing if you can walk away from it," Jim Falls once said, referring to the fact that you can't make a smooth landing upon big snow drifts, wild water, or rough ground. You just make the best landing you can. Jim never walked away from his last landing, though—he didn't even get out of what was left of the airplane.

The lanterns now hurried to show me where the house was and I taxied to the tie-up ropes protruding from the snow. It was the happy end of a day's work.

It took half an hour to tie down the airplane, drain the oil, put on the control locks, and put it to "bed." Then I stepped from the world of darkness and snow into our snug tent home under the drifts. Martha had it all neat and dinner ready. Tears of happiness shone in her eyes and I noted that Jim had my old plaid jacket tucked up on his bunk. I had been gone three days on what should have been a standard one-day round trip.

My wife—any bush pilot's wife—has to live with the awful silence, the silence that begins when the sound of the airplane engine fades and increases as the returning time is reached and passed. Then one begins to imagine one hears a distant hum. There is no radio, no contact, just faith. When the hour grows so late that my return seems impossible that night, the lantern is still kept ready and Jim looks for the old plaid jacket. Then sometimes follows another day of silence, and another. There are a thousand logical reasons why I might not be back and then the one really likely one, bad weather. As we always say in making plans, "weather permitting." Yet the thought is always there: *Maybe he will never return.* This at times makes the silence awful. Martha still hears all airplanes first and knows the sound of ours no matter how faint. When a woman visitor once asked Martha how she could tell, her answer was, "I've had tens of thousands of hours of practice listening."

That particular day's work had started on Saturday, October 23. It was −5 degrees and I could see the stars shining as I began heating the airplane engine with the Coleman gasoline heater; but as I was working, a cloud bank came up from the east and spread across the sky. It proved to be a low fog that covered everything with heavy frost. No flying for today, I thought, so I shut off the heater. An hour later the fog lifted and I again started to heat the engine. Jim and I brushed the frost off the airplane and soon I flew to Aivuk Tukle's camp twenty miles away, picked up a load of nine hundred frozen fish, and headed for Barrow. The −5-degree weather had turned to 20 degrees above with the fog, and I should have known better than to fly into it. The ceiling came down like a wedge and forced me lower and lower to keep from icing. By the time I reached Teshekpuk Lake I could see but a few hundred yards and was flying along but fifty feet above the ground. I then turned farther inland to escape the fog. Clear sky still showed to the south, but a high wind was driving snow. I passed Tom Brower's Half Moon Three ranch, where he had once raised reindeer, and I didn't see the abandoned buildings until I was right over them. From there on I didn't see much of anything until I spotted the black ocean southwest of Barrow, but I hadn't realized I would get there that fast. There was much more wind than I realized. Black fog boiled along the edge of the ocean as I made my way back to the prairie. I just headed into the wind, and when I saw the glare spots of freshwater ice below I decided to land. I only hoped the ice was thick enough to hold me up. Once down, the wind began to slide the airplane backwards across the ice until it stuck momentarily in a drift; I got busy chipping tie-downs into the ice. A movement in the drifting snow caught my eye and a second look disclosed a pure white Arctic fox standing a few feet away watching me.

The wind rippled and flattened its fur while its tail pointed downwind like a wind sock. This intent little creature in the world of white made me feel at home. I spoke and it darted away in the storm.

With the airplane tied securely to four ice toggles, I walked about in the storm to examine my surroundings. The lake was half a mile in diameter and frozen eight inches thick, an ideal spot to take off from when the storm cleared. There were quite a few fox tracks on the lake that stood up in relief. When the soft snow had first fallen on the tracks the foxes had made, it had compressed the snow. Then these tracks had frozen into ice adhering to the black lake ice, and the wind had swept away the loose snow, leaving the white, frozen fox trails standing up on the black ice to mark the passing of little fox feet. There were also several regurgitated pellets of snowy owls, composed of lemming fur and bones.

Since I wouldn't be able to see the plane for more than a hundred yards, it was rather important that I didn't lose it. Arctic winds faithfully blow steadily for days from the northeast or southwest. These are the only winds of any consequence on the north coast of Alaska and so accurate are they that you can check your compass by them and, of course, by the snow drifts they create. Thus I steered my course by dead reckoning. First I walked into the wind clear across the lake. Then I counted my steps as I angled across the wind and kept track of my position, so that the same number of steps would again put me back on a downwind course to the airplane. You can use time instead of counting steps, but this requires a watch, and on a short hike counting steps is easier for me. I can explore quite an area and still return straight to my airplane. It might sound like a tedious way to travel—keeping track of every single step or second of travel plus direction and angles—but it is the only practical, safe way; otherwise you risk losing your camp on such a day no matter how familiar you are with the terrain, and waiting out a storm without shelter is boring and uncomfortable to say the least.

The airplane was right on course. Tied facing exactly into the wind, the snow swept around it and it hardly trembled in the storm. (Airplanes are made for wind, and they only ask to face it at all times. Let them have their way, tie them securely, and no storm will bother them.) I unloaded the sacks of fish and stacked them to one side so that the drift they would make wouldn't bother the airplane. Then I wrapped the wing covers aboard the cabin to insulate the glass area and made myself comfortable inside. The small Coleman stove quickly heated the interior, and a little kerosene lantern gave ample light to read by. I made a pot of onion soup from a dry mix I carried and read part of a book by Albert Schweitzer on African missionary work. There is really quite a bit of room in an airplane when you have the seats out, certainly enough space for me to stretch out my six-foot, two-inch frame in my down sleeping robe.

The storm blew all night, and a world of white greeted me on awakening. I had a candy bar for breakfast. Of the prejudices I had when I first came north, I have eliminated nearly all, having found that each thing I dislike is like a bar in my own personal prison; but I still don't like to eat by myself and will go for days eating practically nothing when I am alone—that's why I had only a candy bar for breakfast.

I had picked up a lot of ice during the few minutes of flying over the ocean and more had formed during the night; I began cracking it off the airplane, but more began to form, so I quit and read. Then the fog let up, and I started heating the airplane and cracked the ice from the leading edges and propeller. The wind was still blowing and low clouds hurried past while fogbanks were here and there. With a few skips off the drifts I was in the air, following the beach line toward Barrow. This didn't last long, for I met heavy fog full of super-cooled water that froze on the windshield and leading edge of the wing, leaving me with visibility out of the sides only. There was nothing to do but turn back. I could see the bright sun shining through a few openings in the low clouds. "Portholes into Heaven," my instructor Doug Wallace once called them when cautioning me not to try to use them. These portholes into Heaven are hard to pass up, and can be an easy way to where you are going, for the sun might be shining at your destination; it is easy flying above the low clouds—provided you don't get lost in that world of purest white. If the clouds grow thicker and become a solid mass, you are on top and unable to get down.

I never did learn to fly on instruments. I am proficient enough to keep an airplane straight and level and make a let-down through fog, but what if there is no bottom to the fog? What if the cloud is "stuffed with rocks"?—meaning a mountain peak or hill protrudes up into it. There seemed little use in spending much time and money learning to fly instruments, adding a lot of weight and expensive gear to an airplane, when there weren't any ground facilities where you were going. The portholes into Heaven remained a siren's call to the weathered-in bush pilot. So it was today, and I answered the call and climbed up the bright shaft of sunlight into a world of purest blue and white where a fiery red sun ruled. The fog was just three hundred feet thick. Below there had been motion, snow drifted swiftly, fogbanks moved across the land, and waves beat upon an icy shore. You crabbed to hold a straight course across the land with a side wind, fairly rocketed along with a tail wind, or made slow progress into a head wind. You could see it and feel it too. Here in this beautiful fairyland above the clouds all was still, for there were no reference marks and you became painfully aware of such things as the difference between air speed and ground speed, compass heading, true course, and magnetic heading. I was dealing with elements beyond my control, and I looked long and hard toward where Barrow should be. A half hour later the cloud layer was solid and I was caught in a world of white, so I turned inland where I saw a dark diffusion in the white clouds. This often means a thin spot and as I flew past I caught a glimpse of prairie grass through it, and a flash of black glare ice. I needed a piece of ice to land on, and by rare good fortune I had found it. How big it was, what shape, or just where I didn't know, but the gasoline gauge told me it was needed, and soon. I spiraled right down through the hole, flared out, and landed. Once again I explored the lake, steering by the snow drifts, for there was no wind here. It was awfully quiet, and once I heard the dogs howl in the direction I thought Barrow to be.

Heavy rime had formed during the night and I found it an inch thick all over the airplane next day. The sun shone brightly though, and I spent an hour "roping" off the frost from the wings and body. Frost is dangerous stuff and you don't want to fly with any on an airplane. The flight to Barrow took just a few minutes. The people had heard me over the village yesterday and knew I would be in as soon as the fog cleared. I landed on the Barrow Lagoon, which separates Browerville from Barrow village. The fish all were destined for Tom Brower's store, where the sign above the door proclaims it was established in 1886 by the old "King of the Arctic," Charlie Brower. It is the first and oldest business enterprise in Barrow. Aivuk's father came with his dog team and he hauled the fish up to Tom's store and then hauled back a drum of 80/87 aviation gasoline for me. I carried groceries and mail, and as darkness gathered I had my load made up.

The airplane engine had been wrapped in a blanket cowling cover Martha had made me, so the engine was warm and started easily.

About the time I was ready to take off, school recess let out and a hundred Eskimo children came running to take part in the event. Some were pushing on the tail and wing struts. I cut the engine for fear one would run into the propeller. It was all in good fun, of course, and I shouted to them in a mixture of Eskimo and English to stand back. They obediently made a little smiling circle around me and left an opening ahead of the airplane. Again I started the engine and began to move away. This was just too much for half a dozen of the bolder ones. When they saw the skis break loose and begin to move, they ran and jumped on the skis' tails. The propeller blast pasted their parkas tight to them. I let them ride for a hundred yards and then stopped again. Here they stepped back and finally I was on my way home, a hundred and eighty miles to the east.

The Arctic is a delicate land of gentle changes. Even the sunsets are quiet, colorful, and lingering. The twilight lasts for hours, and I would have had almost enough twilight to fly home in if it hadn't been for a cloud layer that covered the eastern sky a few miles from my destination. The first stars faded into the overcast, and I was again searching for a landing spot in the dark, but tonight I would have ground support, for Martha and Jim were waiting with the lanterns to mark the landing spot if I could figure out all the variables and find it. Then I spotted the light and there was home. It was like Little Joe, an old Athabascan Indian, once said when I came into his camp, "I am happy as a bird in springtime; it is like a thousand men come for me." I couldn't have felt happier if a thousand airport beacons had suddenly flashed on. At such a time, you sit a little straighter and laugh a little more than necessary, you see things a little kindlier, and you are twice as cautious, for it is the end of a day's work and you "want to walk away from the landing."

2

EARLY DAYS: OUTPOSTS
AND TRADING POSTS

All of interior Alaska was pretty much an unknown area until just before the turn of the twentieth century. The Russians had explored a little of it and in the process had nearly wiped out all the sea otter along the coasts. The Americans and the British had also traveled all around the coasts, and even the most remote sections of the Arctic coast had been visited by the whalers in search of bowhead whales for baleen. The entire interior, inland only a few miles from the seacoast, remained a quiet land of lakes and rivers peopled by Indians and to the north by a few Inland Eskimos. These folks made their living from the fish and game, living entirely or nearly entirely upon a meat diet.

Then gold was discovered in the Yukon Territory of Canada and the stampede was on. Curiously, it was called the Alaskan Gold Rush. Perhaps it was because the stampeders went into Skagway, Alaska, and across the Dyea Trail through Chilkoot Pass into Canada, or perhaps it was because the stampede took place in the Yukon Territory and there was a Yukon River in Alaska that people thought the gold rush was in Alaska; but places like Dawson, Whitehorse, and the Klondike region, are all Canadian. So it was, and still is, that the geography of the North was pretty vague in the minds of most people. The Yukon River rises way back in Canada and is a major river when it enters Alaska.

The gold rush to the Canadian field attracted thousands, and of course few found gold. Many whipsawed lumber for boats and set out down the Yukon River into Alaska, where they began the first settlements. They were a hardy breed of people; the Canadian writer Robert Service described them as men "half mad for the muck called gold." They were resourceful too and tried to make a living at about anything they could. Some found gold in Alaska, and places like Fairbanks, Ruby, Wiseman, Bettles, and Hughes became permanent towns.

These men populated the whole interior of Alaska. It was a sparse, far-flung population of prospectors, but I don't believe there is a creek in all Alaska that some prospector didn't venture up. I have been up or down about every creek in Alaska north of the Yukon by canoe, dog team, and, of course, by airplane, and I never cease to marvel at the places those early prospectors went. No matter how remote the spot, you are likely to find the remains of a small cabin. In one such place also I found the story of what must have been a tragic ending, for inside the fallen logs were left the rifles, cooking gear, and part of a tobacco supply, as if someone had stepped out and not returned.

In my mail I sometimes get letters from relatives asking me if in my travels I have ever met their "Uncle John"; he left for Alaska fifty years ago and has never been heard from. The letters and the old cabins tie in, but it is likely no one will ever know how. I did get to know some of these men quite well through the Indians and Eskimos and, of course, by following their trails and at times by living as they did as well as by spending many hours talking with men like Jack Sacket, who ran a little trading post at Cutoff on the Koyukuk River.

These men left their marks on the map; they founded the first civilization and they were the bush pilot's first customers. Many gave up prospecting and turned to trading with the native people for a living. Many intermarried with the natives and called Alaska home. They had a fierce love of the vast land and never left it.

It might seem strange but the interior of Alaska was much more thickly settled forty years ago than it is today. There are more people there now, but they are concentrated in the towns. In the early days there was a regular network of dog-sled trails that tied all the villages together and every so often a roadhouse along the trails. Mail moved all winter by dog team. The freighting was by river in summer, and of course all towns were on the rivers except for an occasional mine operation back in the hills.

Alaska, isolated by distance from the South Forty-eight or "outside," as Alaskans called it, strove to be self-supporting. People tried hard with some success to farm and produce things needed locally. When everything moved slowly by riverboat or dog team, farming made sense and everyone tried to cultivate a garden; with potatoes at a dollar a pound, even if you raised only a few you coud succeed.

This, then, was interior Alaska right after World War I and set the stage for the advent of bush flying.

No traders played a more important part in developing flying in interior Alaska than have the Jameses at the little town of Hughes, tucked below the hill on the Koyukuk River. The Koyukuk is a big, clean river that drains the south slopes of the Arctic Brooks Range and is one of the major tributaries of the Yukon, merging with it at Koyukuk Station. As you ascend the river you pass Huslia, near the old site of Cutoff, Hughes, Alatna, and Bettles. This was the end of river navigation by barge-pushing riverboats. On upriver were Cold Foot and Wiseman. Into the Koyukuk flowed several tributaries, like the Alatna, that led to the mountain passes to the west, the north Pacific, and towns like Kotzebue and Nome. The tributaries like the John led to Anaktuvuk Pass, the Arctic prairie, and the Arctic Ocean to the north. The gold seekers came up the Koyukuk from the Yukon and searched out every last creek. They had many permanent camps that became little villages and later faded back to the wilderness again. You can hardly find a trace of them today. The old Indians know where they once were, and if you look closely you can find the old cabin sites, but that is about all.

Once I followed the old gold seekers' trail by canoe, first from Fairbanks down the Tanana River to the Yukon, then down the Yukon to Koyukuk Station. Here Dominick Vernetti told me of the Koyukuk River, its moods, and the best way to travel it as far as Cutoff, where Jack Sacket lived. Jack Sacket would direct me on to the Arctic, for Jack knew it first-hand.

Dominick had come to Alaska from Italy as a boy of fifteen. He had picked blueberries and cranberries around the mining camps of Wiseman and Bettles, making enough money to start a little trading venture, and he acquired the nickname of the "Blueberry Kid." He had eventually ended up at Koyukuk Station, married Ella—a lovely Indian princess from the Bering Sea coast—and raised his family there. Dominick ran the Standard Oil works and unloaded the riverboat freight from the Yukon River steamer. With an Italian's love of fresh fruits, Dominick imported them from the outside packed in sawdust; he also raised vegetables in the greenhouse. Cooking up a meal for me himself, he told of how he had camped, prospecting on what later became a favorite gold mine, only he dug around his tent. The next prospector dug where Dominick's tent had been and struck it rich. Dominick sold me a Winchester Model 12 shotgun, saying, "Boy, I tella you, you're gonna need her where you're going." He was right—I did.

The Koyukuk wound and twisted a couple of hundred un-inhabited miles past, or rather around, Roundabout Mountain, for the river really goes all around it in a horseshoe, past where Huslia would later be built when the present village of Cutoff flooded once too often and was abandoned.

Here I met white-haired Jack Sacket, who was then already in his eighties; he was destined to reach nearly the hundred mark. Jack had remarried and had a small son. He read without glasses, and he told me of the land to the north, about the head of the Alatna River where he had prospected for a whole year with Big Charlie, living on meat alone.

"Did you never get hungry for other food?" I asked.

"Well, yes, at times; I thought most of a baking-powder biscuit," Jack said. "Nothing much else though. Meat alone is a fine diet."

Jack talked on about the land and about prospecting. As he talked, I could visualize the vastness of the territory and the beauty of it. From the door of his log-cabin trading post it rolled away and the Koyukuk River whispered on its way coming from all those places heading to the Bering Sea. Jack showed me where the last high-water flood of breakup had left its mark halfway up his living-room wall. What did he do when the water rose? Well, he moved up into the cache, cooked on the Coleman stove, and waited until the water receded.

As we waited at Cutoff, Les James came by on his riverboat. He was freighting supplies for the winter from Koyukuk Station to Hughes and we hitched a ride with our canoe that far.

Les was in his late fifties, and he spoke of the future of the Koyukuk with as much enthusiasm as Jack Sacket had spoken of its recent past. There wasn't a landing field in all interior Alaska aside from Weeks Field at Fairbanks, and Les was going to make one at Hughes. He had ordered a Caterpillar for the job and would haul it in himself. He and his wife, Patty, were changing things at Hughes. Les was so enthusiastic that it was catching, and a few days later we pulled up below the riverbank at Hughes. Every person in the village was there to welcome us. Up on the bank, nestled below a long ridge, sat the trading post, and on each side, in a neat row, were the cabin "town houses" of the Indian people, for each family had his trapping grounds and summer fishing camp. They were only in town for special events. Johnny Old Man was the chief of the people, and he welcomed us with kind dignity.

Here we met Patty, and from that day on Les and Patty have looked after us, helped and guided us, forwarded our mail, and have been a steady source of inspiration. It would have been impossible for the bush pilots to have operated and built a flying economy in Alaska without the Jameses and a few people like them.

Sam White told me of a visit he made to Hughes just before the Jameses' time there. It was a cold evening, and he landed his ski-equipped Bellanca on the river ice. There wasn't a soul about, and he walked up to the dilapidated log building with some misgivings. Inside he found the aging trader ill from some kidney ailment, for his whole body from the waist down was swollen out of all proportion. It was cold inside, and there was no fire. Sam stayed the night and got the place as warm as he could. He also cut a supply of firewood and stacked it near the stove and carried in a little water.

"You didn't take him to the hospital, Sam?" I asked.

"No, he wouldn't leave. Claimed an Indian would come in in a few days and look after him. I hated to leave him there, but that was what he wanted. So I did."

It was a miserable-looking place with "big locks on each door."

At that time Les and Patty James had been working at Utopia Creek for L. McGee. Patty cooked for the mining crew, and Les ran the dredges and heavy equipment there. Patty often told Martha of the early days of cooking in the mining camp. Patty had been a beauty operator in Seattle before she married Les; afterwards they came to Alaska, first living around Anchorage, then Utopia Creek, and finally they decided to buy what there was of Hughes. So Hughes and the Jameses became as one and have been ever since.

Their son, Johnny, was in grade school and the rest of their children were grown and married. Life at Hughes meant teaching Johnny by correspondence courses. (Johnny told me later that his first toy sled had been a broken airplane ski.) He studied in the upstairs room in the back of the trading post. Johnny grew up with bush flying, so of course when he returned from the Army after World War II he purchased his own airplane, a Stinson Station Wagon, and flew for several years out of Hughes.

It was the end of the gold-rush era of civilization for Hughes and the beginning of the age of bush flying. What Les and Patty had to begin with was an empty log trading post where, no matter how you fired the wood stove on cold days, water would freeze on the floor; it was a tumbling-down cache with a few dozen steel traps in it, and a big lock on the door. There were a handful of rundown Indians, a place on the bank of the lovely Koyukuk, and winter was at hand.

Les and Patty often must have felt discouraged when they looked at what their savings had purchased. Furthermore, the trading post carried with it a responsibility to supply and care for all the people in a vast area.

"What was the first thing you did?" I asked Les one day.

"We called the folks together, and I told them that there would never be a lock on any cache again in Hughes and we threw the lock away. Then, as it was the beginning of the trapping season, I distributed all the steel traps among the trappers. Next we threw away the 'book.' The people all walked a little straighter from that day on."

The "book" was the system of bookkeeping of the gold-rush-era trader. When a purchase was made, it was entered in the "book"; when furs were sold, they were credited in the "book." A few traders learned to always balance the books in their favor, for the illiterate people never knew the difference, and so they were kept in debt at all times. There were also two sets of prices for "whites" and "natives." Traders weren't dishonest in reality since the native people had little concept of a money economy or money uses and really had to be handled like children with an allowance for what they did. The Europeans knew money and paid their bills, while the natives often didn't pay and rarely had money so they had to have their needs cared for on a long-term credit plan. It was simply a time-payment plan, and the trader handled it according to his ability and moral values. Nearly all traders treated their people most kindly.

The main, and for some only, source of income for the Indian people was from the furs they trapped. These had been sold on a lump-sum basis and the fur buyer had to deal with each trapper and buy at the lowest figure possible in order to show a profit as well as protect himself against a drop in fur prices. Les and Patty instigated a new system of selling the furs at auction and taking only a small commission on each sale. In this way full value was returned directly to the trapper. By using air freight they could get furs right out to the market and top prices. The furs from the Koyukuk area are among the world's finest. At times a fur buyer would drop by and he could pay a much better price for furs because he need not travel to each trapper and the Jameses had the latest market quotations and knew honest values too. It seemed to the Indians that they were dreaming when their furs brought in so much more than they had expected.

The Jameses put in a modern bookkeeping and receipt-for-purchase system. The first year there was no way to get supplies in from Fairbanks by river, so the things that were most needed were brought in by air. Pollack hauled them in at four hundred dollars a trip from Fairbanks, landing upon the river ice and in summer on the gravel river bar across the river from the trading post. About once a month an airplane would come in.

This was a very big event. The first person to hear the plane cried out, "Airplane!" and all took up the cry until everyone in the area knew about it and hurried to the river landing. Meanwhile the thin hum that had set off the stampede became a roar and Pollack's old Bellanca came over the ridge or from up or down river, depending upon the pilot's navigational skill that day. It is hard to hit Hughes exactly when coming from Fairbanks because it is hidden by the ridge until you are right on it. Therefore the pilot often hit the Koyukuk River above or below town and followed the river to Hughes, just hoping he was going the right way. So it was that his audience on the ground could tell what luck he had in his navigation by the direction from which the plane came.

The early airplane arrivals were always unannounced. Radios usually didn't exist, and if they did they seldom worked. By now the pilot had "drug the area" a couple of times, looking for obstructions on the place where he intended to land and also giving the people time to get children or dog teams in hand. You could see the pilot looking all businesslike and yet with time to take a mittened hand from the controls to wave. After the flight across uncharted lands, often through bad weather, the pilot had arrived. Each landing and take-off was a challenge frought with unexpected hazards. Here was the aerial actor now, the barnstormer, in an audience-participation show, bringing not only the entertainment but the goods as well. The little show served its purpose too, for it gave the pilot the feel of the air, a close-up look at the landing ahead, making every landing as if his life depended upon it—because it did! The best way to describe a stupid pilot was to say he just popped in.

Once down, the pilot handed the cargo out the door and it was carried up to the trading post. After a cup of coffee and a little talk, the pilot uncovered his engine and started her up. A half dozen people pushed on the struts to start the skis sliding and the airplane was on its way. The pilot came back past, waggled his wing in farewell, and disappeared into the vast distance.

The first winter Patty ordered many of the supplies the people needed from Sears Roebuck, and medicines were top priority. Patty became the doctor and cared for all the villagers' problems. Les put in a diesel electric plant, a small one, but it was power enough for a radio and they purchased a two-way radio. Quite an expense to say the least, but it was and is the most dependable in the whole Koyukuk River area. In all interior Alaska there is no more dependable radio than in Hughes, and in all the world no more dependable nor more efficient radio operator than Patty James. If any pilot ever needed radio help, Patty never failed, or if anyone needed a message put through, Patty got the job done. In a land where radio isn't too efficient this is saying a lot.

Hughes became our home address and still is, although our nearest home is about a hundred miles from Hughes, and our furthest nearly four hundred miles away. Yet Hughes is the closest post office to Walker Lake and these are our nearest neighbors. So it is that we are often in Hughes.

The Jameses' straightforward way of living and speaking have taught many. Martha and Patty were talking about cutting hair one winter evening. Martha had never cut hair, so Patty took her in the back room, got out a dairy calf skin, the barber's tools, and gave her a lesson in using barber's tools. Patty had an apt pupil too, for Martha can cut hair as well as anyone today.

When Jim trapped his first ermine, he took it along to Hughes to sell. Les sent the rest of us out of the room while he and Jim got down on their knees and examined the pelt on the floor "like we always did in the old days. People don't want an audience either when they are doing business." So Les and Jim talked furs and eventually got around to the price of the ermine pelt. Ermine were bringing about seventy-five cents, and Les paid Jim a dollar. It was a typical Les James fur purchase. He always paid as much or more than the pelts were worth.

Among the bush pilot's first customers were the fur buyers. Furs were the main cash crop of the early bush-flying era. There were trappers almost everywhere, and the native economy of the land hinged on trapping. The fur buyers wanted to get the pelts as soon as possible and get them on the world market. The Arctic furs from Alaska always were the continent's finest, so the fur buyer would charter a bush pilot to take him to the villages, and here he would purchase the pelts, usually from the trader or trappers. Since this was during the dark days of midwinter when the sun hardly peeps over the horizon and the coldest days are here quite often, the pilot and fur buyer would be "stuck" at Hughes by storms or cold. The bush pilots had −40 degrees as their stopping point. Past that temperatures airplanes just hated to fly, and they broke easily. The snow became like sand and skis wouldn't slide.

Since it cost so many dollars an hour (from fifty to one hundred and fifty dollars, depending upon the airplane), the customer usually had the airplane loaded with everything it could carry, and the pilot, knowing the dangers of an overload, was most critical of any extras one picked up en route.

One winter day Sam White and the Tonsuns were stuck at Hughes during a snowstorm and the Tonsuns saw some cans of special sardines on the trading-post shelf.

"Where did you get those sardines? I haven't been able to get those in years. May I have a dozen cans?"

"Oh, no you don't," cut in Sam. "You don't add another ounce to that airplane."

After dinner when Sam was out checking on the airplane, the Tonsuns came down from their room, purchased a dozen cans of sardines, and put them in their suitcase. A few days later when they were back in Fairbanks, Tonsun said, "Here, Sam, have a can of sardines."

"I thought the Stinson Junior used up an additional ten feet of that river ice getting off," Sam said.

It wasn't an idle statement either. The pilots knew their airplanes so thoroughly that they could tell you almost to the foot the amount of runway an extra pound of cargo would require under a given set of conditions.

Les likes to tell of my early days flying out of Hughes

when I was hauling building materials back into the Brooks Range, using a Cessna 170 floatplane. Of all airplane flying, a float airplane requires the most know-how to get its fullest benefit. I would look at the temperature, wind, river current, and the feel of the air, and then make up my load. There is always a question with a floatplane of whether it can get off with its full load or not. I could tell in the first ten seconds of the run if it would climb up on the step or not. Any load the Cessna would put on the step, it would take off and fly safely with. If I had too much of a load I would taxi back to shore and, as Les put it, "give me a handful of nails and away he would go."

It was usually a ten-pound packet of nails, so close could the pilots judge their loading. Airplanes always operated at their maximum carrying capacity, and I might add, pilots with their maximum skill too, using every trick they knew.

One hot summer day I had a load to take out of Hughes that was about fifty pounds more than the float airplane would put on the step. I could have divided the load in half and made two trips, but I knew that as soon as the cool midnight air came on, the airplane would easily handle the load. I had dinner with the Jameses and then Johnny and I went fishing for grayling. (Patty is very fond of fish and so I have brought her fish from all across the Arctic.) You could just feel the air come to life about ten thirty as the sun rolled into the north. Any engine will deliver more power of an evening than during the day. So it was that the floatplane easily came up on the step that evening, and away I went doing the job that would have been impossible just a few hours earlier, unless I made two trips. Knowing that little trick had saved me flying all day, quite a few dollars' worth of gasoline, unloading and loading cargo twice and, besides, I had had a pleasant visit with the Jameses and had gone fishing.

Two events happened in the early 1950's at Hughes. Andy Anderson flew in one day from the Tanana Hospital with a small, carefully wrapped box. Inside was a newborn baby with a bottle in his mouth. Alice, his mother, was in the Tanana Hospital, too ill to care for him for a long time. Les and Patty, with all their family grown, married, and with full-grown grandchildren even, now had a newborn baby boy to look after.

They called the new baby Timmy. Timmy's parents already had several children and even after Alice came home it seemed only natural that Les and Patty should keep Timmy.

He knew no other parents than them and so when he was one they legally adopted him.

Perhaps it was the realization that they would soon have another child in school that caused the Jameses to set the second event in motion. They had always dreamed of a school in Hughes, and Les said if the Territory of Alaska would furnish a teacher he would build a school, maintain it, and board the teacher. This is the same system that built schools all across frontier America and it still works wonderfully. That fall school opened at Hughes. After Alaska became a state the Jameses helped to set up and operate the new modern schoolhouse and teachers' quarters. Alaska's school system today is one of the best in America.

Timmy has grown up amid the changing cultural pattern of interior Alaska brought about by the Age of the Air. Patty writes that Timmy has surely been a blessing to her and Les and has repaid them many times for their care, kindness, and love.

Les has never flown an airplane, but he has known machinery since he was a small boy. He also has paid for many a flight, for hauling everything from cement to the North Dakota basketball team. Les was born and raised in North Dakota, and many years later when the University of North Dakota basketball team played the University of Alaska, Les, now in his eighties, said, "Those boys can't know Alaska by seeing the cities." So he chartered the Wien prop jet F-27 airliner and flew the entire team to Hughes and Alatna so that they might see the land he loved.

Les has used airplanes as tools in business, and he has also ridden many miles in them. Les has ridden through many really tough spots, but in all the years he has been in but one crackup. He had gone to Fairbanks to purchase supplies. It was in the early spring, and such things as bacon were running low at Hughes. Cliff Everts was flying a 6000 B Travelair NC 9844. It was quite a good airplane but very touchy about frost on its wings. Les eyed the frosted wing and didn't like its looks a little bit. Les doesn't mind speaking up, and I am surprised he ever got into the airplane. Down the runway at old Weeks Field they went and into the air, but not for long. One wing stalled out, and they flipped, neat as you please, landing upside down. Bacon, canned goods and Kickers (outboard motors), eggs and whisky spilled out. Les and Cliff climbed out, and they had to round up another airplane and pilot to take Les back to Hughes. Not an egg was broken, but the whisky was busted and gone.

Les worked away on his runway, clearing away brush, filling holes, improving it step by step, year by year. Then came the winter day when the first DC-3 landed at Hughes. I happened to be there, and we all stood about watching the airliner come in. It marked the end of an era. No longer would the old Bellancas, Norsemen, Stinsons, and Cessnas haul the cargo. It would come by the ton now. A single pilot wouldn't buck bad weather and cold to deliver the goods. Airliners would arrive on the radio beams and on schedule. Les was pleased he had seen one of his dreams come true.

But it was also the end of the era of the independent bush pilot. I hadn't realized how much so until the next fall when I happened to be in Hughes to pick up a hunting party. It was a beautiful autumn day as only the Arctic can produce. Les's runway was in fine style, and the airliner came in. Several tourists got off and wandered about looking at the people. Little Arthur was there to meet them all. One old chap walked up to Little Arthur and asked, "Does it get cold here in winter?"

"I don't know," Little Arthur said quite honestly, for he hadn't given it any special thought.

The airliner was gone, and Les came over to where I was pumping gasoline. I could tell he was burned up.

"How does that runway look to you, Bud?"

Well it looked ideal and really was. That it wasn't paved was about all you could say against it. Any pilot worth the name could have landed a C-46 on it, and for a DC-3 it was a "piece of pie." I told Les so.

Les isn't a profane man by any means, but he swears as naturally as an old mule skinner. "That G—d— pilot radioed Fairbanks and said the field was soft. I tell you what the H— is soft. It is that G—d— pilot."

Les stared off down his runway. I knew he could see the many years of hard, hard labor and perhaps the long line of bush pilots and planes that had asked only for a fighting chance. Yet to the new Wien pilot with all his fancy training and ratings, used only to hard paving, coming out of Fairbanks International Airport where the big jets now land, it had felt soft. He had had to use a little more brake and be a little quicker with the throttle to turn or taxi, and so he had filed his report matter-of-factly, giving his opinion, "Soft runway at Hughes." He had been right in doing so too, for he and those who followed him were not of that breed of men who stood alone. They needed to know the answers, to follow the marked trail and be told when and where and how to fly.

Les had reached a similar conclusion by a different route. "I tell you, Bud, times have changed. The fight has gone out of the dog. Next thing a pilot won't want to help unload his own airplane."

He was right about that too, for a couple of years later I heard a pilot grumbling because he was helping to unload his airplane, saying he wasn't getting paid for it.

I was glad Les or Patty didn't hear him. They belong to that generation of people who did the job because it was there and needed doing. When help was needed they gave it. They didn't ask of the land what it could do for them but looked to see what they could do for it. Money was a tool to use, not a reason for doing a job, and to them and their kind belongs the joy of living.*

* EDITOR'S NOTE: The Hughes Trading Post and buildings burned to the ground Nov. 30, 1966. It was a complete disaster and the Jameses lost everything in the fire. A faulty oil furnace started the blaze early in the morning and the Jameses were lucky to escape unharmed. They moved into a small cabin nearby and are busy now rebuilding. The mementos, treasures, and belongings of a lifetime were gone. Courage and faith remained to start them rebuilding again. It is examples like theirs that break the trail for the rest of us to take heart again and follow when times look hard.

3

LANDING FIELDS ARE WHERE YOU FIND—OR MAKE—THEM

The local ball park usually became the first landing field in any area and so it was at Fairbanks, but since there were few ball parks in the interior, the first pilots had to look elsewhere. There was also no farm land nor pastures. River bars became the first series of landing fields across the interior, or in all of Alaska for that matter. This coincided happily with the fact that nearly all the people lived on rivers too, and all inland towns were located on them.

Necessity being the mother of invention and early airplanes being unreliable, there seldom was a long flight that didn't have a forced landing, and when the motor quit you picked a landing place fast. You played a steady little game with yourself as you flew—Where would I land if the motor quit? Could I glide to that river bar? Would those birch trees be better to land in, or the spruce?

Fortunately, the motor seldom just quit. There were usually plenty of little warnings, and you were always alert for them. In fact, so in tune with the problems of the airplane was the pilot that in listening to the engine run he was like a maestro listening for some off-note during a symphony. Every hum, rattle, squeak, and squawk meant something, and of course so did the gauges. Of them all, the gas-tank gauges gave us the most problems, for when they said empty you had better find a landing field fast.

The passengers too felt as if they were part of the flight crew and kept an ear open for any strange sounds and a steady eye upon the gas gauges. The passengers were often quite helpful not only in handling the airplane on the ground but also in keeping a watch for things in flight.

Since every person in all of northern Alaska was a customer, from the most remote Eskimo to the biggest mine operator, the pilots had a chance for the first time in history to get to know a vast and unmarked land without having to make ground trails all the way. To service this vast land required three types of landing gear: wheels for the land when you could use dry gravel bars or clearings; floats for landing upon water; and skis for landing upon snow or ice; and you might need all three sets of gear to do one job. It is true there were amphibious aircraft, and some were even tried in the interior, but none proved at all successful. They didn't handle skis well, they were expensive, and almost all were twin-engined, which of course ruled them out for a bush pilot. It is hard enough to heat one engine and keep it going in winter without having to look after two!

The doctor had predicted the baby would arrive in early May. We were at Walker Lake, which lies about a hundred miles north of Hughes, and we wanted to get into the hospital at Fairbanks. We had no radio contact, but I knew there would be no snow to land on at Fairbanks, while at Walker Lake we had five feet of it. I would have to change from skis to wheels. To do this we had to fly north to our place on the Arctic Ocean and pick up the wheels. The runway at Umiat had been dragged all winter and was a sheet of hard-packed snow, suitable for either skis or wheels, and we landed here where I blocked up the airplane and made the change. It took me about three hours to do this. It was snowing softly and was daylight all the time in early May. We headed right on for Fairbanks, but it was white with no horizon. The caribou on the plains seemed to float in space. We followed the dark line of willows along the Anaktuvuk River until we ran into very heavy snow-fog and I had to go around it. The Brooks Range in a snowstorm looks pretty much alike, and I flew along it searching for Anaktuvuk Pass. I felt sort of naked now coming back across this snowy land on wheels with no place to land except some cleared landing field or overflow glacier. The latter was formed by a creek freezing to the bottom, breaking out, and flowing on the top until it freezes again, making a patch of glare ice that can be used to land upon with wheels if you read the ice right. If not, you can come to a fast stop by breaking through thin ice or by breaking through shale ice that the water drained from under after it froze.

I somehow missed Anaktuvuk Pass, and the first spot I recognized was Chandler Lake. Once oriented, I turned back, and this time we managed to hit the Pass, but gasoline was low and I picked out a safe spot on an overflow glacier where I had left twenty gallons of gasoline on the way up. From here on we could see the spring breakup unfold as creeks began to flow, and in many areas the ground was already bare of snow, but we couldn't get on into Fairbanks. Low clouds just blocked us and we picked up ice at each encounter, so we turned on down the Koyukuk River and landed at Hughes for the night. The Koyukuk River had just receded from the breakup flood stage, leaving the field at Hughes soft mud with cakes of ice here and there, but it was the only place to land and we landed spattering the airplane with mud.

After our busy day we were doubly glad to see Les and Patty; we spent the evening talking of the past season and enjoying the smell and sounds of early spring, bird songs, running water, and growing things.

The weather still didn't favor us next day, but we didn't want to delay, so we headed on for Fairbanks into gray skies. It was a fight all the way with icing conditions and low clouds. We seesawed back and forth looking for open passes and eventually squeaked through until the muddy Yukon running at flood stage lay below, and we followed it to the Tanana River and on up it to Fairbanks. Here the stormy skies lifted and the flowers of early spring greeted us as we landed upon the dusty runway at Phillips Field. The left brake had given out, and we taxied in circles up to the hangar. Here we left the *Arctic Tern* to be changed to floats by Jess Bachner, while Ann, his wife, took us up to the Fifth Avenue Hotel. We went right on to St. Joseph Hospital and made arrangements for a room—Martha and I were both mighty happy to be there.

Two days later Mark Harmon weighed in at an even eight pounds. It was a happy ten days we spent in Fairbanks, enjoying the early summer, eating all the foods we liked, visiting friends. The *Arctic Tern* was on her floats resting upon the Chena Slough, and when Mark was ten days old we loaded up and headed for home.

It was evening as we came over Hughes, and the people recognized our plane at once. As soon as Mark was born the news had gone out over the Wien Airlines radio. These radios are for air traffic use only, but the coming of a new baby is an event all the Arctic is interested in. There aren't many of us in that area, you know, and each is rather special. We could see the people gathering at the riverbank, and as we taxied up the whole village was there to greet us and welcome the new baby. It made us feel quite proud and needed.

We had dinner with the Jameses, purchased some groceries, gassed up the *Arctic Tern,* and headed on across the quiet land for home. The land had been bare of snow at Hughes, but as we went north snow appeared, and a few miles from Walker Lake it was solid white. I saw a nearly white wolf running across the ice on the lake. The land looked just as we had left it. We were on floats though, and there wasn't any open water, so we just had to land upon the ice.

The sun shone from out of the north, giving the world a dreamlike, rosy glow as we circled, picking out the best spot to touch down. Melting was progressing rapidly, and I could tell there was slush upon the ice. The *Arctic Tern*'s big floats touched the ice and we slid to a stop a few yards from the house in the exact spot from where just two weeks before we had taken off. Martha was busy tucking Mark in to keep him warm until I had the fire going. I wrote down my data in the logbook and as an afterthought added, "Mission accomplished."

So it was that you often needed all three kinds of gear to carry you through a single job. It was always a problem having the right gear on the airplane for the landing conditions. At Bettles Field they often would bring in an airplane loaded with supplies from Fairbanks, where there was no snow; change to skis at Bettles, where there was snow; then fly the cargo on to its destination, where only a ski landing was possible.

It was always good if you knew the spot you were going to before you took off, but many times this wasn't possible. Some customer in town wanted to go home to his mine or cabin, and so you asked him questions about the landing area. Nearly everyone had some sort of a spot near his place where you could land. The clincher question was: Who has landed there before? Then, if the pilots named and the airplanes used were in your estimation equal to your airplane and ability, weather permitting, away you went.

In taking trappers and miners back to isolated cabins, a bush pilot soon learned to have them show him exactly where they lived on the map before he took off. Of course the maps were inaccurate, but you generally knew the country pretty well by heart, and you wanted to know where the exact spot was before you left, for often your passenger didn't recognize his own house from the air!

This surely wasn't always the case as Harry, an old Eskimo, proved to me once. Harry and Aivuk ("Walrus") wanted to go prospecting back in the Brooks Range. It was quite a flight from Barrow and, as none of the places were named and my map didn't even show a lake or river where they said there was one, I would have to go on faith. I was flying a floatplane at the time and was doubly cautious about the lake's size at high altitude. Aivuk and Harry sat drawing the route in the sand and I had a fair idea of where it was. Harry had heard talk of where there was gold from the "Old People" and he wanted to take a look. Aivuk is one of the most reliable men I have ever known, and when he assured me that Harry could remember the route although he had seen it only once as a teen-age boy forty years ago when his family had traveled that way, I believed him. Aivuk had never been there himself.

I, of course, knew the general area and flew the first three hundred miles direct to a branch of the Nanushuk River. Here Harry took over, saying, "Take that branch," then a few minutes later, "Go over this ridge, fly to that hill, now turn up this valley." After about an hour he said, "The lake is around behind that hill." Never once had he hesitated, and when we rounded the hill there was the lake, exactly as he had drawn it in the sand and just the size he had said too! It was as if he had flown the route many times and was following an accurate map. Yet he had only walked over it once forty years ago, long before any airplane had come to Alaska. I have wished I had a memory like his many times since.

I left them there at the wild, beautiful unknown lake and marked it on my map. I was to bring in some grub in a couple of weeks and leave it at a rock by the lake shore. There would be a note for me there. Two weeks later I was back, and there was a note. "Found no gold. Having a fine time. Will walk to Negilik [Arctic Ocean spot where my fish camp is]. See you at freeze-up there, Aivuk." So I flew the grub onto the Arctic coast nearly three hundred miles away, the way they would have to walk it, across three big rivers.

Just before freeze-up they walked in. They had been living on parka squirrels and caribou. They had made a little boat of willow sticks and caribou hide to cross the rivers and had a fine time all summer. They hadn't found any gold, but they hadn't expected to, nor, I believe, had really wanted to. Their "gold" had been in being where they wanted to be and doing what they wanted to do. You must truly love a land to remember every tiny detail of it forty years later.

This was true of all the old bush pilots. They really loved the land and they remembered the tiny details. Sam White was right there with the first, and Sam surely loved the land and speaks of it in small, detailed ways. Sam used many a trick in his landings and was the first I know of to use caribou as field markers in a whiteout on the prairie.

A whiteout is when you lose your horizon and the light is so evenly diffused that all the world is white and you can't tell literally up from down while flying. There isn't any reality in your world and you are in trouble. It is just as bad as total darkness, except for one saving grace—when there is a dark object you can see it. Sam was flying north of what is now Umiat across the rolling hills of the Arctic prairie just before it turns into the coastal plain. It was early spring, when whiteouts are most likely to occur. The weather had just been marginal all the way, and Sam finally was in bad trouble when he saw a herd of caribou floating in the white world ahead. There were several hundred head, and Sam made right for them. The caribou had trampled down the snow, making a good landing area.

"There wasn't any time for smart flying," he said. "I just supposed those caribou were standing on land, and I set the old Bellanca in right among them. Caribou went past both wings, and I damn near hit a couple. I didn't dare circle 'cause I couldn't see and there were hills all around to hit. Those caribou saved me that time. I was plenty scared, too!"

I have used the caribou many times to show me where the land is and to land among them as Sam did. It is a real friendly sight to see caribou at any time. And a caribou gave me one of my biggest surprises in flying and one of the fastest warnings too.

It was a white day and I shouldn't have been flying, but I wanted to go home and was trying to get through Anaktuvuk Pass. Ice, fog, and whiteouts had plagued me steadily. I had followed the few dark willows up the John River and then I had a pure white stretch in the pass before I picked up the dark willow line in the Anaktuvuk River. I was flying just a few feet above the ground, knowing full well the hills rose up above me a few yards back from the stream's edge. There is an Eskimo settlement in the pass now and Wien's has a landing field there, but there wasn't anything there to guide by that day, though, and I just hoped I was in the center. I thought I was through, for time seems awfully long under those conditions, and I was trying to pick up the first willows of the Anaktuvuk River when a caribou appeared, standing looking down at me from a little to the left of dead ahead. I surely brought the ship around hard to the right in a climbing turn and steadied down, for I could have plowed head-on into the mountain. I can still see its graceful form just yards from me and the surprised look as I banked away from under its nose. Beyond the line of caribou lay the dark willows and in a few minutes I was out into the clear blue skies of a lovely spring day. Weather often piles up on one side of the range, and the other side can be clear skies.

Vic Calcattera of Detroit was with me when I made the fastest forced landing of my flying career. Vic and I had been hunting the pack ice north of our home in very cold, clear spring weather. The pack was hard to hunt that year and we had ranged far afield. Although I have flown to within a few miles of the North Pole, I usually don't take hunters out beyond the crushed-up open lead. There isn't any need to run this risk on a hunting trip that is for pleasure. Vic had wanted to see the broken ice, and since we hadn't seen any bear signs where we were, I took him out over some of it. We were about one hundred and ten miles north of Alaska, it was −30 degrees and the open water in the leads smoked in the cold air. I was flying at four hundred feet when the engine started revving down. I quickly changed fuel tanks but it revved on down and stopped. I had turned for a smooth piece of ice at the first loss of power, and as we glided around, I worked the gas selector, carburetor heat, throttle, and starter, but to no avail. The smooth piece of ice was young ice surrounded by pressure ridges up to twenty-five feet high. I used full flaps to just lift us over the pressure ridges and felt the tail ski click as we glided down the far side for a smooth landing. It had taken forty-five seconds from the first sign of trouble until we were down. Neither Vic nor I had spoken a word until we came to a stop. I jumped out and tested the ice with an ax and found it plenty thick. All around our small ice pan rose the pressure ice, and there was open water on one side.

I wrapped the engine up as soon as I tested the ice. Salt

ice is tough and rubbery, and you can walk across salt ice you can't stand still on. Had this ice not been thick enough it might have supported our airplane five minutes before letting it through, and in that time we would have had to take out all of our emergency camping gear.

Vic and I walked around our landing field and found it about four hundred feet long as its best, with a ten-foot ridge to clear at the end. The ice was under pressure, crushing and moving slowly as the pressure ridges formed. We then tried the airplane engine and it ran beautifully. Apparently frost had formed in the carburetor screen and completely cut off the fuel flow; and the heat from a wrapped-up engine had cleared it out.

We worked the airplane back into the pressure ridge as far as we could and took off smoothly, for luckily there was a little wind down the long way of the ice. Vic felt it had been one of his most fascinating experiences. I was pleased it had all come off as well as it did, but there had been not a split second for indecision, and I was mighty glad Vic hadn't had any questions in that awful silence.

There was hardly a day of flying that didn't have its anxious moments or funny side. I used to run one tank dry on a long flight before switching to the other tank. This practice worried my friend and editor, Angus Cameron. He flew to get where he was going and not for the love of flying. He felt if an engine quit it was the end. Yet he loved the wilderness, and flying was the only way to get there. We were on our way to Hughes one day when I saw a black bear and circled to show it to him, and as the nearly empty tank in the right wing rose in the turn the engine starved. It just took an instant to change tanks, but in that silence he had a chance to express his feelings. He did, and his exact words were a quiet "Oh dear."

Barrow had one of the worst landing spots. We used to use the beach between Barrow and its twin sister, Browerville. The Barrow Lagoon was on one side and the Arctic Ocean on the other. The beach itself was pea gravel that won't pack and was torn up by storms and land traffic such as tractors. I hated to use the spot and didn't very often, for I was usually flying floats in summer or skis in winter; but in the fall I had to use wheels before the ice was thick enough to hold up the airplane. We didn't have radio contact, so Reverend Wartes (Bill), the first missionary to fly this part of the Arctic, would hurry down to point out the best-looking spot and I would land. You didn't have to worry about rolling far because you couldn't in that pea gravel. It was even hard to walk on. But at all times you had to worry about children or dog teams running in front of you, and you had to drag the area to clear out the ground traffic.

Such a problem proved Walt Bear's undoing at the Barrow landing. The lagoon ice was thick enough that day and we were landing there. Walt had put in a good season of flying and was going back to visit his family in the States, as we called the South Forty-eight then. He had a bit more flying to do and was returning from Wainwright. When the wind is from the northeast, your final approach is across the Arctic Ocean. It is often open water here as late as early December, cold gray water in the sub-zero air dotted with loose ice cakes. There was a dog team on the landing area the first time Walt came around and he had to make a second approach. He was on his final leg a few hundred yards short of the lagoon, all "centered down" and concentrating on that landing, when something went wrong. The airplane just pitched head-long and vanished forever into the open sea. None of us could ever figure out what had happened. As Bill Wartes said one day when we were talking about pilots we had known in the early days—only two were left of the nineteen he had known—"They didn't all make it, you know."

Sam White was one who did make it, though, from the very first to the last. In December 1932 Sam flew into Hughes in a Swallow open-cockpit biplane arriving in a blizzard. As Sam put it: "Couldn't tell where it was safe to land. Finally a man with a red shirt walked down and stood still. I figured he was marking the end of the runway. I landed so close to him he was startled, but I needed him; he was the only thing I could see. He turned out to be Gus Wagner, an old-timer who cooked at the Model Café in Fairbanks. There was no one else in town. He was 'bushed' to see someone. We tied the ship and went to his cabin where he cooked up moose steaks, pies, and cakes. Gus was an excellent cook, and I really enjoyed my stay for the next four days while the blizzard blew itself out."

The kind of a landing field you watched for as you flew along depended upon the gear you had on the airplane. If you had on wheels you watched for river bars or mud flats and open areas. When you were on skis you kept an eye open for any open stretch covered with snow or ice, and when on floats you had your pick of almost anything except heavy brush or mountains, for you can land a float airplane safely upon any surface you can land any type of airplane on. Now getting it off again is another matter; but when you are just thinking of a safe landing, you take care of first things first. You must handle each problem as you get to it, and then there is plenty of time.

In the summer the sun doesn't set in the Arctic. It varies from just one day of steady sunshine at the Arctic Circle to six months of steady sunshine at the North Pole. The north Arctic coast of Alaska has continuous sunshine from mid-May until mid-July and you get a bit careless with its use. It is a pleasant, unhurried land and the old bush-pilot phrase "trading daylight for dark" doesn't apply when you loiter along your way. As fall approaches you nearly always get caught short, especially if your flight takes you straight south.

Once Martha and I were flying from our Arctic coast home to our place at Walker Lake, getting things in order for a fall hunting party. It was a little over a four-hundred-mile flight, and our *Arctic Tern*, a Cessna 170-B floatplane, would make it in about four hours. Being used to the steady daylight and rather wasteful of it, we took our time. On the trip south one progresses from the flat, open grasslands of the Arctic prairie a hundred miles across to the rolling, grass-covered hills of the Arctic plateau that rise to some two thousand feet and extend another hundred miles to the Brooks Range and the opening of Anaktuvuk Pass.

Anaktuvuk Pass is a beautiful spot and reminds one of the fabled Khyber Pass of Kipling stories. It is the gateway between the interior of Alaska and the fantastic stretch of Arctic plateau and plain used by ancient man, as his abandoned artifacts show. It also separates the interior Alaskan weather from the Arctic weather, and, like a wall, this particular night the storm clouds of the interior lay waiting along with a hundred and fifty miles of the roughest mountains.

Into the rain we went while darkness began to settle. We twisted and turned, following the streams up one river drainage and down another, and all the while darkness deepened. When we passed Inukuk Lake I could see the water through the rain. Water runs up over an airplane's windshield and you have only side visibility. We were but a half hour out of our Walker Lake home now. Twenty minutes later we met solid fog. It was impossible to go on. Nothing was visible. I had been keeping my direction and altitude by the light in the western sky and the dim mountains through the side of the airplane. We were well down in the mountain canyons, and I had to turn back. We would make it to Inukuk Lake. It was almost dark now, but I could faintly see the mountain peaks. Bush flying was almost all done by the seat of your pants, since even if you could fly instruments and had them all working, you wouldn't dare use them at such a time; it would have been a fatal mistake. There are no instrument ground facilities and to just be able to fly straight and level is of little use when you have to get down. So we kept ground contact at all times. Often it was so little that I wonder and marvel that the flights succeeded, but it was always there; however, if you lost that tiny sliver of visual contact, you had had it. Many a pilot has "bought the farm" moments after he lost that sliver of visual contact.

As we came over where Inukuk Lake should be, it was dark but the mountain peaks were darker than the sky, and knowing their pattern I could figure out where the lake should lie. There was rain and fog over the lake. Martha said nothing, and now that I had determined what the course would be and where I felt the lake lay, I turned on the instrument lights and set the airplane in a glide, using instruments now. I could see Martha's face in the red glow; she smiled at me and turned back to staring into the black, rain-splashed night as if it required both of us looking to see ahead. Bosco, our sled dog, who was in back, whined apprehensively. There was no need to turn on the landing light, because in the rain over calm water it would just blind me. I was glad the lake was nearly ten miles long, for it gave me a bigger target to hit. The red warning light of the stall indicator blinked on and off as I settled slowly just above stalling speed. The sound of the stall warning set Bosco off howling mournfully; he made a terrible racket. Bosco's mouth was right by my ear and Martha knew I had all I could handle already, so she quickly rammed her hand into his mouth and it shut him up. It seemed like an hour as we settled, but it was only a few minutes before I felt we weren't flying and I could hear spray from the floats. I snapped on the landing lights and a feathery wake boiled up from each side. The landing had been so smooth that we weren't aware we were down!

We taxied to shore using the landing lights now, and I

realized we had landed right in the center of the lake. Bosco was happy to be down and wanted to go right out on shore. When I had finished tailing the floats up on shore, I opened the door and let him out. He jumped about in the sand and then sent a long howl out into the black night. From right back in the brush a few hundred yards away came an answer from a family of Arctic caribou wolves that put Bosco's howl to shame, raised the hair on our necks, and sent Bosco under the tail of the airplane for the night. Bosco didn't say any more, nor did the wolves howl again. We slept in our seats while the rain drummed on the metal airplane.

Morning came with a bright, warm autumn sun, and we were on our way home to Walker Lake. How beautiful the mountains were, and how happy a man can be when, in looking back, he realizes the last decision he made was exactly right. It doesn't give you an exaggerated opinion of yourself or your ability, though, for you can clearly see you never would have made it through The Valley alone.

On one of his first training flights at the start of World War II, the Reverend Wartes was flying a trainer over a city when his motor quit. He could have parachuted to safety and let the plane fall on the city, but he decided to ride it down and try to save those below. The airplane glided "like a bucket of bolts." Bill knew he couldn't handle it, so he just said, "Lord, it's beyond me. It's in your hands; show me the way."

A big barn caught by the expanding city loomed right ahead. There was no way of missing it, so Bill pulled back on the stick. The heavy trainer surged up, just clearing the barn. A woman was coming out the barn door with a basket of eggs and Bill saw her throw up her hands, and the eggs went flying. The airplane then went under a power line, over an irrigation ditch, and stopped in a small cow pasture. A man came running up to Bill and shouted, "If my cow loses her calf, the government will pay damages for it."

When the crew came to dismantle the airplane and take it away, no one could figure out how Bill ever got an airplane into such a small yard.

In Sam White's long flying career he has had many landings, and each in itself was an adventure. As Sam once put it, each was just a controlled forced landing, for there weren't many marked-out places to land.

Late one fall Sam was flying a party of Coast and Geodetic men into Fairbanks when darkness and falling snow caught him. He was on wheels, so he had to land on a river bar; but in the dark and falling snow it was an awful job just telling what a river bar was. You get impressions of an area in the fading light, and Sam thought he had passed a good bar some ten miles back down the Tanana River, so he headed back for it. About all you can do is hope you are in the right area. Sam did his best to figure out where the river bar was and not to go into the thin ice of the river or into the trees. When he stopped rolling there was a big pile of drift stumps on either side. By their flashlights they could see Sam had not only missed all the stumps but had landed in the only possible safe spot. The passengers all thought Sam had some sixth sense, that he could see in the dark and had flown about each obstacle. Sam said it was pure luck, and in the daylight he had a job just taxiing back between them.

One the prettiest sights I have ever seen is that twin row of lights that marks a landing field. Once on a flight from Whitehorse, Yukon Territory, to Edmonton, Alberta, we were caught in an unexpectedly heavy snowstorm—the kind where the flakes are big and fat. Darkness closed in like a shutter, and I wasn't sure just where we were in that mountainous land. Then, looking like a lighted Christmas tree, we saw the runway lights of Teslin; each set of lights as we came over them was fuzzy through the snow. That landing field was beautiful just as we found it.

A problem all bush pilots face in winter is that of frost forming in the gas lines, which slowly cuts off the fuel supply. The best insurance now is some fuel additive, like Ban Ice, but we didn't have this in the early days. This has caused many pilots to pick landing fields or make them.

One time on a flight from our Colville Delta home to Fairbanks I had the whole family along. We had a pleasant flight to Bettles, where I gassed up and headed right on for Fairbanks. It was a beautiful night and I climbed higher than usual for some reason. Altitude is like money in the bank and I sure needed it before the flight ended. We crossed the mighty Yukon and Fairbanks lay but forty minutes away when I changed from the nearly empty tank to the full one. The engine soon began to rev down and at last almost quit. I knew at once that the line was nearly closed with frost and would likely close altogether. We had forty minutes to go, a three-hour fuel reserve, and but ten minutes' flying time in the one tank! There wasn't a single lighted field we could reach in ten minutes.

"Let's land on the river," Martha suggested in a questioning voice. It looked so easy and safe lying ten thousand feet below in the moonlight.

"We have a good chance of going through the ice at this season," I told her.

I rocked the plane, and from the way the gas gauge moved I figured I had maybe fifteen minutes. I changed to the full tank and the engine ran for about a minute before it started slowing down, but it took four minutes before I had to switch back to the open line to hold the plane up.

If the shut-off valve were tight and I was actually burning from the frosted-line tank I could, by switching back and forth, just make it to Fairbanks before the free-flowing tank went dry. I would climb during the minute I burned on the open tank and then hold all the altitude I could as I ran on the nearly frosted-shut tank; but I lost altitude steadily. Up and down like a roller coaster we went, me watching the gas gauges, my watch, and the map—figuring, calculating, praying as all pilots pray, losing altitude as a miser loses money; Martha watching my face, looking for landing fields in a landing-fieldless land; the little boys sleeping, the pet cat curled up, the parakeets asleep in their cage, and that big Arctic moon shining down. It was an awful temptation to land on the big lake in Minto Flats, for I felt I could land safely there, but then the Search and Rescue would be alerted. I would have to look after the family in sub-zero cold, which could be done safely if we didn't have a mishap on landing.

The gas gauge read empty now, but I knew I had five minutes left. I should be in Fairbanks in ten, if . . . ! In using the calculated risk you always hedged where you could. Thus, if I used two minutes of the usable tank and what I could get out of the choked-up tank flying toward Fairbanks, I could then turn back and still make the lake if I hadn't passed the halfway mark. Wind wasn't a factor, for the air was almost calm. This would also let me know if I had enough altitude to get over the last range of mountains. It is when you reach the end of your allotted time that you squirm and wonder. I figured we would make it, so on we went just above the trees and then it was downhill. The beacon light of Fairbanks was beckoning, and those beautiful twin rows of landing lights at Phillips Field. The gas gauge didn't even waver any more. The tank was empty; as we flared out and touched down the motor quit. We sat a moment while fuel trickled into the carburetor, then started up and taxied to the hangar before the motor could starve again. The children woke up and asked if we were in Fairbanks. Bill Ackerman came out and helped us tie down.

"You folks coming in from the Arctic coast for a visit?" Bill asked.

"Yes, we are in for a visit and a little shopping."

There was no need to tell Bill how happy we were to be there. It must have shown in our faces. This was one time we didn't have to make the landing field, nor find it either, for we knew right along where it was; the problem had been just getting there.

4

THE WIEN BROTHERS

In interior Alaska, and in fact in all of Alaska, the most famous name in aviation is Wien. It is with good reason too, for the Wien brothers were first in almost everything in the flying field, and they stayed first. Their fantastic combination of determination, skill, kindness, and courage led them from that summer day of July 6, 1924, when young Noel Wien flew his Hisso Standard J1—which he had assembled for Jimmy Rodebaugh—from Anchorage to Fairbanks, marking the first flight between those towns to the present time, when the vast complex of Wien Airlines offers scheduled airline service to all interior and northern Alaska as well as daily flights to Juneau with turboprop planes.

There were a few flights in Alaska before Noel Wien flew to Fairbanks from Anchorage that day in 1924, but all were of the exhibition type. Noel had spent the month previous to his departure for Fairbanks in flying passengers about Anchorage, which was the first flying ever done there. An Army party of four had flown from New York to Nome. Ben Eielson had purchased an old Army trainer and had given a few joy rides about Fairbanks and also did a little commercial flying, having flown the U.S. mail for the first time. Then Jimmy Rodebaugh had a pilot named Art Sampson who was doing a little flying, taking passengers mostly on joy rides or to nearby Livengood or Tanana. Art Sampson left a month after Noel arrived, leaving Noel Wien the only pilot in Alaska north of the Alaska Range, and almost every flight Noel made was a first. He was the first man to fly across the Arctic Circle when, on October 8, 1924, he attempted to fly from Fairbanks to Wiseman but low clouds turned him back. His official Circle crossing date was not recorded until the following spring when he finally completed the flight. Today all the passengers who cross the

Arctic Circle on the sleek Wien jets receive a certificate signed by their pilot showing that they have crossed the Arctic Circle.

Jimmy Rodebaugh formed the first airline in Alaska really. Jimmy was a railroad conductor who visualized the future of aviation in Alaska. He formed the Alaska Air Transport Company and Noel Wien flew for him. Jimmy was a quiet man with unlimited faith in the future of aviation. Jim did solo and made a few solo hops around Fairbanks. He acquired very few hours and once nosed up on landing, but he was often a passenger with Noel on history-making flights.

That first season of flying Noel piled up 138 hours of air time in the single Hisso Standard, which was surely a record in itself under those flying conditions, for about every other trip the engine had to be taken apart and overhauled. Even with Jimmy Rodebaugh's faithful backing, the Alaska Air Transport Company passed out of the picture when, in the winter of 1924–5, a group of Fairbanks businessmen formed the Fairbanks Airplane Corporation with Jimmy Rodebaugh as its manager. Noel Wien was given authority to purchase a cabin plane for the company, and he scouted the States. He found the only cabin plane available was a Fokker F-3 monoplane built in Amsterdam in 1921 with the German-built BMW 234–250 h.p. engine. The plane was shipped from New York via the Panama Canal to Seward and via the Alaska Railroad to Fairbanks on two flatcars at a shipping cost of two hundred and seventy dollars. Noel Wien returned to Fairbanks as the only pilot of the new company, and his older brother, Ralph, came with him to serve as mechanic.

On June 3, in the full flush of an Alaskan summer with its twenty-four-hour daylight and soft warm days, the Fokker monoplane arrived. Noel and Ralph assembled it there at the ball park and then test-hopped it. Nearly everyone in Fairbanks went out to the ball park to see the new airplane. Soon they had the Fokker ready, and Noel test-flew it. Airplanes, though, were expensive to buy, to maintain, and to operate. But the public was enthusiastic about airplanes in Alaska and willing to help in every way they could. It was quite a change from the South Forty-eight, where people were afraid to fly and regarded flying as a stunt and pilots as untrustworthy individuals.

As soon as the Fokker was test-flown, Noel loaded three passengers and his brother Ralph aboard—for on any flight the mechanic was as important as the pilot—and they headed for Nome. The charter rate for this flight was fifteen hundred dollars. It is interesting to note that the charter rate for a Wien airliner of the C-46 type today is about the same price for this run, but the payload has been upped about twenty times and the flights are routine.

This first flight of the Fokker wasn't to be a complete success, though, for on its first landing at the Ruby ball park in rain and fog Noel hit a soft spot in the ball diamond and nosed over. Nosing over was a rather common occurrence in those days, and often a spare propeller was brought along just for such landings. The engine would break the wooden propeller to splinters as the airplane went over on its back. This time Noel didn't have a spare propeller and the Signal Corps at Ruby telegraphed Fairbanks for a new one. Dick Woods, president of the airline, headed for Ruby with the new propeller, first by railroad speeder to Nevana and then by gas boat (as gasoline-engine-powered boats were called in Alaska) to Ruby. The three passengers apparently decided that the day of the airplane had not yet come, for they left at once by gas boat for Nome, leaving Noel and Ralph to repair the airplane. When Dick Woods arrived with the new propeller, the Wiens repaired the airplane and, instead of returning to Fairbanks, they went on to Nome.

The Nome people had expected the flyers a few hours after leaving Fairbanks, and they waited all night at the fairgrounds to welcome them. They had all the trimmings for a greeting, including a brass band. But as the second day began they all drifted off home. Four days later the Fokker came in and the people knew that the towns of Alaska were linked together at last by fast transportation. It was the first commercial flight between Nome and Fairbanks and at the same time marked the beginning of the end of the dog-team transportation. The passengers arrived by boat two days later. Poor weather at Nome held up the return flight until June 20, when Noel, Ralph, and Dick made the return flight nonstop in six hours and fifty-eight minutes, Nome to Fairbanks.

People immediately put in a request for airmail service between Nome and Fairbanks. Noel put in 255 hours of flying in the Fokker that season. It was real pioneering "bush flying." None before had ever had the level-headedness, courage, or kindness to accomplish what he did, and he blazed the trails all the others would follow. It was under the toughest conditions, where a man stands alone all the way; and perhaps the greatest test was that he did it all without a serious accident.

We have been talking about Noel Wien and his early flying. It is about time we learned more about the man himself. As to his flying ability, the years of constant flying speak better of his skill than anything I could say. Sam White, whom Noel taught to fly, summed it up when he simply said, "Noel was the best." Speaking of his own flying one day, Noel told me that he used every precaution he could, did his best, and when he needed a little help from the Lord he asked for it.

After his successful year of flying the new cabin plane, Noel spent a year in the States barnstorming with Snyder's Flying Circus, but in March of 1927 he landed back in Fairbanks, this time accompanied by his younger brother, Fritz. Fritz was a mechanic by trade and went to work with a gold-dredging company. Noel had taught Ralph to fly and it wasn't long before Fritz was working with his two brothers as the mechanic of Wien Alaska Airways. Slowly the Wien brothers were acquiring the skills necessary to operate an airline. They purchased one of the Hisso Standards from the Fairbanks Airplane Corporation in June 1927 and began servicing Nome and Seward Peninsula and Arctic points, as well as the Fairbanks area and in-between points.

One of the first commercial flights out of Nome was when Noel took Ralph Lomen out to round up reindeer from the air in that June. In July George Tracey developed blood poisoning in his foot. Noel started for Anchorage with him, but weather forced him to go to Fairbanks where, by a timely operation, George lost his foot but lived. Thus began a long line of mercy flights. Babies have even been born on Wien Airline flights and so their place of birth may be recorded as "ten thousand feet somewhere between Barrow and Fairbanks"! Many a person is alive today because of the timely arrival of some bush pilot.

The Wiens were accumulating a vast knowledge of Do's and Don't's flying in a land of no landing fields with only the rule of common sense to go by. They rounded up reindeer, landed prospectors on top of mountains, and began building people's confidence in and dependence on flying. Noel gave flight instructions in the Hisso Standard, and this must have been a chore since there was only one set of controls in the rear cockpit and both instructor and pupil had to crowd into the single seat. It was a tight squeeze, but several fledgling pilots got into the air in this way and not a single accident occurred.

The Wiens increased their operations at Nome by purchasing the Detroit Stinson from the Arctic explorer Sir George Hubert Wilkins in the fall of 1927, and Gene Miller sold out the small interest he had held in the new company. The name of the company became Wien Alaska Airways beginning in June 1927, but then was incorporated. Noel broke in the new Stinson Detroiter with the first flight ever made from Fairbanks to Deering, on Kotzebue Sound. The 220 h.p. Wright J-4B engine made the flight nonstop in exactly six hours.

The list of firsts piled up during these days would fill a dozen closely typed pages. Almost every flight set a first for something. When Noel left home "field" he had no possible way of knowing what weather he would encounter en route, nor what sort of a place he would have to use for a landing field. It was long before the days of radio. It just took plain good sound judgment to sort out the reliable information you saw, heard, or suspected.

In May 1928 the Fox Film Company wanted to film Arctic life and chartered the Wien Stinson for an expedition to Point Barrow, with Noel Wien as pilot, of course. Virgil Hart, leader of the expedition, also picked Russell Merrill of Anchorage to furnish the other airplane.

This was the first commercial flying in the Arctic part of Alaska, and while Noel knew quite a little about the southwestern Arctic, he was now pushing into the far north, during May whiteout conditions to boot. Russell Merrill was, of course, clear out of his element, being from the southern coast, and, in the white, featureless land, fog forced him to land near Barrow. After living on little lemmings and walking for several days, he was picked up by white trader John Higness and his dog team. Merrill survived the Arctic ordeal and returned to flying operations around Anchorage. On September 16, 1929, he was hauling a shaft for a gold-mining operation when he went down in Cook Inlet and was never found, although part of the fabric of his airplane was picked up in the salt water. Thus while the airplane saved many from accident, sickness, or epidemic, it also claimed the lives of others in their efforts to reach further into the unknown.

March 7, 1929, saw the beginning of more history-making flights and also marked the beginning of intercontinental flights between North America and Asia. In its way it also set the stage for the tragic death of Alaska's first and in many ways most daring and famous pilot, Ben Eielson. The Swenson Fur Company of Seattle chartered Noel and his Hamilton Standard to fly from Nome to North Cape, Siberia, and bring back a payload of 1,100 white Arctic fox pelts valued at a hundred and fifty thousand dollars on the New York market. The Wiens were to receive forty-five hundred for the flight, and the natives at North Cape, Siberia, were to shovel off a 2,000-foot landing strip. The temperature was in the −40-degree bracket, and it took Noel six hours fifteen minutes to cross the broken ice-filled stretch of ocean. He remained overnight and then returned in six hours the next day, concluding the first successful international round-trip flight to the west. Noel received a congratulatory telegram from William P. McCracken, Assistant Secretary of Commerce, for his contribution to aviation development.

While Noel was working with the Fox Film Company, there was of course no news of their work or whereabouts. Ralph Wien, with only ten hours of dual instruction and solo time combined and no cross-country experience at all, made the mail flight to Nome and around Seward Peninsula and returned successfully. I am sure such a flight without weather information, suitable maps, or any navigation aids has no equal in the history of flying.

Ralph Wien undoubtedly would have been one of aviation's all-time great figures. He had courage, skill, and common sense, and he was a remarkably astute businessman. His brilliant career was never destined to develop, however, for on October 12, 1930, while flying a diesel-powered Bellanca for the Catholic Missions of Alaska, something went wrong right after the take-off from Kotzebue and the plane crashed, killing Ralph instantly. It is another tribute to Ralph's cool thinking that even in those frantic last seconds as he fought to control the falling airplane, he had found time to close the fuel valve and lessen the fire hazard.

Wien Alaska Airways continued in business until August 6, 1929, when Ben Eielson, representing the Aviation Corporation of America, bought out all the existing airlines in the interior, including the Bennett-Rodebaugh Company. The Wiens didn't sell their company name or their accounts receivable. They did, however, agree not to fly in competition —for three years—with the newly formed company, which was called Alaskan Airways, Incorporated. Noel flew for the new company until September. One interesting item in Noel's logbooks of that time was that on September 10 he gave Ben Eielson two landing tests. In late September, Noel and his wife, Ada, left Alaska for Minnesota. Noel purchased a Stinson Jr. airplane with a 220 h.p. Wright J-5 engine and went to work doing commercial flying in that area.

In October 1929 a new company was formed in Nome called Northern Air Transport Company, Inc. It was formed with a capital stock of twenty-five thousand dollars, and the three directors were all Nome men—C. M. Allyn, W. H. Sturtivant, and Julius Silverman. Thus the Wien brothers left aviation in interior Alaska with competition developing, companies well formed, and the public dependence upon airplanes an established fact.

Alaska had claimed the Wien brothers, though, and they wouldn't stay away. As a person can feel the call of this vast land in Robert Service's poetry, so the Wiens could feel its call. Cross-country flights weren't at all common to Alaska in 1930, but in December, Noel and his brother Sigurd left Virginia, Minnesota, and flew via Edmonton, Prince George, Telegraph Creek, Atlin, Whitehorse, Dawson, and Fairbanks. It took just fourteen days at this most difficult time of the year to make the flight—the fifth from continental United States to Alaska at that time. Noel went to work at once flying the Stinson under contract for Alaskan Airways, Inc., while Sig, as his brother Fritz had done before him, went to work for the Fairbanks Exploration Company—the F.E., as it is called—dredging for gold.

On August 6, 1932, the three-year "no-competition" agreement in the sale clause lapsed, and the name Wien again appeared in aviation circles, this time as Wien Airways of Alaska, Inc. The company was formed by Noel Wien and his wife, Ada, with Mr. and Mrs. William Arthur, Ada Wien's parents. It operated thus until 1935, when Noel and Ada bought out the Arthurs and became sole owners of Wien Airways of Alaska, Inc. A new Bellanca Pacemaker with a 300 h.p. Wasp Jr. engine was put into service and was used out of Anchorage, Fairbanks, and Nome. There was keen competition now in the large towns, but Noel had the know-how and equipment to handle the work and kept busy even at the lowest temperatures.

It is very difficult to fly at low temperatures, for everything slows down and works against you. Airplane engines burn much more gasoline. The best illustration of such flying that I know of took place on January 13, 1934. Noel took off from Fairbanks for Ophir, Crooked Creek, and Bethel with a temperature of −50 degrees on the ground. On the return trip he landed at McGrath and stayed overnight; next morning it was −70 degrees. At this temperature snow is like sand and you can't move a ski ship even empty at full throttle, so Noel was grounded until the fourteenth, when it warmed up to −60. Once in the air at 5,000 feet it was only −35 degrees, but when Noel landed at Fairbanks it was −66 degrees. January 14, 1934, was the coldest ever recorded at Fairbanks—its 66 degrees below zero still remains the record low there. That is cold, bitter, hard flying no matter how you go about it, and that trip must have set some kind of an all-time record for low temperature endurance of man and machine. Noel had delivered the mail, hauled the produce, and it was no wonder that legends grew up around the man who performed such duties as a matter of routine work.

In 1933, when Wiley Post flew the *Winnie Mae* around the world, he became lost on the Yukon River near Ruby. Noel and Ada were making a trip from Ruby to Fairbanks in their Bellanca when Ada sighted and recognized the *Winnie Mae* in the distance. They knew at once that Post was lost, and Noel tried to catch up to him but the sleek Lockheed Vega the *Winnie Mae* was too fast for the Bellanca workhorse and unfortunately they were unsuccessful. Wiley Post wandered around then looking for Fairbanks and finally landed at Flat, where he nosed over. It was Wiley Post's first accident in Alaska.

Sigurd (Sig) Wien returned to Fairbanks in the spring of 1935 with his A & E (airframe and engine) mechanic's license and went to work for Noel. Noel had given Sig his first basic training in flying back in Cook, Minnesota, in 1923 in a Hisso Curtiss Jenny. The years from 1934 to 1937 were busy ones for Sig as he gained valuable mechanical experience and earned his commercial pilot's license. To us today it may sound strange that there was a vast difference between flying an open cockpit airplane and a cabin plane, but it was true, and many who could fly an open cockpit never did learn to handle the cabin planes. A note in Noel's logbook reads: "Gave Sigurd some instructions. He performed exceptionally well for first cabin landings."

In 1935 the Wiley Post–Will Rogers crash near Barrow closed the logbooks of two of the best-loved Americans, and the world waited for pictures of the crash. It was up to Noel to get the films from Fairbanks to Seattle. In the great flights of history, Noel's trip under pressure and with no preparation ranks with the top. Like Lindbergh's crossing of the Atlantic, it was done in a single-engine airplane, and the distances were nearly the same. About the only real difference was that Lindbergh crossed over ocean and Noel had mountains below him all the way, and Noel had Al Lomen and Vic Ross as passengers. On August 17 Noel left Fairbanks in his Bellanca with the Post-Rogers crash pictures and headed for Seattle. He landed at Whitehorse in the gathering darkness, gassed up, headed on down that vast mountain chain for Seattle, flying the single-engine airplane through the night across some of the wildest country on earth, and delivered the pictures to Seattle the next day.

At about the same time the Wiens acquired their first multiengine airplane, a Ford trimotor NG 8419. Noel flew it back from Seattle, Washington, with six passengers. During the next five years Noel flew the Ford, and it was to establish many firsts in Alaskan aviation since from the start it was the first multiengine bush airplane in Alaska. The landing fields were still river bars or just clearings in the brush after you left Weeks Field in Fairbanks. The average size of a good landing area would be 50 feet wide and 1,200 feet long, and the place might have such a name as "No Grub."

In the meantime the business structure of the airline had developed too. On April 14, 1933, they had amended the articles of incorporation to increase their capital stock to two hundred thousand dollars, with fifty thousand dollars of preferred stock, so the airline was then a quarter-million-dollar enterprise. The airplanes owned by the company were the Ford trimotor, the Bellanca, a Fokker Universal, and two Stinsons.

Up to this point, the three brothers had worked together or independently or for other companies or airlines. Now all joined together to form the new company of Wien Alaska Airlines, Inc., which remained its name until 1966, when it was changed to Wien Air Alaska. In 1968 Wien merged with Northern Consolidated to form Wien Consolidated Airline.

Sig's destiny was to lead him into the far Arctic, and his love of the land and people still remains. He started with managing the Wien operation out of Nome; conducting it would be much more accurate, for he did the flying, too! From Nome he worked north as far as Barrow and tied in that most northern village with Fairbanks and all interior Alaska. The name Sig Wien became a byword with all the Arctic Eskimo people and is spoken with pride and reverence by all to this day. Sig knew that the few scattered people of the Arctic wanted and badly needed air service and he set about providing it. This was and still is aviation's greatest challenge in Alaska. Between 1937, when Sig first went to Nome, and 1943, Sig logged 6,500 hours of flying time. Much of it was in the real Arctic. (Incidentally, Nome isn't in the Arctic at all but lies even a little south of Fairbanks, but because it is far to the west on the Bering Sea it approaches Arctic conditions and many of us tend to think of it as "Arctic.") On May 16, 1940, Sig Wien became president and general manager of Wien Alaska Airlines, Inc., a position he held with great ability until, in 1969, he became chairman of the board of Wien Consolidated Airline.

In 1943 the first real comprehensive exploration of the Arctic began when the U.S. Bureau of Mines sent a party to Alaska to explore the oil resources. Sig Wien did the flying for the group using the company's Bellanca. The oil-exploration camp of Umiat was located on the Colville River, and here I met Sig for the first time in 1944, when I was exploring the Colville River and he landed upon the Umiat River bar landing.

Two major factors had affected all Alaskan flying in the late thirties and early forties that set the pattern for modern-day Alaska and Wien Alaska Airlines, Inc. This first was the development of certified routes by the Civil Air Board, and in the second, the strategic importance of Alaska in the air routes of the world as was so clearly demonstrated by World War II.

Aviation developed much after the first commercial flight made by Noel in 1924, and by the late thirties there were a dozen airlines operating out of Fairbanks Ball Park, now grown up into Weeks Field. Scheduled flights between Seattle and Fairbanks were a regular thing, and even the extended runways at the Weeks Field were too short now. There just wasn't enough business for all the airlines, and not much rhyme nor reason either. Into this complex of growing pains stepped the CAB, and blocked out the scheduled and certified air routes. There wasn't really much that they had to go by, so they awarded the routes to the companies who had serviced the different area during the last few weeks. So it was that the Wiens ended up with the air routes of almost all interior and all Arctic Alaska. This suited the Wiens perfectly, since this was the area they had pioneered and served; but some of the other companies came up with rather odd routings.

During the Roosevelt era there also appeared the many government bureaus that were to bring so many headaches, along with orderly development, to Alaskan flying. These were the FAA (Federal Aviation Authority), FCC (Federal Communications Commission) and the CAB. The laws were of course made to govern aviation in such areas as New York City, San Francisco, Miami, and Chicago, where trucks, trains, and water transportation were also involved. When they were applied to Alaska they often sounded ridiculous, to say the least. But the laws had been passed and the Alaskans were bound by them. The airline operators soon found it illegal to do almost anything except breathe gently.

Right on the heels of the new air regulations and certified routes came the pressure of the war; aviation literally mushroomed. The new federal program of developing airfields went into effect, and every community had a new airfield. Aviation literally surged ahead and then redoubled. The postal department began to send all mail by air, and today even parcel post moves by air across all interior Alaska away from the railroad area.

Wien Alaska Airlines, Inc. grew apace with the need for aviation. Two Boeing 247 twin-engine aircraft were purchased in 1944 but, while they served well, their maximum range was four hours and some close calls were had when dealing with Alaskan weather and distances. Longer-range ships were needed, and in 1945 two DC-3's were added to the fleet, and then a third. Then a C-46 cargo airliner and later two more C-46's. In the meantime literally dozens of Cessnas of the 170, 180, and 195 class were in use on short hauls, along with four Super 18 twin-engine Beechcrafts.

As the airline developed so did communications and a

regular radio network came into being. Great changes have taken place since those first independent days when Noel took off and they heard no more from him until he returned; today, entire central and Arctic Alaska are tied together by a radio network, so that airplanes, ground stations, and the central office are in constant contact when radio signals are good.

Each time there was need for some new project in the interior or the Arctic, the Wiens were called upon to handle the operation. In a vast new land where man yet goes as a stranger, this is no small undertaking. When the Distant Early Warning sites (DEW Line) were built, the Wiens were given the job of hauling in the materials and suppying these early sites, and the same was true with the White Alice sites.

By this time Sig had to spend his days just managing the airline; Fritz was vice-president in charge of operations; and Noel had retired from the presidency (in 1940) but still took an active role in the organization. The Wien brothers were dynamic men who liked the flying part of the business, the first-hand helping of their customers and the development of aviation; but the fast growth of the airline forced them into executive roles. When Weeks Field grew too small, the big airline operation was moved to a site six miles southwest of town. This became Fairbanks International Airport. The advent of the jet age was here and intercontinental travel a routine thing. The Wiens built a large modern hangar at the new field, and this became the flight center for interior and Arctic Alaska.

By 1960 Wien Airlines had 66,000 miles of scheduled certified routes that required sixty-five pilots, a hundred mechanics, with a total of nearly three hundred employees and a payroll of two million dollars—the largest commercial payroll in interior and Arctic Alaska. Two Fairchild F-27 turboprop airliners had joined the fleet of airliners, while the smaller bush airplanes were going out and the DC-3's or C-46's began to take their place.

Scientific studies were being carried out on the Arctic ice near the North Pole, and the Wiens once again supplied the equipment and know-how to service them. They purchased a four-motored Constellation to handle this long-range hauling. The need for better bush ships to care for the many customers who still needed the services Noel had first furnished with his Hisso Standard led Sig and Noel and Ada to Switzerland to take part in designing a new airplane that would incorporate all the characteristics of short-field operation that the old Hisso Standard and Bellanca had. From this work came the Polatus Porter, and the Wiens now have ten of these modern single-engine turboprop bush planes that do all that the old Hisso Standards did, only faster, better, and much more economically. The DC-3 and C-46 are on the way out too, and already Sig has new turboprop-powered two-engine transports ready to take their place, while three new jet airliners now make the runs that Noel and Sig pioneered. When the new route from Fairbanks to Whitehorse and Juneau was added, Wien became an international carrier again.

The push was on into the Arctic in search of oil, and once again Wien airliners broke the trail. This presented the same kinds of problems that the Wien brothers have had to solve since their first days of operation, but this time my family and I participated too.

Ada Wien summed things up pretty well when she said of Sig, "It was and still is Sigurd's belief that the people of the Arctic country want and need air service." This statement can be enlarged to include all of Alaska, and it is even more true today than it was in those early days when Noel laid out Alaska's first air routes with the Hisso Standard J1.

5

READING WATER

A floatplane is really an airplane that uses two covered-over speedboats for landing gear. It is a beautifully made machine, light and strong. There is actually a step on the bottom of each float as there is on a speedboat. When the floatplane is at rest it floats because of the water it displaces, but as it gains speed it climbs upon the step and races along as a water skier does. When it has gained enough speed, the wing takes up the load and it changes from a watercraft to an aircraft.

There are but three parts to the process, but, as in playing a console organ, the trick is to do the right thing at the right moment with the right amount of pressure. Unlike the organist who deals with a fixed set of conditions, the floatplane pilot deals with a continuously changing set. Taking off a seaplane is always an audience-participation show, and even the oldest pilots will gather to watch someone take a load off in a seaplane; for while you can bully a wheel airplane or, to a lesser extent, a ski airplane into flying with an overload by just lengthening its run upon the ground, only skill will get a heavily loaded floatplane off regardless of the runway length; and there is a set point at which even skill can't do the job. The set point varies greatly with altitude, wind, temperature, weather and water conditions, so that herein lies a whole new world for the pilot to explore. And the necessary skills to be a sailor, riverboat pilot, water skier, and airplane pilot must combine to make the floatplane pilot. Anyone can fly a lightly loaded seaplane; it is the easiest kind of flying. But those who can handle a maximum load under all conditions are a rare and exclusive breed. Their performances are worth watching, for no matter how good you are, the variables you deal with will keep you on your toes, and your own ideas about yourself will be cut back to size all too often.

There are even a greater number of variables in landing a floatplane, and a pilot's skill in flying shows up faster here on floats than on any kind of gear. The wheel plane and ski plane have spring gear to cushion a landing, but on a floatplane a set of floats is attached solidly to the plane and there is very little give to water when hit at landing speed! So it is that a floatplane pilot must be able to read his water and draw the correct conclusions from what he sees. And even the best make mistakes, but fortunately for pilots the float airplane forgives us about every kind of mistake and hurts our pride more often than anything else.

Floatplanes opened up an unlimited number of landing areas in the north. Float airplanes were a natural to follow the trails of the river voyagers, and, as summer is the ideal time to fly the north, the float airplanes reached about every remote spot first. They attained their highest degree of usefulness in the forties and early fifties, when nearly all interior and Arctic freight was moved by float airplanes in summer. With the advent of an airport at every village, the floatplanes, like the dog teams, began to decline. The airlines eliminated every floatplane they could, and today they are used only by the sportsmen and by the few who still must go where airfields do not exist. And it costs twice as much to haul freight by floats as by the larger wheelcraft.

I received my floatplane license at the old Sea Wings Airport in Westport, Connecticut. I made a few take-offs and landings, and that was it. The instructor showed me how to hold the wheel full back and use full power to get the airplane upon the step, then how to hold it there until it had enough speed to lift off the water. The inspector then rode with me, pronounced me a seaplane pilot, and I have been flying and learning about seaplanes ever since.

From Westport I headed north across Canada to Alaska flying a Cessna 140, and at each landing I talked floatplane flying with every pilot I met. My first landing in Canada was at the Radcliff Air Base near Ottawa. A gale was blowing, piling up enormous waves upon the Ottawa River, and, what looked even worse, a boom of logs had broken loose, filling the river with logs. It was one of my first chances to read rough water from the air. At first I thought the loose logs really had me shut out, and then I realized that they made the water calm in places, like the ice cakes in the

Arctic Ocean prevent wave action, and I landed in among the logs like a duck seeking shelter from the storm. Once on the water I was able to taxi slowly, avoiding the logs, and work my way through the high waves to shore. The Canadian pilots used to the big government-owned flying boats thought my "little kite" quite a novelty and took good care, of me and my tiny floatplane after their greeting of "Mac, we thought you had it that time. We couldn't even see you at times for the waves, you know."

The little floatplane rode the waves like a sea gull. These planes are extremely seaworthy, but there are several Do's and Don't's in floatplane flying. Don't try to turn downwind with power; it will upset you. Just let the wind blow you around, for a floatplane is the best weather vane imaginable and will point into the wind. Don't try to turn a floatplane at all in a high wind; tack and sail it like a sailing ship back and forth to your destination. Don't try taxiing at half throttle and ruin your engine; either taxi slowly or put the airplane upon the step so the engine will run cool. Keep the nose up so the propeller won't pick up spray or waves and spoil the propeller. Don't make any stall landings upon glassy water, for you can't tell where it is and you may be looking at the bottom of a clear lake or a reflection. Don't drift a ship backwards in a high wind without power on or the tail of a heavily loaded floatplane will dig in and the airplane will go down tail-first.

As the older pilots taught me I tried to teach those who followed, and thus when the Reverend John Chambers came to take the Reverend Wartes's place as our second flying missionary out of Barrow, I went over the essentials of flying with him. He had had only a few hours in the air, and every time I thought of something or some situation that could develop I would explain it to John. He was an apt student, and learned his lessons so well that he flew the Arctic for five years without damaging an aircraft.

One windy day in early fall John stopped by our home en route from Barter Island to Barrow. I was away flying at the time, so my son Jim and he went caribou hunting to lay in some meat for the mission's winter supply. Martha waited dinner until late, and then we ate. I was a little worried as I remarked that I had forgotten to tell John not to drift a heavily loaded floatplane without power in a high wind. It was getting dusky at midnight now, and we were about to go to bed when we saw the Cessna 170-B's landing lights as John came onto the lake.

John and Jim had located a herd of caribou some forty miles away and killed three good bulls. They had dressed them out and loaded them in the *Arctic Messenger*. It was getting fairly late and the dew point was near so that all the windows were steamed. John wasn't quite sure where the lake ended in the fading light and had "chopped throttle" on the first take-off run rather than risk hitting the bank. There had been ample room though, so he started to drift back for a second run now that he knew the way his airplane handled with the load, the size of the lake, and the flying conditions. The *Arctic Messenger* was loaded so heavily that the tails of the floats were under water and instead of rising with the waves they dug in, and the next thing John and Jim knew the tail of the airplane was underwater and one wing tip was in the waves. They were turning over! John acted fast. He jumped out and crawled forward to the bow of the high float while at the same time Jim threw caribou meat into the lake. It is quite a ways from one float across to the other, but John managed to leap from one to the other, back and forth, balancing the wave action, and as Jim threw out the last of the caribou meat the tail came above the waves. The *Arctic Messenger* had taken quite a bath, but all was safe.

Just last fall I almost was caught by the same thing when I tried to get off a big lake at high altitude with a full load. It was windier and rougher than I thought, and we picked up speed drifting more than I realized. Next thing I knew we were starting to heel over and the tail was in the water. I hit the starter and the blast from the propeller righted us quickly. Accidents and tight squeezes have no respect for seniority or hours flown.

In a high wind there is always slack water behind the up-wind shore, so land there. In landing on rough water use a full stall so that you have the least possible forward speed; then it will still be rough enough, but the closer you land to the upwind shore the smaller the waves will be. This leads to the problem of making sure you still have enough space left to stop in. If the bank has a gentle slope, you will end up stuck on shore if you cut it too short, and this has happened to many pilots.

Angus Cameron and I were hunting caribou in the Colville River Delta one windy fall day. We had flown clear across the Brooks Range and ended up in a storm where the prairie and ocean met. In that flat land the waves fast get big near the upwind shore and run way up on the prairie on the downwind side. I cut my landing a little too short and we used up the water. A floatplane has two stopping points: first it skis along on the step, next it falls off the step and begins to float. It doesn't go far after this; but just as we were ready to drop off the step, we ran out of water and went ten feet up on the prairie, stopping high and dry.

A floatplane looks big and stands tall on the land. It took us a half hour to push the airplane back into the water! We had eliminated one problem in that landing, though. When you land on the upwind side it is often quite a job to get the airplane shut off and to get out and up on shore to tie the airplane before the wind can drift it back into the water. You usually can put the floats ashore with a little power and stick them, but it would surprise you how a floatplane can work its way loose. It is about five times harder to hold than a boat, so once on shore you have to tie it and then tie it again. Even this may not be enough.

It wasn't enough that night. When I awoke next morning the airplane was gone! At first I couldn't believe it, but there it was—no airplane. Then I made a frantic search across the water and I saw it on the far shore. I made haste around the lake and found it parked with the float tails driven up on the sandy beach; the faithful *Arctic Tern* was bobbing up and down with each breaker as if bowing to them.

In lakes you have only winds and, of course, shallow water to deal with. In rivers there is current as well. When the wind is high and the river crooked, you meet different conditions at every turn, and on take-off a floatplane will fight like a wild horse as winds throw it one way and currents jerk it another. Again an empty plane is little problem, for it has speed and power to spare. A heavy load, though, comes up slowly and leaves the water at stalling speed. Make one mistake here and you are slammed back to earth or you don't make a turn and go up into the brush.

Once Sam White was taking off in a Travelair NC 9844 on floats from a winding, willow-bordered stream. He had the heavily loaded ship on the step gaining speed. This is the float pilot's happy moment when at last the ship is running on the step, but as Sam came into the last bend the wind and current set him over and the old Travelair, always short on rudder control, didn't have rudder enough to straighten him out, so up into the willows he went for nearly fifty yards.

Nothing was hurt except Sam's pride. It took him the rest of the day to unload and get the airplane back in the water. An empty floatplane will pull itself on ice, snow, and sometimes over wet grass or wet willows. But it gets stuck in sand or gravel.

It is always a surprise to land in shallow water. I never have had it happen to me, for I started out in canoes and learned to read the water before I began to fly. Generally the deep water is along the "cut-back" side and the shallow water on the flat sand-bank side. Vegetation, shore shape, birds, color, and ripples all tell water conditions. You can see into the clear lakes of the Arctic and spot rocks or shallows. Rivers betray the presence of rocks and shallows by the surface currents, but experience with an area is your best guide.

Last summer Mark, my son, then six, called to me: "Daddy, that pilot is landing on the runway!"

That statement would have sounded natural except that the ship was a floatplane, and Mark knew it wasn't the right spot to land. Actually, the pilot was landing beside the runway in a body of water that wasn't four inches deep. The Cessna 180 slid along on the step and just stopped. The shore birds that were feeding in the shallow water flew away in alarm, and we worked all day unloading the airplane and wading through knee-deep mud until the evening, when the tide rose a couple of inches with the wind and the pilot could get the plane moving again.

One windy day on the Arctic coast Martha and I landed at a point on the ocean and I jumped ashore to tie up the ship. As I jumped, the plane recoiled and the wind caught it before I could get a rope on it; the airplane was now out of reach and drifting switly out to sea. Martha had never started up the airplane, and as she drifted away I shouted instructions: "Turn the key to the right . . . turn the gas selector to center . . . pull back the throttle or you will take off: the starter is right of the throttle . . . let down the water rudder"—this I could see happen. The ship was now forty yards away, drifting with the angry sea for the North Pole.

"Now pull the starter," I shouted.

The propeller began to turn, stopped, turned again; the engine fired and kept running. Martha was in control now and she guided the ship back to shore again.

Sig Wien had a similar experience at Cross Island, a tiny sand island that lies some ten miles off the Arctic coast. Sig Wien, Cliff Everts, and a mechanic had flown a Norseman floatplane there. They tailed up the floats on the beach and unloaded the plane. The next thing they knew the Norseman was fifty yards from shore drifting out to sea. The coast of Cross Island isn't regular and it looked as if the plane would drift near the last point, so they all raced for it.

The mechanic reached the point first, stripped off his clothes, and jumped into the ocean to swim to the plane that was drifting on past. Instead of swimming he gave a shriek and floundered back out, turning a bright, cooked-lobster red from the freezing water.

Sig had scouted about and found a small piece of driftwood, which he tied to an empty 55-gallon gas drum, and, taking a shovel for a paddle, he straddled the barrel and paddled to the drifting Norseman. With the mechanic's example of just how cold that water was, Sig sat mighty still on the barrel. When he reached the Norseman he left the barrel between the floats, started up the Norseman, and taxied back to the island, saving both airplane and barrel. He was the hero of the moment, since neither Everts nor the mechanic much relished the idea of being marooned on the lonely island.

Anyone who has ever ridden an oil drum in warm water needs no further explanation as to why I believe Sig's feat in catching the airplane is one of the greatest displays of seamanship I know of, but then too Sig had one of the greatest motives I know of!

Wherever floatplanes operate people will gather to see the show, and there is always a show. No machine can match the sheer beauty and grace of a floatplane, nor the joy of handling one. It is a thing alive that responds to the call of the sea and the sky. To the audience is offered the spectator suspense of the bullfight, the beauty of a symphony concert, and the thrill of a steeplechase as the heavily laden floatplane taxis away, often loaded so full with lumber, furniture, tools, and a canoe or even a dog sled tied to the outside floats that there is hardly room for the pilot to get in. The tails of the floats are awash as he makes his way with idling motor away from shore that often is lined with Eskimo whaleboats or Indian riverboats. The sled dogs howl a farewell.

Now the airplane looks like a toy as it turns into the wind on the far shore. "You can't use the runway that's behind you." Then you see white spray fly as the floats rise under full power and a moment later the fighting scream of a flat-pitched propeller driving its hardest under full power sweeps across the water, shaking the world around you and lifting the hair on the back of your neck. The bull has entered the ring, the maestro has lifted his wand, and the horses are off. The pilot is rocking his ship, making it porpoise deliberately, coaxing it to climb upon the step. If he can get it on the step it will fly. The airplane is steady now. It's on the step racing toward the spectators. The angry roar of the engine and the scream of the propeller fill the air, spray boils away, and a rooster-tail plume of spray follows in the sky. The echoes roll from mountain to mountain, and the plane is abreast of the audience. The spray has flattened out, the ship streaks along; and then with a flip the left wing rises, taking the left float off the water. It hangs a moment, and the right wing rises, lifting the airplane clear of the water. Silvery spray trails from the floats for a moment, and the hard-driving tempo of the engine subsides. The ship gathers speed to fade away across the vast horizon into the big sky, and the spectators go back to their work.

The audience always saw a good show when the old float-plane pilots were operating. You were a good pilot if you knew to the pound what your ship would handle under the existing conditions. The shows were mostly funny, even if a pilot blew a "jug" (cylinder) on take-off. It was funny to see a bunch of boats hurry out to haul the airplane back in for repairs. But there was too the element of danger there, and stark tragedy just one slip away.

The list of those whose floats will rise to the surge of power no more is a fairly long one. Some just vanished across the vast horizon into that big sky and were never seen again, as did Stan Fredericksen, Clarence Hodes and his son, Jack, in the Fish and Wildlife Grumman Goose N-720. Others, like Dick Wien, flipped over, swam toward the bottom of the river, realized their mistake, and headed up the right way to pop out on the surface, scared, nearly drowned, but able to climb up on the keels of the floats until picked up.

There is a marker, about fifteen miles southwest of Barrow, in memory of two great floatplane pilots whose show for their Eskimo spectators didn't come off as planned on that cold, foggy day of August 15, 1935.

Wiley Post spent quite a bit of his flying time in Alaska lost, or perhaps confused is a better way of putting it. So it was near Barrow that day. He and Will Rogers were trying to find Barrow, were low on gasoline, and had sighted a tent on the Arctic Coast. I have often followed the coastline into Barrow on a foggy day, and if you know which way the town lies you can fly along just above the grass, following the coastline with only a few hundred feet of visibility. But you do have to know which way to turn, and Wiley Post, not being familiar with the area, had to ask; so he landed and asked Claire Oakpeha. The Eskimo pointed out the direction to Barrow, and Post took off again. They had landed upon a lagoon and took off toward the sea. Fog was low, and in taking off toward the sea they must have run into a completely horizonless world, for instead of turning to the right along the coast for Barrow, they made a 180-degree turn and came right back for the lagoon. With vision in only one eye, the odds were all stacked against Post, and in that land of unreal distances he was in real trouble. I'm sure he would still have handled the situation okay, but he was low on fuel; and as the wing rose in a turn, the engine starved and quit. The *Winnie Mae* was not a good float ship and hard to handle at best even with power; it was a plain killer in a turn at stalling speed with a dead engine. In that awful silence Wiley Post didn't have a chance.

The *Winnie Mae* flipped over and whipped into a graveyard spiral to crash just short of the sand spit into the lagoon with such impact that Post and Rogers never moved from the wreck. The Eskimos waded out to the wreckage and found both men dead. All the little problems, elements, and caprices of Fate had combined in that grassy land where the sea loons call, the ice pack drifts in and out, the freezing waters of the Arctic Ocean lap on the pea-gravel beach, and the prairie wind blows.

Claire Oakpeha ran the fifteen miles to Barrow to carry the news to Charlie Brower and it was relayed by radio to a startled world. Joe Crosson, Wiley Post's old friend and one of Alaska's all-time great pilots, made the flight to Barrow for the bodies of his friends. The Eskimos chanted the death dirge as they rowed back to the wreckage site in their ugrugskin boats. They were afraid to pose beside the wreckage for pictures. Mrs. Post wired Charlie Brower to destroy the entire airplane except the motor, which was to be shipped back to the factory.

Young Tom Brower carried out her wishes. It is ironic that the beautiful aviator's watch Post wore had quit on impact while the simple dollar watch Rogers wore was still running. The burnable parts of the airplane were burned and the rest were sunk in the Arctic Ocean. Nothing was left except for the registration numbers of the *Winnie Mae*. Tom Brower couldn't bear to burn them, so he cut them away with a patch of fabric. Eventually Tom framed the numbers and they hung on the wall of his father's old home now turned into a museum, until a wild storm in 1964 tore out the walls and angry seas carried the numbers away. In the summer of 1965 two little boys found the piece of fabric where the storm had thrown it. The museum was rebuilt and once again the numbers hang on the wall there beside the Arctic sea.

Joe Crosson had flown thirteen hours through bad weather to bring the bodies to Fairbanks in his floatplane. There was a move to award him the Distinguished Flying Cross and the Congressional Medal of Honor, but he wouldn't hear of it, saying that the Eskimo who ran fifteen miles across the prairie had done just as hard work as he and that the whole idea of medals was unwarranted and not in keeping with what he had done. In reality, Joe Crosson's flight to Barrow and Noel Wien's flight south with the pictures (which I recounted in an earlier chapter), which were performed under duress and sorrow and with but scant preparation, rank as two of the greatest flights ever made.

Joe Crosson was said to have been the last man to have talked with Will Rogers before he left Fairbanks. The great humorist Will Rogers' last wisecrack was, "Well boys, I hope we have a forced landing. I won't feel like a sourdough until I Siwash it."

On the shore near that "forced landing" stands the monument built in their memory. It reads, "Will Rogers and Wiley Post, America's Ambassadors of Good Will Ended Life's Flight Here August 15, 1935." I'm sure both old flyers would have approved.

6

TRADING-POST HOPPERS

Wherever gold was discovered a town soon came into being; but this happened only in two major areas, Nome and Fairbanks. The former is on the ocean and was serviced by ships, while a railroad was constructed to serve Fairbanks. There was gold at scattered places on the upper Koyukuk, too, but by the late twenties all that remained were trading posts. The economy of the land was dependent upon the traders and the people they served in their areas. The trader was the head of the community and ordered the necessary goods for his people a year in advance. Whatever came in on the summer boat had to last until the next year. When freeze-up came, traffic stopped. The traders and people welcomed the bush pilots with open arms. The airplanes meant the end of isolation and a continual flow of commerce. Noel Wien was the first to develop a business among the traders, and it is Wien Consolidated (the old Wien Alaska Airlines) today that now carries out almost daily flights to interior and Arctic Alaska. In between there was a long list of pilots, each trying to make a living and make flying pay. Flying attracted all sorts of personalities, among them the renegades who just kept a jump ahead of the law and still do.

Sam White recalls how in the early days, whenever pilots gathered, there was always talk of "hot fur." Actually there was plenty of business waiting to be done without dealing in illegal traffic, and there really wasn't much to be gained by trading in illegally taken furs. But here are some who would rather make a dime illegally than a dollar honestly, and the renegade was always a part of the frontier. Prohibition gave the renegades a real boost, and such men were able to sell liquor at a good profit, exchange it for legal or illegal furs, money, or what have you. Of course all people and all business dealings are known in Alaska. Although it is often thought by the uninformed that Alaska would be a good place for a criminal to hide, in reality it is one of the worst, since everyone is well known and distances are so great that a person's business and reasons for being there are known by all.

The renegades were the tramps of the air, going wherever they could turn a legal or illegal dollar. The airplanes they flew were marvels to behold, whether they were begged, borrowed, or stolen; the only requirement was that they be able to get into the air. Of course, these pilots were but a small percentage of the total, but they filled a need by bringing transportation to a few, entertainment to many, and by giving the rest of the pilots the job of trying to find them—for they were also the "lost" generation of flyers. Some of them were lost so often that it seemed routine to be searching for them. Most were really skillful pilots—they had to be able to keep the airplanes they flew in the air—and would have been able to hold top jobs with the airlines had they just settled down; but they couldn't or wouldn't.

Up until World War II there was one law of the land that not even the renegades violated, and this was that a cache was sacred. Anyone could put up a cache of gasoline, food, or supplies anywhere and it would not be touched by anyone else. The pilots had caches along the routes they flew and depended upon them in times of emergency. Almost anyone would go out of his way to repair someone else's cache.

In Barrow I always shipped in my fuel on the steamship *North Star*. I just left it stacked up on the beach near the mission. There never was enough gasoline in town, but I didn't lose a single gallon. One fall a big storm washed in and my entire year's supply was washed away. The storm scattered drums for twenty miles up and down the beach. I wasn't even in Barrow, but the Reverend Wartes wrote me about it right away. When I returned to Barrow in early October I was surprised to find every battered drum back in place beside the mission. The Eskimos knew my aviation gasoline drums, and when they located one they hauled it in with their dog teams. Most of them just left the drums at my cache site and never even mentioned it, so that I was only able to thank a few of those who took part in the operation. And none would accept any pay for what was often a day's work.

It was quite a contrast to the postwar era when the aerial polar-bear hunters and wolf hunters descended upon Barrow and stole the mission gasoline from beside the mission itself. A drum of gasoline left unguarded in Barrow today doesn't last long. The modern-day renegade has ignored the last taboo; no gasoline cache, nor any cache, is safe anywhere in Alaska from him. He still deals in all sorts of traffic. "Hot fur" always was a myth, and with the decline in the fur prices and a shift of the economy, almost no one traps any more; so there is hardly any legal fur for sale. But a new boom in easy big-game hunts is on, and so the renegade deals in hot big game now whenever he can—along with his other sidelines. He still furnishes entertainment for all, although sometimes it is a little hard to see the humor in it, and he still keeps all the rest of us looking for him; for, like his predecessors, he is still a skillful pilot, but he cares little about his aircraft except that it fly, and the airplane cares little about him too and lets him down regularly.

There were a few pilots like Bill Lavery who used their airplanes to service the trading posts, trappers, miners, and prospectors and who were really a delivery service for their own store. Bill Lavery's first busness was running a store, and flying fit in with this. They were the first generation of pilots. Today Bill Lavery flies the same air lanes his father pioneered. The Jameses' son, [Johnny], tried to use flying in connection with the trading post at Hughes, too, after World War II. He was moderately successful. He purchased a Stinson Station Wagon and hauled produce from Fairbanks, delivered orders along the Koyukuk, and finally loaned his airplane to his friend Billie Levy at Kotzebue. Bill flew it for a year, trying to make a go of bush flying, until he was killed in a crash during a bad fog near Shishmaref. It was the time of scheduled air operations expansion, and the end of the trading-post hoppers. Johnny and I used to talk flying in the trading post at Hughes before he learned to fly even. Before he loaned his airplane he said, "If you can't lick them then join them"; he was referring to the steadily increasing scheduled airline service with lower and lower rates. In a few years the air-freight rate dropped from twenty cents a pound to seven cents, Fairbanks to Hughes, and from thirty-five cents a pound to fifteen cents, Fairbanks to Barrow. So Johnny hired out to Wien Alaska Airlines and flew out of Kotzebue for a few seasons. In the meantime he had married Agnes, the pretty nurse at Kotzebue. Johnny kept on flying the bush, but as their children came along Agnes liked less and less to have Johnny flying. The dangers of bush flying loom up out of proportion, but the fact remains they are very real, and the radio messages are hard for a wife to live with. When her husband is delayed a few minutes she is afraid to listen to the radio, and when the minutes become hours she suspects every person or group of having a message for her that she doesn't want to hear; and so she keeps after her husband to find some other work. Johnny gave up flying in the mid-1950's and joined the FAA.

There were all sorts of pilots in the early days, and traders too; and then there was and still is Archie Ferguson.* Most are remembered in the North because of the things they did, flights they made, or enterprises founded. Archie could be remembered for any of these, but he isn't; he is remembered because he was "Archie Ferguson."

The Ferguson family came to Alaska in 1917 when times were hard for them "outside." Archie went back "outside" as far as Seattle a few times, but each time headed right back home as fast as possible, not caring "nawthin' " for the rattletrap, hurry-up lives and people he saw there. "Oh God, I'd die outside" were Archie's words about that "snarled-up mass of humanity."

He was a little fellow as size goes—short and built like a potato, with an unruly shock of hair, dimpled cheeks, a determined smile, and boundless energy. Couple this with a keen mind, an iron will, and a bubbling-over love of flying and you had Archie Ferguson. Into that short, solid frame went the courage and humor that would have been enough for a dozen ordinary men. Archie was literally afraid of "nawthin' "—man, animal, machine, country, or any combination thereof.

Archie and his brother, Warren, worked in mines, drove dogs, and trapped far into the Arctic. Both married Eskimo women. The entire Ferguson clan was hard-working and finally they settled at Kotzebue, where they opened trading posts, built a sawmill, tried mink farming, kept a cow, tried raising turkeys, opened a motion-picture house, bought a motorcycle and put it on skis and went tearing across the sea ice between villages, opened gold mines, ran a restaurant and hotel—in short, they built an empire. They brought the first automobile to that part of the world and ran it on the

---

* EDITOR'S NOTE: Archie Ferguson died on February 4, 1967, at the age of seventy-two, and is buried in Kotzebue.

sea ice between villages. In 1939 Warren came to a tragic end when he went through the ice in the automobile and drowned. Warren and his parents are buried at Kotzebue.

Archie says he first decided to fly when he was riding the motorcycle across the sea ice. He came to an open crack four feet wide. There was no way across, so he made a ramp of hard-packed snow, backed up, and hit it full speed. The motorcycle sailed through the air and lit ten feet on the other side.

Archie took his first airplane ride in 1926 with Noel Wien in a Hisso Standard. It was an open plane. Noel looped the loop, and Archie felt sure he would fall out; he had gripped the sides so tightly he could hardly get his hands loose even after they landed. In Archie's words, "Christ, I was scared."

In 1931 the Fergusons bought a Great Lakes Trainer and had it shipped to Kotzebue. Pilot Chet Browne of Colorado had run an ad in a magazine and they hired him to teach Archie to fly. Then followed sixty hours of instruction, and Browne felt Archie still needed more; but Archie felt he knew enough about flying and was ready. Chet Browne wasn't sure how he would ever get his student back down again, as Archie "just loved to fly" and might stay up until he ran out of gasoline. So he put an alarm clock under the seat telling Archie to land when the alarm went off. Archie made a nice take-off and flew about over town having a fine time and, as Browne had suspected, plumb forgot about time and his landing instructions. When the alarm clock went off Archie almost bailed out; the plane nearly got away from him, and he was very frightened because he thought something was wrong with the airplane, so he landed upon a sand bar instead of the airfield.

From here on Archie went at flying in the same way as he had every other enterprise, only flying was an obsession with him. He didn't take the time to learn to fly because he was so busy flying. It woud be about right to say that Archie was the worst pilot and the "flyingest" man in North Alaska. But Archie had one big advantage over all other pilots: he knew the land, for he had driven a dog team or run a river-boat over it all. He understood the weather like a sea gull, and he knew machines. He had so many things going at the same time that it was no wonder he just started using airplanes and never learned to fly.

Archie handled his vast enterprises like popcorn in a popper. One evening I landed in Kotzebue and Archie was there with a little Caterpillar and a load of gasoline to fuel up my ship. Soon I found him at his restaurant and he served me dinner and talked, steadily hopping from behind the counter up to a stool and onto another stool while keeping up a stream of questions, answering most of them himself. He was at the hotel when I registered, and later that evening in the movie theater the picture suddenly sagged as the screen fell down, and when the lights went on Archie was already tying the loose end of the screen back in place. When I went to bed about midnight Archie was feeding some turkeys he had in a pen ("goin' to raise mah own Thanksgiving"), and a moment later he was driving his pickup loaded with gear down the beach in the red rays of the northern sun. I was up at 4 A.M., ready to depart, and Archie was already out working. All the rest of the town was asleep. An Eskimo village sleeps until noon or later, and unless you are careful you develop the habit of always getting up late. Archie's pilot was still sacked in and Archie complained, "Oh Jeezus, that Zulu could have made a trip already; he's snoozin' when there's work to do."

Archie's first commercial flight was to set the pattern for his flying. He took Jimmy Donovan from Kotzebue to Shungnak, where the elder Fergusons were operating a trading post. Archie wasn't sure of the wind, but he tried to land on a smooth spot in the Kobuk River, overshot, and hit the next bend. Every landing he has ever made was a controlled crash, and as Archie once told a radio operator during the war when Archie asked for uncoded weather and the operator said he couldn't give such weather except in an emergency, "Jeezus Christ, any time I'm up in the air it's an emergency."

Out of that first commercial flight Ferguson Airways developed. More pilots were hired to teach Archie to fly and to fly for Archie. "The Ferguson College of Technical Knowledge" saw a steady stream of pilots. Money was always "sumptin' to buy with," and Archie paid his pilots well. Archie didn't do anything without pay, and he didn't expect anything done without paying for it. His yearly income climbed toward the quarter-million-dollar mark from his enterprises and it poured right back into the country again, for Archie spent the money right where he made it—a rare thing indeed in Alaskan history, for nearly everyone wanted to make a fortune and then leave. Archie was strict with his pilots, too. He knew what all the successful ones knew—no pilot could handle liquor; it always handled them. And smoking and drinking Archie didn't do and didn't allow.

The British system of government allows for and hires its opposition to oppose any project. In the Arctic it wasn't necessary to do this, for it had Archie Ferguson, as the officials of every big government-founded project soon discovered. Listening to the stories about Archie was always inspiring and fascinating because he represented that fresh approach to life that reminds one of a barefoot boy crawling through a fence with a can of worms and fishing pole although a sign posted reads "NO FISHING" and "BEWARE OF BAD BULL"; in the distance you can see the bull and the sheriff, but you know the boy will get around it all and go fishing—he is on his way.

The first government agency to cross Archie was the FCC. Archie and his brother built their own wireless sets out of old Model T Ford spark coils, hooked them up to antennas; then they and their Eskimo wives learned the Morse code and went on the air. Other ham stations joined in. It was a happy time in the Arctic, and gossip, curse words, and news crackled across the Arctic skies, but the powerful homemade sets blanked out the rest of Alaska too, and the marshal made them give up that enterprise.

About then Archie printed his own money, too; not counterfeit—Archie never imitated anything or anyone. He printed his own trade money, a big coin with "FERGUSON STORES" printed on it, and some are still floating around the western Arctic.

It was about time for flying regulations and some navigational aids in Alaska, and the CAA set them up. In its officious way the bureau crossed Archie at every turn, and in each encounter it came off second best. Radios were for talking over or for carrying on the argument with his wife that he had started in the morning; Archie would dispute with her all day by air. Hadley, his wife, the granddaughter of an early chief, could handle a radio with the best; she also ran the Ferguson Trading Post and the airline too, although she had little use for Archie's flying (she would go tearing about the ice pack with him on the motorcycle, but never in an airplane). With an Eskimo's complete innocence of profanity, and Archie's complete disregard of it, they turned family spats into a regular airway's comedy, while monopolizing a quarter of an hour of public air space at a time. Archie would call this station or that and begin to chat, just as if he were in an old saloon. If some station were a little slow answering, he would read them out: "What'cha doin', boozin' it up? Snoozin' it up down there, or God knows what you're up to. The weather's fine up here, I'm flying right up the Kobuk River . . ." And he would go on describing his trip as if it was the most interesting thing happening in Alaska at the moment—and it usually was. He might end with, "Jeezus it's hot today. I'm thirsty . . . wish I had a watermelon . . . Christ I love watermelons."

Scientific air navigation and radio beams were so much rubbish to Archie. He never trusted them, never used them, and didn't believe them. He didn't mind telling the CAA (later the FAA) that their damn radio towers, wires, and gear around the airfields were "one helluva hazard" to flying. They made the real navigation aids like crooked streams and dogteam trails dangerous to follow! "If the CAA keeps improving the airways with their damn towers and wires, the only way we can fly in Alaska is underground," he wrote.

When the Army descended upon Alaska, Archie didn't like it one bit and made the "brass mounted boys" say "uncle" at every turn. One Army engineer started building a power line right across Archie's airfield. Archie jumped in his little airplane and headed right off to see the general. Work was stopped on that project promptly.

The big military airports were a farce to Archie. One time he landed at Galena. He tried to follow the regulations, and they held him up an hour getting weather information and red tape by the basketful. He got so much unwanted help that he was afraid it would get dark before he could get out. At last they gave him a clearance for Fairbanks, but he didn't know what to do with it. He asked a half dozen people to take it, but none wanted it, so he gave it to a ditchdigger and departed. When he arrived in Fairbank they jumped all over him for leaving Galena without the proper clearance. "Oh Christ. If I ever go back there again I'm gonna land on a sand bar," he told them.

The precise air-navigation logbooks were something Archie paid no attention to. While men like Noel Wien and Sam White loved the airplanes and flew them as a concert violinist plays a violin, Archie used airplanes as a bass drummer beats a drum. Airplanes were repairable and replaceable. Flying was a thrill, airplanes a way to fly. He went through a dozen airplanes in less than a dozen years! Archie would crash an airplane in the way a Hollywood stuntman might, while such things as a 40-pound battery and cargo flew past him like bullets. Yet in all his crashes he never killed a passenger or hurt himself beyond repair.

Aside from the dozen busters where the airplanes were complete wrecks, there were litrally dozens of near-smashups. Archie was a mechanical wizard. He knew machines and what can make them perform, not for the machine's sake but for performance's sake. Landing upon thin ice once, he broke through and knocked four inches off one end of a wooden propeller. Archie just took his ax and carefully cut an equal amount off the other end of the blade to balance it; this made the passengers nervous. The airplane took four miles of river ice to get off, but it flew and took him back to Kotzebue safely too!

Once Archie landed his Cessna on a short river bar at Kiana. The water rose and soon the airship was underwater and the airplane belly-deep. With the help of some Eskimo women he managed to work the airplane up on a small river barge. They blocked the wheels and tied the Cessna tight. Then the women climbed upon the barge, Archie started up the engine and, old riverboatman that he was, he took this airplane-barge hybrid roaring up the river to an unflooded bar, where he docked, ran the airplane ashore, and took off again.

He tried wolf hunting from the air and shot the end off the pinning propeller the first crack. The airplane crashed and Archie had another repair job. Archie used an airplane like he used a riverboat; he made it perform, not by careful shepherding love and skill but by making the damn thing do what he wanted it to, when he wanted it to!

He darn near "bought the farm" and all the rest one winter day when he tried to bully an ice-laden plane under full throttle through fog across from Fairbanks to Kotzebue. Patty James likes to tell about it, since she played an important role in it. It is known as "The Rescue of the Swearing Parrot," although there wasn't even a parrot aboard.

Archie had ordered the bird from "outside" and it had been trained by sailors, so it knew every cuss word in the English language. That was several years before the accident. Archie and his pilot, Maurice King, were flying from Fairbanks to Kotzebue when they ran into what Archie claimed was the roughest air he had ever seen, and it must have been bad. Maurice King was fighting the ship to keep it from being torn up while Archie was just busy trying to control the parrot. The parrot was screaming and calling them every name imaginable, blaming them for the rough air. It never did forgive Archie and hated him to its end, which came fast when Archie's big black dog, Sunday, caught it and ate it three days later.

It was in the winter of 1941 that Patty heard Archie radio: "Hughes Radio—put the coffeepot on."

"Hello, Archie—where are you?"

"Never mind where I'm at. Put that coffeepot on."

Hughes is hard to find on that flight, and Archie didn't know for sure where he was "at." He thought in ten minutes he would have figured it out, though, so he hopefully sent the message. Meantime he was tearing along all iced up at treetop level in ice fog. Before the ten minutes were up, Archie couldn't hold the airplane any more. One wing hit a tree, the plane swung around and crashed out of control in a flat half turn during which the wing sheared off and the engine ripped free of the airplane.

Archie sat unconscious, crumpled against the instrument panel, his broken arm sticking out the windshield and dangling where the motor used to be. Oil from the departing engine had spattered him like blood, and there he sat, the picture of sudden death. His two passengers, a doctor and a restaurateur from Fairbanks, thought he was gone. And Archie, not one to be still long, came to as they were talking about his being dead.

"Christ, I thought they were right and I really was dead."

Then he reached to shut off the switches and saw he didn't have a workable arm to reach with; and on second thought there wasn't a switch to turn off, for the radio had torn loose with the engine.

On taking stock, 'most anyone else would have decided they were better off dead. They were a hundred miles from Hughes or anywhere else, there was no grub, one sleeping bag, no gun, and one pair of snowshoes in deep snow at 20 degrees below zero. Luckily no one else was badly hurt. Meanwhile Patty James was calling steadily, and soon other stations hearing her plea took up he calls. There was urgency in the calls now. All the stations called again and again. Someone might reach him, someone might find his whereabouts. The minutes drawled into hours, and the silence lengthened. At last the gasoline-on-board limit was passed, and all knew Archie was down somewhere. That it was a crash no one doubted because of the radio silence, and so the coffeepot boiled dry on the stove. Darkness comes quickly in midwinter, and all in interior Alaska wondered. At a time like this you are a little edgy. The children have to be quieter than usual, for at any moment a faint radio signal might come through, for somewhere out in that great white world help is needed. You know it for sure, but where?

As soon as Archie found he wasn't dead, he was his old cheerful self, even with the broken arm. He began chopping trees and making a snowhouse. When the weather cleared, he realized he wasn't anywhere near where he had thought he was. The days passed and the search planes looked around Hughes, where, of course, Archie wasn't. They all got plenty hungry, and Archie started looking for a bear's den and somehow lucked onto one. This was surely quite a feat, since you might spend a lifetime in that area and never find a winter bear's den. Archie couldn't very well handle the bears alone with but one arm, so he took the doctor and restaurateur back with him. They cleared away the brush and prepared for battle. Archie got a stick and gave one man the ax. Then Archie got up on the den and began to punch the bears. "There's two of them," he yelled. "Oh Jeezus, here they come."

The passengers never knew if there were bears in the den or not, they didn't wait to see. They stampeded back to the airplane. Archie was indignant and floundered after them. They were even more outraged.

"You got us into enough trouble, you're not going to get us into any more," they emphatically told him. And they refused to go back to the bear's den again.

Archie decided the only way out was by using the torn-up radio, so with his one good arm he slowly retraced the currents and patched the radio back together. The battery was frozen solid of course, and a frozen battery is useless. Archie remembered his riverboat days when he had heated a battery to get a last gasp of life from it. He lit a fire and carefully heated the battery, and it worked. His radio repair job worked too, and a voice from Fairbanks answered, "Archie, we hear you. They are searching for you. What's your position?" He tried to answer, but the battery had given its all.

Archie knew that a battery that sits a few days will also pick up a little charge if you can keep it warm, and so he waited a few more days. The grub was all gone and the men wouldn't tackle the bears. They were still awfully hungry. Archie knew that the law of "pecking rights" starts at the bottom and, being the smallest, he got to thinking his passengers might decide to eat him. So he kept the snowshoes handy in case they tried. He knew that with him on the only snowshoes, they would not be able to catch him. He lay awake all night too.

On the fifth day, Archie figured the battery had reached its peak and it was then or never. "Tell Maurice King we are where we had the trouble with the parrot." It was all the battery was good for, but it worked. King never forgot the rough air at that spot and the profane parrot. The search planes flew directly to where the wreck lay.

There are not many who could have cared for the passengers, repaired a radio, and nursed a frozen dead battery through. Even if some could have surmounted the first two obstacles, they wouldn't have had the self-control at the last moment to run the calculated risk and make every word count.

Archie was determined to salvage that airplane. He hired a crew of Eskimos and sixty dogs, and the cut a trail two hundred miles across the wilds to haul the entire plane back. The motor was unhurt; Archie rebuilt the wings, ordered parts from the factory, and had her going good as new. His arm healed in the meantime and then he was back in the air.

I was in Duane Wallace's office at the Cessna aircraft factory in Wichita, Kansas, one day. The aircraft business was slow and they were even making office furniture to keep going. Soft-spoken, Abraham Lincoln-like Duane Wallace was carefully guiding his company along. We were discussing a picture he had under the glass top of his desk: it was of Sig Wien in a Cessna 195 and me in our Cessna 140 on the shore of the Arctic Ocean. I was on floats tied up to the land. Sig had landed on the beach and taxied up beside my plane. Sig thought Duane would like to see the two explorers' Cessnas together, took a picture of them, and sent it Duane. It was the first time I had seen the printed picture.

"You have a pilot up there at Kotzebue who uses quite a few Cessnas too," Duane went on. "I had a letter from him a little while ago. Do you know him?"

"That must be Archie Ferguson," I said. "Sure I know him."

"He must be quite a fellow. He wants to buy a dozen airframes of the Cessna 195, and instead of the 300 Jacobs engine he wants to bolt a 450 Pratt and Whitney on. I'm afraid the CAA wouldn't go for it," Duane said thoughtfully.

Archie didn't care if the CAA or anyone else didn't go for it. He never broke the rules; he just didn't bother to find out if they were there. He knew what many years later former President Dwight D. Eisenhower put into words: "I simply don't believe it is possible to make laws centrally that can completely and wisely govern a nation as big as ours."* This making of arbitrary laws for the South Forty-eight and applying them to Alaska has been the hardest burden the North Alaskans have had to bear. Archie instinctively knew these laws were made without even knowing about the people who were there. He paid those laws and the officials who tried to enforce them just as much mind as they had him when they passed those laws.

Archie was a practical joker with a purpose, an industrial genius, the "trading-post-hoppingest" pilot of them all, a breath of fresh air in a crowding world, and, in his own words, "Jeezus, he just loved to fly"—and, like the little red hen, he did.

7

JACK-OF-ALL-TRADES AND MASTER OF MOST

The development of a new land requires many people with a variety of skills. It is said that in the early days of the Old West a mountain man stopped to talk to a wagon train. The wagonmaster said they were going to a new land in Oregon and further mentioned that there were skilled artisans of every trade in the train. Each man could start a new business in his own field, and every man was useful. As they stood talking, the mountain man tried to figure out what one old man here possibly could be useful for, since it didn't look as if he would do much more than make it to the end of the trail.

"What's that old fellow good for?"

"Well, he has a place, too. We're going to start our graveyard with him."

In the bush pilot all the necessary skills had to be combined in one man, and if he proved not to have the qualifications they enlarged the graveyard with him—that is, if they could find him.

A review of the Congressional Medal of Honor awards shows that nearly all have gone to men from ranches, farms, or very small towns, with almost none from large cities. The same thing is true of Alaska's bush pilots; nearly all came from the farms, ranches, or small towns. The reason for this is simple; it is these environments that teach self-reliance and initiative, and out of these come courage.

Central and Arctic Alaska was the toughest, most hostile, and vastest land Americans ever entered—not because these qualities were inherent in the land, but because the newcomers did not understand it. Dr. Vilhjalmur Stefansson, the most important Arctic explorer of them all, called the very toughest part of Alaska and Canada "The Friendly Arctic." Stefansson was the greatest explorer because he brought understanding to the land. He found a way not only to cross and explore the land but also to live there with what the land had available. In so doing, as he many times pointed out, he only succeeded in accomplishing what the native people already had done since before the advent of recorded history. This is exactly what the bush pilots had to do, each in his own way; each had to fit in his airplane, care for it, and make it pay.

Sam White's flying typifies the skills needed to make a trip in the early days. Sam left Fairbanks for Wiseman and returned in his Swallow biplane NC422N. It was one of those trips when almost everything goes wrong. It was cold and in the dark days of winter when it is hard to dress warm enough in the −40- to −60-degree air to keep warm walking, and to keep warm in an open cockpit airplane is a real chore. As Sam puts it, the Swallow's range and his freezing-up point were about the same.

Ice fog often hides the country by day and north of the Arctic Circle where Wiseman lies the sun doesn't rise in mid-winter, so it is just as easy to fly by moonlight after the twilight day is past.

That day Sam picked up a load of mail and some gold-dust pokes to take back to Fairbanks, and then he headed off. He was flying along peacefully, enjoying the flight and the moonlight beauty of the Arctic as only an old dog driver can, when the motor quit dead. Sam was flying near the Koyukuk River and a couple of miles back he had passed a trapper cabin, so he picked the most likely looking spot, squeezed across the trees, and plunked into two feet of powdery snow in the below-zero air. The bar was too short. The Swallow was on skis, and it plowed over the bar across a frozen river channel and up on another bar, stopping as pretty as you please. ("Couldn't have done better with a tractor" was Sam's comment.) Sam climbed out, took stock of the situation, and headed for the cabin on his snowshoes. It was just 11 P.M. when he knocked upon the door of his old friend Pete's cabin.

It was a snug cabin of ten by twelve feet built of spruce logs in a lovely setting. Pete had a bad leg and was well along in years. By the light of the candle Sam saw a battered Yukon stove in one corner, a bunk across the back, and a table. The Yukon stove was burned through in several places on top and flattened-out tin cans were laid across the holes. You could regulate the draft in the stove by moving the cans, and you had to be careful in your cooking not to dislodge the cans and burn up your wood too fast. Pete was living on rabbits mostly, and for breakfast next morning Pete and Sam ate up the last of the "store grub," which consisted of a few hotcakes and some "Bayo beans." Sam had a good supply of grub in his plane. After breakfast he walked back to the airplane and tied her down tightly, trapping wooden toggles in the snow to tie her in the same manner we tie up a dog team or anchor a wolf trap. Then he tied the control surfaces on wings and tail so a wind wouldn't damage them, and covered the open cockpit so it wouldn't get full of snow. Then he took the pokes of gold, some gear, grub, and headed back toward Wiseman ten miles up the river.

At Pete's cabin Sam left the grub and paid Pete thirty dollars to cut a cord of dry spruce wood and stack it beside the airplane. The ten-mile walk to Wiseman wasn't much of a problem, but the heavy poke of gold was. No matter how Sam packed it, the solid lump was hard to carry, and it whacked Sam at every step. Two days later an airplane came into Wiseman and Sam was lucky to get a ride back to Fairbanks.

Herhm Joslyn was one of the famous early-day pilots who in later years flew for Pan American. He took Sam and a new motor; Ted Hoffman, a master mechanic; and Johnny Paul, a Weather Bureau man, back to the bar, where he landed them right beside Sam's Swallow. They had taken along sleeping bags and a big tent. Herhm Joslyn left soon after, before his engine froze up. The crew got busy and pitched a big tent right over the engine of the airplane, set up an airtight heater, and moved into the other end of the tent. Sam had taken along a gasoline lantern, and with the dry wood Pete had cut they had a good fire and a snug camp. Spruce boughs made good beds with their sleeping bags over them. In the quiet Arctic night they could hear the wolves howling around the camp.

The next day the motor was all warmed up nicely and they soon had the old engine off and the new one in its place. Sam started the ship up and then moved it and all the camp gear up to Pete's place. Pete had gone up to Wiseman for a while, so they set to modernizing Pete's cabin with the new airtight heater and Coleman gasoline lantern. Sam's willing crew did this while Sam was checking over the airplane and making it safe for the night. He walked back to the old camp to gather up gear he hadn't been able to bring in the airplane.

When Sam returned he found a real frenzy of frontier log-cabin cleaning going on. When the new stove was fired up, the cabin was heated nicely as never before, and an awful stench rose from the floor. The gasoline lantern lit up the scene as Pete's candle never had, and it revealed the source of the stench. Rabbit entrails, heads, and hides were trampled into the spruce-bough flooring, so that the entire floor of boughs had to be hauled out and new, fresh-smelling ones replaced them. The blood-soaked table top defied all efforts to clean it up, so the crew just planed off the plank surface with a sharp ax. With the housekeeping job all finished, they cooked up a good meal and slept snugly as the airtight heater kept the cabin at an even warm temperature all night long.

The next morning Sam flew the men to Wiseman and left Pete's cabin all slick and neat, with a good stock of grub too. Martin Slisco ran a roadhouse there, and he decided to have a dance in honor of Sam's getting his airplane back in the air, all in the manner of frontier fun. This was easily arranged by just ringing the big bell, and all in the village gathered. Someone played an accordion, another played a violin, and a third a guitar. There were but two unmarried native girls in the village, and they never left the dance floor. After the dance Martin served free lunch.

The next day a plane came across from Fairbanks, so Johnny Paul and Ted Hoffman caught a ride back to Fairbanks, Herhm Joslyn remained at Bettles awhile, and Sam started back for Fairbanks by way of Bettles and Alatna, expecting to go right on across. This time the weather caught Sam at Dahl River. The Yukon was all "socked in" with ground fog on the hills and a heavy overcast toward Fairbanks, so Sam found a hole through it and landed at an old cabin on Dahl River. Ten minutes later it was solid fog everywhere.

Sam once again tied up and put his ship to bed and then got the old cabin all warmed up. He just had things nicely under control when two Indian trappers came by. They had shot a lynx, which they skinned and cut up on the table. They cooked up the meat and ate without the benefit of washing their hands or cleaning off the table. Lynx cats have fleas, and Sam felt all "ten million fleas" migrate to him. They chewed him up worse than the cooties of his trench-warfare days in the A.E.F. Luckily, lynx fleas won't live on people; they just chew them up for a half day and then leave.

The fog was thick as ever the next day, but Sam didn't care for the trappers or their lynx fleas, so he walked the six miles to Stevens village and spent the night with the honest old trader Dave Drolette. Dave was happy to have company and served up some excellent moose stew along with tales of the early prospecting days and life along the Yukon River. One story told that the big pike in the river often ate full-grown muskrats and young ducks. Sam doubted this a little at the time, but later events proved Dave right, for during Sam's years as a game warden he found full-grown muskrats in the stomachs of large pike.

The next day a wind blew the fog away, and Sam walked back to the airplane, heated it up, and flew into Fairbanks without trouble. Sam told his wife about the lynx fleas, but she wouldn't believe his story that after a few bites of him the fleas dropped dead and he had to go through a full delousing campaign.

In bush flying you had to make do with what there was at hand in order to get your airplane back safely. One pilot landed at Tanana and tore some fabric loose from his airplane. It was way below zero and he didn't have any glue to fix the rip with, so he took a piece of bed sheeting, some warm water, and froze the fabric in place. It held until he reached Fairbanks.

If the airplane or the pilot didn't need some special attention along the route, the customers usually did. There was always something that needed fixing or some problem to diagnose. The spring breakups often flooded the villages, putting everything under muddy water. Since ice jams usually caused these floods, the water rose fast and about all the time the people had was enough to get camp gear up in a cache or to the nearest high ground. When the water dropped it left its ring of mud to mark its highest point, and everything was wet and covered with river mud. Washing machines, refrigerators, light plants—whatever is used in daily living I have had a try at fixing. All we pilots got a world of on-the-job training, and we rarely failed to get the machine running or the necessary parts ordered. Everyone liked to have a pilot stuck by weather for a few days so that the odd jobs needing tending could get done. The native people have a great deal of faith in the spark of a magneto, and any time a motor wouldn't start it is the magneto that gets taken apart first. I sometimes feel as if I have looked at every magneto in North Alaska!

Bettles was quite a prosperous little village until 1943, when the CAA decided it would build an airfield there; but no suitable site for a modern airfield could be found. The final decision to build the airfield across the Koyukuk River and six miles upriver spelled the eventual end of Bettles.

I first saw Bettles when I was on my way to the Arctic coast in 1943. A construction crew was busy tearing up the land with bulldozers and carryalls, hauling gravel and making a runway. Their camp was upon the riverbank and the crews worked the day-round. Bettles Field, as the new settlement was called, was a link in the airfield chain into the Arctic. At the same time airfields were being built at Umiat and Barrow, tying this part of the Arctic in with Central Alaska and opening the way for the oil exploration work to follow.

The new airfields also spelled the end of the old breed of bush pilots, for DC-3's and C-46's appeared on the scene to take over the freighting between towns now as modern airfields appeared. The Wiens purchased their first twin-engine Boeings and a DC-3 soon after.

Wien Airways put up a new air station at Bettles Field to service the surrounding area and haul freight up and down river. They put up log living accommodations combined with a roadhouse. James L. Anderson ("Andy") and his pretty wife, Hanna, settled down there to run it. Andy came from a farm in Pennsylvania and Hanna had been born at Bettles. Andy had come to Bettles with the CAA. He took over the bush flying, and in a sense he could be termed a bush pilot. Andy is of that breed of men who would have been one of the great early pilots, but he came into a new era. It wasn't long before "Andy" became a byword, synonymous with dependability, to everyone in the Koyukuk region, from the oldest trader to the youngest Indian. The Hamilton Standards and Swallows were gone; the Norsemen and Cessnas had taken their place, and it was with these last two types of airplanes that Andy serviced his district. No pilot in all Alaska put in more flying hours each day than Andy, and none took a more personal interest in each person in his area. When you asked Andy a question, you got a direct and accurate answer. If he told you he would be there at a certain time, you could almost set your watch by his arrival, "weather permitting," and with Andy weather was nearly always permitting.

Andy's day began early; you might hear him fill his flight plan from Bettles to Hog River and Kotzebue at 6 A.M. as he took off, and all day long you would hear Andy flying. That evening as you were ready to go to bed, you would hear Andy still in the air somewhere heading for Fairbanks, perhaps to exchange an airplane at the Wien hangar for a freshly overhauled one.

The remarkable thing about Bettles Field was the organization of the entire setup. Hanna managed the hotel, which was the nearest thing to an old-time roadhouse left with the air-age twist. Hanna also managed the radio at times. Bettles Field sits back in the brush away from the riverbank, and there is nothing to recommend it aside from the neat gravel runway and the row of neat FAA buildings on the east side, with the equally neat Wien Station at the north end of the buildings. Andy kept the place just like that, too —neat and orderly. In all the years I have known Andy never have I seen him idle. With his mechanic and helper, "Canuk," and his loader, Frank Tobuck, Andy ran the most efficient bush operation Wiens had. And it stayed that way. Andy brought sound business management to the bush flying operation and it was the beginning of a new era of flying. Unlike Archie Ferguson, who understood and loved the land like the native-born and flew without ever taking time to learn to fly, Andy was a superb pilot who used every modern means of navigating and flying and never did learn to like the country. His heart was always in his beloved farm in Pennsylvania, where he wanted to be from the time he started flying in Alaska. But as the love of gold held Robert Service's Sam McGhee "like a spell," the vast Arctic held Andy's flying interest. So it was that this jack-of-all-trades took a new gravel CAA strip carved out of the Arctic brush and a few small airplanes and built it into a solid, sound business enterprise, ending forever the day of the bush pilot and opening the door to the future.

8

WEATHER EXPERIENCES

Pilots still put on shows for their audiences. The people of all Alaska admire the pilots who serve them and take pride in their accomplishments. It is also sort of a sport and, as in the bull ring, the closer the matador comes to the bull's horns without getting hooked the greater the suspense—and so it was and is with the pilots. The pilots, unlike matadors, certainly don't plan it that way; they like nothing better than calm, clear flying, but days aren't always fair, and frequently they get called out of their element.

The weather of the Arctic regions around the world is a paradox. For the high-flying airliner it is the easiest and smoothest flying anywhere in the world the year-round, with the smoothest, clearest air possible, and this can be the case on the ground. Thunderstorms and the violent cumulus clouds are absent, as we don't have the extreme fronts to create them. Tornadoes and violent storms are absent, too. There are steady winds sometimes, but not violent weather as in the south and central climates. So it is that those who fly the airlines of the Arctic ride smooth, storm-free air.

The bush pilot who makes his way over the rough terrain meets other problems. When the prairie winds sweep inland and go tumbling across the mountains, it creates air as rough as a waterfall for him and his small airplane; the shifting fog of the sea can roll in, blanketing his world with "soup" a few hundred feet deep and impenetrable to vision. The temperature inversion that makes it colder at ground level than just a few hundred feet up makes him operate in way below zero conditions, while the airliners ride the smooth, warmer air aloft and the bush pilot's small airplane is leaving contrails above the treetops. Then the whiteouts of spring and winter leave him groping through a world of such brilliant light that he can't see anything. Added to this is the fact that the early pilots used landplanes, seaplanes, and ski planes in a land that has the greatest temperature variations of all—from 100 above to 80 below zero—and light conditions that vary from continuous daylight in summer to continuous darkness of midwinter. It is a land of contrast and change. It is no wonder that the old pilots were all weather-wise.

It didn't take the first pilots long to realize that frost on the wings would keep an airplane from flying. It looked so harmless and on a cold morning in early fall a pilot might just ignore it, but after a few airplanes went into the brush instead of flying at the end of the runway, the pilots made wing covers and put them on each evening, and took them off just before take-off. If this wasn't done, you roped the frost off by working a rope back and forth across the wings and sweeping until all was smooth. Frost on the wings gave Noel Wien his most embarrassing accident when he ran the old Fairchild 71 (10623) out through the spruce trees at Chena Hot Springs. It took to the air but wouldn't stay there and settled right back into the trees. All that Noel hurt was his pride, but the airplane was all beat up.

Once when Sig Wien was flying his mail run from Barrow to Kotzebue in midwinter in the Travelair and he was ready to leave, they pulled off the wing covers, but frost settled on the wings as he ran up the engine. When he had about reached the end of his take-off run, he realized that the airplane wouldn't fly; so he cut the gun and taxied back again. He got out his rope and broom and they polished up the wings; then the airplane took off as smooth as you please. This wasn't the end of the frost problem, though; on the first landing at Wainwright, light frost had collected in flight, the wings stalled out just as he was ready to touch down, and the airplane slid around ending up crossways on the runway—but neither the plane nor the pilot was hurt. They cleaned off the frost again and Sig headed on for Point Hope. As he approached the field this time he was ready for the frost stall and set the airplane down in full flying altitude so the skis were on the runway before the wings stalled. All went well until he began to lose speed and lower the tail. At this point the wings stalled—unequally—the right wing stalling before the left one, and it acted like an air brake. The controls were taken right out of Sig's hands and the ship swung right around again, stopping crossways on the runway, undamaged.

Some airplanes were much worse about frost than others, and Sig recalls fondly that the old Bellanca would pack any amount of frost and still handle smoothly.

Jim Freericks came to Alaska with the CAA right after the war and drifted into bush flying for Wien Airlines. The Cessna 170's were the main airplanes of the bush flights at that time, and while they were and are wonderful airplanes, perhaps the safest ever made, they weren't made to handle the heavy loads that were put in them. Jim had been waiting to make a flight north up the coast and inland to a little mining strip in the hills. The low clouds just sat over the land, but by afternoon Jim figured he could make it. He had a caterpillar track aboard that made for an awful overload, and after he got off he could hardly climb; but he headed along the seacoast, following the beach and gaining altitude as he burned up gasoline. He still couldn't see back up the canyons and couldn't tell what the pass was like. Jim had been wanting to deliver that "cat" track all week, knowing full well that the mining season was short and they needed the track, so he finally convinced himself the pass was clear and he could get across. As quickly as he turned up the canyon he realized his error—the pass was socked in with fog. The heavily laden airplane couldn't turn in that narrow canyon, and there was only one way to go—straight ahead into the narrowing pass.

During the winter the miners freighted across the pass using caterpillars, and in the pass between the two creeks the tractors had scarred the prairie sod, making a road of sorts. Jim knew this, and he felt that if he could follow it across, the other side would be clear. As the stream gave out he saw the dim road and followed it just feet above, tearing along in zero-zero fog with the canyon walls on each side and the only chance for life that dim old trail that comes at you out of the fog a yard at a time. Time is nothing—it extends forever. You are scared so bad that you aren't aware of it. Your eyes strain to see your landmark, the dim trail is given to you not in hours, minutes, or seconds, but in fractions of a second, and your life hangs in the balance of those fractions. You don't think about much of anything except how mad you are at yourself for getting into such a mess. For those who make it through, there is the sudden glimpse of clear trail ahead and then open sky. So it was for Jim; he popped right out into the clear above the runway and landed. In recalling the incident Jim said,

"You know, I'm glad there wasn't anyone there to meet the airplane, for after I landed I just sat there with the motor running. It took me five minutes before I could control my hands enough to reach the switch and cut it off."

That is the kind of skill it takes to fly weather. You have to do your shaking after you land. And those are the men you want at the controls when things go wrong. Yet many of your closest calls you never even know about, like the time Sam White came back into Fairbanks. We all landed at Weeks Field in those early days, and the ice fog that settles over Fairbanks at about −45 degrees would completely blanket the town and field so that the tops of big trees and some buildings would be showing above. It would be a beautiful day all over, except that your landing field was just socked in by an opaque-white, still fog. By lining up with landmarks you could usually hit the field. Anyway, you couldn't stop flying just because you had closed your airport by fouling up your own air!

Sam had left in the morning, adding his gasoline fumes to the "soup." When he returned he lined up the old spruce snags that were visible above the sea of ice fog, figured out where Weeks Field was, and settled into the fog. What Sam didn't know was that a single-motor Ford had been stalled and was sitting in the center of the runway! Sam's luck was good, though, and he missed the center of the runway enough to somehow miss the unseen stalled airplane. Then Sam thought he knew where the hangar was and taxied about in circles, still missing the stalled airplane, until he came upon the back side of the hanger.

There is always something funny in the weather situation you find yourself in either for you or for those who try to help you get into the field. On one of Archie Ferguson's first flights he got into trouble because he couldn't tell which way the wind was blowing. He told his mother to put something in the stove to make smoke every time he flew over, so he could tell the wind direction. The next time Archie came over all sorts of smoke boiled up from home, but his dad didn't come out to meet him as usual. When he reached the house, he found his father looking everywhere for his pants. Now that Archie was safe on the ground, his mother stopped worrying about him and realized that in her haste to help him she had stuffed Papa's new pants into the stove!

Weather flying always brings up visions of fog, snow,

storms, or high winds, and these are the ones that give the most trouble, too. It was a clear, bright, beautiful day that ended Ed Badten's career of selfless service to all he met. Sam White described Ed Badten best in the least words: "He was a man of highest principles." Ed Badten came to Alaska on his own as a missionary to help the native people. He preached on Sunday and worked all week. Ed settled at Fort Yukon and, seeing the need for houses, built a sawmill. He decided to learn to fly, and Sam recalls Ed's first solo attempt. He took off on a cold, clear day in a Taylor craft and climbed a thousand feet. At this point the motor quit and Ed wasn't experienced enough to handle the situation. Down he came and smacked the Yukon River ice right in the center. The airplane was all torn up, and Ed had a hard time untangling himself from the wreckage. He was ready to give up flying at that point, but Sam gave him a pep talk and Ed continued to fly. He went on to become one of the best. Like nearly all the top pilots of interior Alaska, Ed was soon flying for Wien Airlines.

Ed was flying the Norseman out of the Kobuk and it was full summer when the few fluffy fair-weather clouds hang in the air, it is still and hot in the canyons, and the peace of the world rests upon the vast Arctic land. Martha and I were at Walker Lake at the time and I did what flying I had to do late in the evening or in the early-morning hours when the sun hangs in the north and the air is "alive again," for during the heat of the day the air is dead. A floatplane with a heavy load just can't climb in it.

The impatience of your passengers is one of the worst hazards a bush pilot has to face, for it can tip your judgment the wrong way. But you can hardly blame the men who hire you to fly; their desire is to get where they are going on time with all the freight they can haul. Ed Badten knew he had more load than he should haul on such a day, given that the air was dead. Still, the people wanted to go, the day was beautiful, and the Norseman came up easily with its load. They swung away from Shungnak and headed across the rolling hills and on up the canyon. The pass could be seen clearly; one could see on forever. But the Norseman wasn't climbing, it was settling! The oil temperature gauge hung on the edge of the red, and Ed still had to increase the power setting. The ground rose faster to meet them and Ed kept looking back, hoping for a thermal to lift them. The air speed wouldn't build up, and more power was needed. They couldn't make it. Ed knew it for sure by then. The canyon walls were near, but there was room for a turn, with a little luck. He swung the ship as near to the right wall as he dared, and under full power he brought the ship around. The heavy ship just wallowed in the dead air of the tight canyon, and Ed could feel the buffeting of the controls as the stall shook the ship. Yet he dared not straighten out; there wasn't room. Courage and skill can't achieve the impossible, but they can hold the ship to the very last. The Norseman still lies there where she struck, shattered beyond repair. All of Ed's passengers survived, but Ed didn't have a chance to protect himself; he flew it to the last and died in the crash.

Weather problems most often come at the end of your day's flight. This caught Martha, Jim, Mark, and I once. We had to move our camp gear and equipment each time we went from one of our Arctic homes to the other. This time we were coming from our Colville Delta home to Hughes. It was late fall, when the sun has set and there isn't much light at best, yet it is a five-hour flight. We had left in the dark, and it was a pleasant, smooth flight all the way. Now the darkness gathered; we were but ten minutes out of Hughes when the airplane just plummeted earthward on a violent downdraft. The climb indicator recorded a 2,000-foot-a-minute drop. Then as quickly it recorded a 2,000-foot-a-minute climb. I reduced the power, for you can tear an airplane apart in rough air. From then on it was a battle just to hold the airplane. Things were rolling and flying about. Jim was upside down in the back seat with his feet sticking up front. Martha was doing her best to protect the baby. Dirt floated in the air. I tried to line up with the runway, but the wind threw me about like a feather. I missed the runway entirely on the first try and all the people came running out to the field. The spruce trees twisted and struggled like grass in the wind, and I had to go ten miles before I could set up another landing approach. Martha kept trying to hold on to the seat and finally tore one side of the seat loose. Jim had just settled down under the pile of duffle. A downdraft can't go into the ground, and there has to be an updraft near—you tell yourself this, but it is hard to believe it as you drop near to the trees and can't get free. Finally I pulled in toward the field. The ship skidded and dipped, then shot up, and I brought it back down. At last I managed to hit the runway near the trading post, and the spectators got hold of the airplane.

"It sure was nice of those people to run out and help me land," I told Les.

"Run out to help you land, hell! They came out to pick up the pieces. Don't you know the airliners had to stay grounded all day, and Andy Anderson tried for half an hour and couldn't get near the field, and then you—you have to land here in the dark, too. Of all the damn fools, you take the prize."

Thus Les read me out as he brought up his catepillar grader to lash the airplane to so it wouldn't blow away. I can always tell from how Les greets me how rough the flight was.

Many of my tightest squeezes came from trying to get home after some flight. If I couldn't get home straight across the country, I would follow the streams, flying just a few feet above the surface. You must know every creek and canyon to do this and recognize them in the fog, rain or snow. Then you don't always get in. I have homes and caches across the Arctic so I can usually get in to one, but one fall I got stuck. I tried to make it from Hughes and you couldn't see the tops of the hills. The good smell of fall was in the air, of wet berry bushes andl spruce needles. I flew low up the Koyukuk River, and the visibility worsened. Rain turned to wet snow but it didn't ice up the airplane, and I turned up the Alatna River to follow it. It was the first snow of the year, and flakes like golf balls fell thick and fast. Visibility was down to a hundred feet and I had to follow every turn of the river in that narrow valley, even the oxbow loops, for I didn't dare cut across. I was on floats and could have landed except the river was low and I was afraid I might not get off again. How it did snow, and I tried to just push through to Takahula Lake, and did too, except I couldn't see the familiar turnoff and didn't dare to take a chance. The snow increased in intensity, and I was afraid now to try a turn. The canyon was narrow here, but I had to. Then I remembered a place where the river had cut through an oxbow loop just a little farther on, and I would be able—if I recognized it—to make a circle here safely and head back downriver. If I missed it, I would be in real trouble. Then I saw a moose standing like a traffic policeman in the old river channel. One side of him was covered white with snow; he was just plastered with it.

He was a big old bull, and he never moved as I went past just a few feet above him. It was my turnaround, and I followed it closely. As I came out of the loop, there stood the moose. He hadn't even moved an ear, and he looked like a bronze statue all snowed under.

It was just as bad going back downriver, except that I knew I had been through once and would be able to get back. The storm just poured it on, and a foot of snow fell in a half hour. It was flying like piloting a riverboat. You went as slow as you could and still keep flying speed, and you were but fifty feet above the trees at best. You didn't dare lose contact and you had to remember the high banks of the river so you didn't fly into one. The snow had moved to Alatna by the time I reached there, and I landed to tie up beside the mission's boat. Reverend Randy Mendelsohn cam out and helped me dock.

I was happy as could be just to be safely down. We went up to the mission for dinner. It was dark and snow fell fast. I was still uneasy from the storm and went out to look at the airplane. She was down in the water with the tail half under and water pouring over the top of the left float already. The weight of the snow was pushing her under! Randy ran for a rake. I started knocking snow off as fast as I could. The floats were taking water through the air vents in the top, and it was half an hour before we had the airplane safe. It was midnight before the storm let up and all was secure. Next morning it was a beautiful day and I flew home in the prettiest sunshine ever.

The fall weather wasn't through with me yet though, for a few days later Martha, Mark, and I started for Fairbanks. It was rather overcast, but soon snow began to fall. At last we were in fog and snow so thick we couldn't see. I headed for Alatna but I could not see the town, so I lit in the first piece of river water I saw and shut off the engine. A moment later Lindberg, one of the Alatna people, came up in his riverboat and we drifted back to the tie-up at the mission boat.

It was the first real freezing weather and, mixed with snow, the river temperature fell fast. When the storm let up three days later, it was near zero and the river was running bank to bank with ice! The pans bumped and lifted the floatplane as they came past. I had to get it out of there fast. In taking off a seaplane in freezing temperatures, you must take care that your controls don't freeze tight.

I cleaned ice off as best I could. Luckily, there was a bright sun and the wings were clear. We loaded up and worked our way out into the river amid the ice pans that came turning and floating past. There was no choice but to take off across them. The *Arctic Tern* reared back, lifting her floats' bows under full power, and we went sailing into the first pan. We hesitated for a moment, and the ship went on the step as we shot across it and into water on the other side. We went for half a mile before I gained sufficient flying speed to stay in the air. I have nothing but admiration for the tough quality of those Edo floats. I gave them a beating that day, and I can say the same for the Cessna airplane that carried them. They both took a beating, and yet there wasn't a mark on either. As we climbed out, I kept shaking the controls so they wouldn't freeze up, while below the pans of ice swung in majestic ponderous procession downstream, sealing the river with ice for another year.

The freeze-up and breakup always gave us some of the worst weather flying. You had to try to outguess the weather and this was something no one has really mastered yet. When you add to this the fact that freeze-up and breakup take place at different times all across Alaska depending upon the distance north, the altitude, and local conditions, you have problems.

When we think of weather flying, we have visions of snow, fog, rain, high winds, and stormy skies or the nothingness of a whiteout, and yet I believe the warm, clear, dry days of mid-summer produce the worst conditions of all, as many a pilot has found to his surprise. Those warm dry days dry out the vast spruce forests and forest fires begin. The dry mossy land is like a wick and the fires eat slowly away. On Noel Wien's first Alaskan flight from Anchorage to Fairbanks it was forest-fire smoke that gave him his worst problem. Forest-fire smoke closed down Fairbanks' modern international airport and the small aircraft and big jets alike couldn't land for days.

Any pilot who has flown the north for long can tell stories of forest-fire smoke hazards. The season of 1958 was one of our worst. It stayed dry and small thunderstorms that were hardly more than a single cloud would drift across the land, setting fires with their tiny lightning bolts on every ridge like meteorological pyromaniacs. This added to the usual thoughtless smokers and careless ones who kept forest fires burning all over interior Alaska.

It was the first time I have seen smoke in the air on the Arctic Ocean for luckily the vast Arctic prairie won't burn and the smoke had to spread across two hundred miles to get to the Colville Delta. My father was visiting us, and I wanted to take him and Mike Wynd back to Walker Lake. It is about eight hundred miles round trip and normally takes a day. This time it took a week, and I should have waited a month until the fall rains put out the fires and cleared the air. We had a good flight all the way across the prairie, but at Anaktuvuk Pass we began to meet smoke. Visibility slowly closed down. The sun shone from a coppery sky and the world became featureless. I dropped down in the canyon to keep contact with the John River, and each mile visibility grew worse. As visibility closes down, your speed seems to increase. I slowed the airplane to seventy miles an hour and put on one notch of landing flaps to give me solid control. Luckily, we were on floats and therefore the infant John River would grow into many landing strips farther on and at last there would be the mighty Koyukuk with unlimited landing places—if I could get that far. But right there in the bottom of the John River Canyon, flying a few feet above the trees to keep contact with the tumbling water, I didn't have room to turn around. There was only one course—straight ahead. Fortunately, the water flowed my way and I couldn't make any wrong decisions about which fork to take when the wrong move would put me in a blind canyon. Following water uphill is infinitely more dangerous than downhill. The rivers flow together, the stream gets larger, and for a float airplane there are landings then and you are going downhill so you needn't keep climbing.

The chances are slight of meeting another airplane under such flying conditions, but you surely could and so keep this in mind and stay on the right side of the river, keeping close contact with the river below while once again your route is given to you a split second at a time and you are but a split second from eternity all the way. The only thing comparable to that kind of flying is driving in express rush-hour traffic in fog.

Mile by mile we made our way down the John River to the Koyukuk at old Bettles. I had burned up so much gasoline that I had to pick up more there, and since I had a big load in the floatplane and was now at higher altitude, I could only take on one tank or I wouldn't get off the river.

The smoke was awful. You couldn't see across the river even, but we took off following the big Koyukuk River now just a few feet above the surface. You have to know your river-banks very well to fly this way and even then you can get turned around. Sam White said that he once flew around a big river island three times before he realized it. Alatna is my port-of-bad-weather call, and I landed there to borrow ten gallons of Bishop Gordon's gasoline before trying to work my way up the Alatna River. I had hoped the smoke would lessen, but it stayed the same. In two places I flew past where the flames were burning, and in the gloom visibility was about a hundred feet. There wasn't a chance of getting across Help-Me-Jack Pass, for with no stream to follow it was impossible, so we went on and I followed the river and at last a tiny creek into Takahula Lake. When I crossed the lake the stream vanished and I felt sure we were over the lake, but it was impossible to tell because you can't see dead calm water in smoke at all. Dad and Mike never said a word as I just let the ship settle. No time for hesitation, no time to check things out. Ahead reared Takahula Mountain, five thousand feet of it. The lake is surrounded by mountains. There was no way out for me. The float ship touched the glassy water so gently that I wasn't sure we were down until I saw the spray flying from the floats. It was like a shower of rare jewels all colored from the smoky light, and a shower of jewels couldn't have been more useful either. It had taken nine hours of flying to get that far on what was normally a four-hour flight, and we were still a half hour from Walker Lake. We had a sack of corn-meal and that all-important item—more aviation gasoline to go on with.

It was a week before the smoke lifted enough for me to make it across and fly back to the clear air of the Arctic coast again, and the last half hour of that flight was through swirling fog where I went down the Colville, following the low riverbanks, holding the airplane at a landing altitude all the way until at last I couldn't see and just landed to taxi on downriver a few miles home. When you near home, you shut off the engine and listen for your dogs to howl or for the sound of your diesel light plant and then taxi toward it again until finally the familiar tie-up is there. If you have a radio at home, your wife listens and tells you where you are and directs you in.

But you didn't always make it home. Weather often

turned you back or put you down. In the early days before radios, this happened more often. Yet even a radio won't always help nor get through either.

On this particular occasion, I had been in Fairbanks getting the *Arctic Tern* checked over and ready for a polar-bear hunt. I purchased a planeload of fresh produce and eight goldfish in a jug. The weather was poor at Fairbanks and all across the Brooks Range, but at the Colville Delta it was good. I didn't get away from the hangar as soon as I would have liked, and for me it was a five-hour flight home. Fortunately, I had good radio reception and talked with Martha all the way across. I landed at Bettles, where Andy Anderson helped me gas up, and then went right on. There were low clouds and ice fog all the way but clear skies at home, and I kept on following the willows along the Anaktuvuk River, then the Colville. Just ten miles from home I broke into the clear in time to see the sunset in the bank of fog while at the same time I faintly heard Martha on the radio: "Fog is moving in fast." I answered, and she couldn't read me now. I tried again. There wasn't enough gasoline for much more flying. It was getting dark; fog was everywhere. Then I hit the wet fog that now blanketed home.

"Fog . . . impossible. . . ." I couldn't make out the rest and yet I wasn't but eight or ten miles from home, but where? I tried the radio and there was no answer. I could hear Martha calling in the background. The ship was all iced up. I couldn't see out at all except to the side. I couldn't see down. Visibility was gone. Three caribou floated past in a world of white to my left, and I let the ship down with full flaps. We touched, bounced, and stopped.

In the silence the radio antennas began to whine and cry as they do when frost is building at times.

"Are you safe? . . . Are you landing?" I could faintly make out a few words. I tried to answer and although the radio worked perfectly, signals were gone.

". . . 48 Delta . . . 48 Delta . . . Wien Colville . . . 48 Delta, give me a series of Rogers if you are safe."

I tried, but no one could hear me at all. Martha couldn't ever hear my carrier signal.

"Where are you, 48 Delta? . . . Are you safe? We heard your engine once. Are you all right? . . . Give . . . series . . . oger." Then the signals were completely dead. The radio antennas ran up and down the scale crying and moaning in the darkness. In my pen-light beam the thermometer read 38 below zero.

I blocked up the skis so the plane wouldn't freeze down and then wrapped up the engine, using my sleeping bag. I put my lighted kerosene lantern in with the engine to keep it warm—a trick we often used on the farm to keep a well from freezing—and I wrapped the wing covers around the cabin to insulate it. Then I started up the Coleman gasoline stove, left a crack in the windows for ventilation, and went to sleep sitting up in the pilot's seat.

The next day broke so bright and clear I felt as if I could see right on forever. The engine started easily and the radio worked perfectly.

"We have you in sight, 48 Delta. . . . Be careful of the caribou upon the runway."

Happy words from home. I had them in sight too, and the caribou looked up as I landed nearby. The trip was over, the job done, and not a goldfish lost nor a pound of fresh produce frozen.

That is weather flying. It is something you avoid as much as possible. It has given the bush pilots their biggest problems. It has taken the lives of more pilots than all other factors combined, caused more search missions, and worst of all left more people waiting for the sound of an airplane that will return no more. For those who flew it and won through, weather flying taught us respect and humility. In the quiet of evening when airplanes are tied down and all is safe, then there is time to remember. And as Andy Anderson put it so well: "Time to be scared."

9

THE MACHINES THEMSELVES

The first airplane in Alaska as far as the records go was built in 1912 at Nome by Henry Peterson, an eccentric gray-haired old chap who was a superb craftsman. It was powered by a French-made rotary engine where the crankshaft stood still and the pistons revolved! In the spring they pulled it up the hill and everyone paid a dollar to see it fly. The Eskimo word for airplane is *tingoon,* a cry that used to drift across the Arctic prairie every time someone heard the hum of a distant airplane in the sky. Few even bother to look up anymore when an airplane flies past. The first *tingoon* never did fly at all, for although it roared and plowed up the snow, it never took to the air.

The first airplane to fly in Alaska was a small tractor biplane flown by James Martin from the ball park at the log-cabin settlement of Fairbanks on July 4, 1913. Restaurant owner Art Williams and two other merchants had hired Martin to put on an air show; they paid his fare, his wife's fare, and freight on the airplane all the way up from the States, plus a salary. They were going to charge five dollars a ticket to see the show. They felt sure everyone in town would turn out to see it, and they were a hundred per cent right, for everyone did—but not at the ball park! People figured that if the airplane flew they could see it from anywhere, and so they crowded the roofs of cabins and all high points in the area, but few turned up at the ball park to pay five dollars. No one was disappointed either—except for Art Williams and his backers, who lost heavily—for after one false try, James Martin took off and circled over Fairbanks at an altitude of four hundred feet. He didn't get far from the ball park but he did fly for nine whole minutes and made four flights in all.

James Martin was one of aviation's early pioneers, a

close friend of Billy Mitchell, and the inventor of the first successful tractor biplane in 1911. After his flight in Alaska he returned to his factory in Long Island, New York. But the sourdoughs of Alaska knew that heavier-than-air craft would fly.

It wasn't until 1920 that General Billy Mitchell sponsored the Army's four open-cockpit DeHavillands for a flight from New York to Nome, thus crossing Alaska for the first time by air. The people waited for the Black Wolf Squadron to appear about all summer, but they only missed their ETA (estimated time of arrival) by three weeks. The people at Fairbanks cut brush from around the ball park and the fire chief laid a white cross on the ground to show them where to land. An observer perched on top of the power-company buildings saw the airplanes coming first, and a shout went up from the crowd. The squadron circled the field, putting on a good show for the spectators, and landed, swinging around to shower the spectators with dust. Nobody minded that at all. One old prospector ran forward shouting, "Broken trail . . . broken trail."

The trail had been broken and the continent spanned. The pilots had also broken about every breakable thing on the airplanes in the process. The Liberty Engine-powered De-Havillands had made it across, though, and the old prospector who had spent years backpacking across the land saw the vision of easy transportation, and air travel grew in Alaska and is still growing there as it is nowhere else on earth. General Billy Mitchell had foreseen world air travel as clearly as the old prospector had seen it for Alaska, but Billy Mitchell's vision led to friction among the higher-ups and a court-martial for Mitchell, because he saw the future and believed. In Billy Mitchell's defeat the lid came off the sealed box; people began to share his dream and what he envisioned is today a reality.

The airplanes weren't up to Alaskan requirements yet, though, by a long ways. A military flying expedition across Alaska didn't add up to air travel for the prospectors yet. Clarence Prest tried to fly a Jenny to Alaska in 1921, but a storm wrecked his airplane on the way. In 1922 he shipped a Standard powered by a Curtiss OX5 engine to Juneau. The *Polar Bear*, as he called his ship, quit several times on the way to Fairbanks via Dawson. Everyone gave him a hand and even passed the hat to help him pay expenses, but he didn't make it. He weathered several forced landings but finally cracked up for good on the Seventy-Mile River. He wandered downriver, where search parties found him, leaving the airplane where it had crashed. Prest said he would return next season but he never did, although quite a few others tried and all met with failure. It is interesting to note that in spite of the equipment and scanty facilities none of the pilots' lost their lives or were seriously injured in any of these early attempts.

Even Roald Amundsen, the famous explorer, tried an early flight over the North Pole from Wainwright. He shipped two airplanes, a Junker and a Curtiss Oriole. Lieutenant Omdal and Roald Amundsen were going to fly the Junker over the North Pole, but on its intial flight they landed upon the rough sea ice and the ship crumpled up. Neither was hurt, but the expedition was off, and in Amundsen's opinion the aircraft wasn't up to carrying two men across the North Pole. He was right, too, for the machines weren't ready to handle the Arctic just yet.

In 1922 Roy Jones flew a Curtiss MF powered by a 180 Hispano-Sueza engine to Juneau. He flew his flying boat, the *Northbird*, about that area all summer but lost it in an accident on Wild Lake in the fall. Jones recovered but the plane was a complete loss. That same year Otis Hammontree brought an old Boeing Amphibian to Anchorage. It was Anchorage's first airplane, but it soon plunked into Cook Inlet and that ended that.

In the summer of 1923 C. F. La Jotte brought an airplane to Nome and flew it about until he lost his way in a fog and wrecked the airplane upon the prairie. There people were willing to fly, but the airplanes weren't up to the jobs at hand, nor were the pilots yet.

Ben Eielson came to Fairbanks in 1922 to teach school, but he really came to study Alaska and fly there. Ben was already a pilot. He had won his wings in the U.S. Army, purchased a World War I Jenny and flew it about North Dakota until he hit a telephone wire. The resulting crash had wrecked the Jenny but not Ben's desire to fly. He had gone on to finish college and get his degree, and Fairbanks was his first teaching job. Ben was of Scandinavian descent, as have been the majority of Alaska's great airmen. Ben Eielson studied interior Alaskan flying and went about promoting it; by spring he had enough backing to purchase a Jenny with an OX5 engine. It was the home-grown project of the local schoolteacher, the townspeople, and a vast new land. It was the first sound flying project in Alaska, and with friendly backing and a man like Ben Eielson it was bound to succeed.

Ben flew about in the Jenny during the summer. He was far from a skillful navigator and got lost easily, but he thought out each problem and solved it. It took several hours' work on the ground to keep the Jenny in the air one hour. All the flying was done in the warm days of summer and was of the exhibition type of joy-riding variety. But joy riding and exhibition flying wasn't what Ben wanted; he wanted to make the airplane pay and to develop aviation. To this end he worked until he had a contract to haul the mail at two dollars a mile between Fairbanks and McGrath, a trip of a little over three hundred miles. The post office gave him a contract for ten bimonthly flights in the winter and shipped him a DeHavilland powered with a Liberty engine to do the job. Wheel airplanes wouldn't work in the deep snow of winter and this was the beginning of ski airplanes in the north.

Charles Schiek, a local carpenter, made heavy flat-bottomed wooden skis that weighed over three hundred pounds a pair, and the local mechanics assembled the airplane. It was a community project with each person giving his best. It was all new too, for none had tried winter flying here before. It took a lot of courage to fly that airplane into unknown conditions. They heated it in a makeshift hangar using wood stoves for heat, pushed it out onto the ball park, and loaded five hundred pounds of mail aboard. Ben took off in a cloud of flying snow. It was February 21, 1924, and the days were growing longer. Ben had planned to just leave the mail and return, but the people of McGrath had a banquet prepared so he didn't get started back until mid-afternoon. Ben lost his way and wandered about. An airplane doesn't give you time to stop and think. You have your fuel reserve as your time limit and you had better be where you are going when it is exhausted. It was pitch dark before Ben finally saw the lights of Fairbanks. The people had lit several bonfires to mark out the field, but Ben missed it completely and went into the trees and the plane turned over on its back. Ben was unhurt and the airplane was repairable. The local people hoisted him up on their shoulders and carried him into the hangar where the mayor presented Ben with an engraved gold watch.

The DeHavilland was a rugged ship, but it landed fast

and almost every third landing was a crack-up of some sort; each time the local people repaired the plane—until late in the spring when Ben wrecked it beyond the ability of local repair. Ben finished the first successful season of Alaskan flying. Ben had two more mail flights to make to finish his contract, but the post office refused to send a second plane or finance the repairing of the wrecked one and ordered what was left shipped back to the States.

Ben had shown what the machines could do even in the winter and he had broken a new trail. Ben Eielson wasn't a bush pilot in reality. He was an explorer, promoter, and his field of aviation was in reality the world. Fate had started him in Fairbanks, Alaska, where all the people had faith in aviation and in Ben Eielson's ability. Noel Wien was the father of bush flying, big, kind-hearted, brave, and skillful beyond measure. The highest compliment that could be paid a bush pilot was to say he flew like Noel Wien. Noel knew his machines and he made them perform in his skillful hands. The Hisso Standard J1 was the first bush ship ever used. It had a payload of five hundred pounds and carried its passengers right out in the weather. The ship had no brakes, could take off or land in six hundred feet, and was really quite a good-performing airplane. It was a biplane, and struts were bound and wired with piano wire. It was said of all these old ships that as they approached a stall the piano wires played "Nearer My God to Thee." It took understanding and steady maintenance to make even a short flight, and the engine needed a major overhaul about every twenty-five hours of operation.

The first cabin plane in the interior was the Dutch-built Fokker F3 with the German-built BMW 250 h.p. engine. Almost all the airplanes were fabric-covered and the engines were liquid-cooled. Sig Wien recalls how the engines used up water and one had to land every so often to pour in water. The pilot was out of the weather for the first time.

The development of the radial aircraft engines such as the Pratt and Whitneys, Wrights and Jacobs in the early thirties put bush flying upon a solid basis, and airframes such as the Fairchild, Cessna, Bellanca, and Stinson Pilgrims were designs that made bush flying both safe and practical. In fact, the basic designs—e.g., the Bellanca J6, which Sig Wien flew—have never been surpassed as bush airplanes for rough Arctic usage. These airplanes cost anywhere from ten to fifty thousand dollars apiece and were expensive to keep up. The pilots could lose one in a moment's carelessness. Insurance rates were prohibitive. No one could afford insurance.

The successful pilots were expert mechanics and they kept their airplanes in top condition. The success of Wien Airplanes is due in great measure to the high standard of maintenance that was initiated by Noel and carried on by Fritz and Sig. The bush planes were pretty machines but they were entirely functional; there wasn't a single frill on them. Every piece of equipment had to be useful. There never was a machine designed in which the importance of the weight to its usefulness was judged more critically. Even the paint had to be lighter than usual or it wasn't used.

Winter flying took the most work because of the frost problems, dark days, and often extreme cold. A ski plane had to be blocked up; if it was left standing out it would freeze to the snow and you couldn't get it started moving again. You had to cover your engine up as soon as you landed so it wouldn't freeze up, and if you intended to stay long, you drained the oil so you could pour it in hot for the take-off. In addition, the rudder, aileron, and elevator controls had to be locked each time so winds wouldn't damage them. Of course the airplane had to be tied down or it could literally blow away—in one storm at Barrow a pilot lost his airplane and they never did find a trace of it. You had to take the battery indoors or it would freeze up and wouldn't work. All switches had to be off, all doors closed tight, and by the time you had an airplane properly put to bed, you had spent two hours. It was the same in the morning, for you spent two hours heating it and getting ready to fly. There just weren't any short cuts and the successful pilots followed their routines religiously. I had a little short cut that I used which saved me draining the oil and it worked well for a few seasons, but it cost me an engine in the end and put me back to the old tried method of draining the oil.

I was flying a Cessna 170-B on skis into Barrow in late November, hauling in frozen fish. I had a good insulated blanket engine cover and a small Coleman gasoline stove that was really wonderful. I would go to the plane before breakfast and start the heater; by the time breakfast was finished and the airplane loaded, the engine was nice and warm, as was the battery, so it started as easily as in midsummer. I had used the system for several years and it worked fine. I was leaving Barrow for Colville with a load of groceries and one passenger. It was a frosty day of low overcast and I usually just got away as it began to get light. Everything went well as we took off across Barrow Lagoon and I climbed up through the overcast heading east. All below was a solid blanket, but above it was clear and open. The black fog comes in from the ocean and blankets Barrow. When you are climbing up you can see the light clear sky above, but once up top it generally is at four hundred feet, depending upon its height that day, and you are in the clear and below it is opaque. The first moments of take-off are busy ones and so is the climbout. Then you relax and the heater starts warming up the cabin. I had just reached that happy state when I saw the oil-pressure gauge begin to drop! There were two alternative possibilities—either the gauge was faulty or the oil pressure was going. The almost instant rise in cylinder-head temperature showed the latter to be true.

At the first sign of trouble I had turned back for Barrow, but just where was Barrow? It lay below the fog; if I overshot I hit the ocean like Walt Bear had, and if I undershot I hit the village. There wasn't enough snow upon the prairie for a safe ski landing yet. By now the engine had begun revving down and the temperature gauges were in the red going out of sight. The ship was fully loaded so we settled fast with me using full power to just keep the engine going. We popped out of the overcast and I realized I had overshot. I was over the ocean. I swung back for the lagoon only a mile away. The engine was so hot it smelled like a new stove. The smell of melting bearings and the clatter of connecting rods coming loose filled the cabin. We were close to the beach but I saw we wouldn't make it. We were going into the ocean just offshore, but we were still gliding fast. The motor had given its all yet it was still firing slowly as the waves reached for the skis. I came back on the flaps and the big flaps of the Cessna caught, lifting us in a little crowhop a hundred feet farther, and we plunked down right at the edge of the beach. The momentum carried us over the sandspit onto the frozen lagoon, but both skis marked the sand from waterline on up and the tail of the ship had salt water on it while the engine quit without needing to be shut off. The engine popped and snapped and fried as it cooled out and the Reverend Bill Wartes came hurrying down to tell me it was a short landing. The answer was simple. I had seen it happen in quart oilcans and should have taken the warning.

You can put a quart of oil on the stove that is at −30 degrees and heat it until the can bulges and is so hot you can't pick it up. Then shake it and there is still a lump of frozen oil inside. It is surprising how long it takes to thaw out that lump. This had, of course, happened many times in my own engine, but the warm oil had circulated easily until the whole mass was liquid. Somehow today the oil lump hadn't stayed put but had drifted into the intake and plugged it up, starving the engine for oil.

I set up a tripod of two-by-four planks and took out the engine, then sent it into Fairbanks on the Wien airliner to Jess Bachner at the Fairbanks hangar. Here Eldred Quam gave it a major overhaul and sent it back ten days later. I had the Wien bush pilot fly to Colville and bring Martha and Jim, and we spent Thanksgiving with the Warteses. It was cold, dark work putting in the new engine on the Barrow Lagoon where the wind blows, but step by step Bill and I fitted it up and finally it was done and ready to run in. You start a newly overhauled engine and run it at slow speed for a few hours, slowly increasing the speed until it is ready to fly. The airplane was good as new again and we all headed for home. From then on I drained my oil each time until, years later, we got a diesel electric plant and could keep the engine warm with an electric heater continually.

The pilots and the airplanes were closely tied together. You grew to love those airplanes. I was talking of buying a new airplane once, and Martha said that was fine but I had better be able to afford two airplanes, for I couldn't ever sell this one; it was part of the family. In reality, there is no wearing out a bush plane. They require constant maintenance, new engines, and a few new parts, but their usefulness and value remain pretty much unchanged. Strange as it sounds, there still isn't an airplane made that will do all the jobs that those old bush planes did under the same conditions.

Don Hulshizer was one of the best of Wien's bush pilots, and he now flies the airliners. I often think of his remark about bush flying: "Bush flying is long hours of hard and monotonous work interrupted with moments of stark terror."

You worked with the airplanes, checking out every part of them until you knew every part inside and out. You repaired them with frozen-tipped fingers when the metal burned your bare skin like hot iron at −40 degrees; you spent more than you could afford on their upkeep; when the storms blew, you couldn't sleep until you had walked down to see how the airplane was riding the storm. You looked after it as if you life depended upon it because *it did,* and then when the going was rough, the chips were down, and it had given its all, there was still a little extra left under full landing flaps to lift your skis above the waves and set you safely on shore.

10

THE BUSH PILOT AS A HUNTING AND FISHING GUIDE

The largest percentage of the people who came to Alaska and stayed did so because they liked the freedom of a vast new land and its game and fish. Almost all who visit Alaska today do so for exactly the same reasons. Take the game and fish from Alaska and nine tenths of the people would move away and ninety-nine per cent of the tourists would go elsewhere! It was natural, then, that the early pilots became guides and showed their customers the land and the game. The pilots held the keys to the big games areas. In his daily flying he became familiar with the country and the animals so that he could recognize individuals and tell what they would be doing at almost any time of the day or year.

Like most other pilots I love the animals and this new land, as does our whole family. I had spent quite a few years in flying and exploring the Arctic and had taken out a guide's license so I could show some of my close friends the Arctic. We often lectured in the South Forty-eight in the winter, and we were in Ithaca, Michigan, one night when Art Williams called up and asked us to dinner. Art is a kind man and a direct one. We talked about the Arctic and the game, and he asked me if I would take him hunting. I answered that sometime I would.

"These sometimes never come about. Let's set a time and place," Art said.

I explained then the facts of $2.50 per gallon gasoline, vast distances, bad weather, danger, and problems.

"Well now, it looks as if you survived pretty well, and

if you can put up with us, we will just put up the price, so name the amount, the time, and the place—unless you are just trying to keep all that pretty country for yourself," Art added.

"Well now, that's not the case, Art. I want to keep the country pretty for sure, but not just for myself, so the price will be $5,000 for a month's hunt, the place will be Hughes, Alaska, and the date August twentieth, when the sheep season opens."

It was the start of a lifelong friendship, and this has been true of every hunter we have guided since. The flights into Hughes were made but once a week then and so it was that I finished up my summer's flying by a trip to Barrow, Barter Island, and headed for Hughes across five hundred miles of prairie and mountains to land our floatplane upon the river just as Wien's DC-3 landed upon Les James's new runway.

For the flying guide, the pile of gear that had to be flown in and the meat and trophies that had to be transported out were always major problems. There were four in our party, Dr. Dean Hart, Leo Beard, Cliff Collin,* and of course Art, plus myself. Our Cessna 170-B, the *Arctic Tern,* would haul about five hundred pounds at a trip on the long flights, so the crew kept camp and all pitched in to work while I did the flying and guiding in the field. It was a wonderful hunt into completely unhunted lands. An airplane enables you to get into new country but, once there, you are on your own, with a minimum amount of camp gear, and it takes a lot of hard work plus ingenuity to complete such a hunt. For a month we wandered the Arctic mountains, seeing a fantastic amount of game and beautiful country without end. We shot a few head of game, just enough to keep us fed and a trophy or two for each hunter. It was the greatest hunt of a lifetime for four men, and a guide can't ask more than to have made such a trip possible.

In looking back across more than twenty years of Arctic guiding, I often wonder what was the most interesting hunt I have ever made, and the answer is that each has been the most interesting because each has been so different. I have never made but two or three hunts a season and in so doing we have been able to make each hunt something special.

Our hunters have come from all walks of life. Some have spent their life's savings to make just one hunt, and others

---

* Cliff Collin died in a crash when his engine quit and he struck a steel tower trying to land in the dark in 1967.

have been among the world's most wealthy men. All have ben great sportsmen and always a pleasure to be with. Friends often ask if I don't get some real stinkers for hunters. The answer is no. The Arctic weeds those out before they ever get here. There is something about pitting a very small airplane against the immensity of the Arctic that lets you know the game is played for keeps and the first mistake will be the last. Only those who will play the game fair and pay the price of understanding have ever made it to our home here.

The requirements of a guide's airplane are first that it be safe and dependable for use in rough landing areas. It must use skis, floats, and at times wheels for year-round operation. It must also be fairly economical so you can afford to use it. The Cessna 170's filled the bill best, being perhaps the most dependable, safest, and most economical airplanes ever built for this type of work. The Super Cubs are small, but they, too, are very useful in getting into rough spots and are the favorite of many. Many other airplanes were of course used; in fact, almost every kind has been tried.

The airplanes allowed sportsmen for the first time to spread hunting and fishing pressure across the entire land. Always before when men went into a new land they killed all the game as they advanced into the wilderness; where the roads and trails went, this hunting pressure increased as days passed and more people came. And by the time the land was explored, the big game was all gone. It wasn't a question of cropping an annual big-game harvest; it was a mopping-up operation. This was the pattern all across America and on into many parts of Alaska until the airplane arrived. Airplanes allowed the spreading of hunting pressure across the entire land and a regulated harvest. Airplanes also allowed the careful policing of all areas by the Fish and Wildlife Department.

There were and are some mighty poor examples of sportsmanship by airplane hunters, but this cannot be blamed on the airplanes, for sportsmanship doesn't depend upon the mode of travel but upon the people involved.

Angus Cameron and I once made a hunt for sheep into a little lake that lies on the north slope of the Brooks Mountain Range. It was early fall and there isn't any more beautiful land than the Arctic at this season. We flew in across three hundred miles of prairie that ended in mountains and landed upon a little lake that had never seen civilized man before. It was a small deep lake set in the mountain walls, and as we set up camp a ewe and lamb came over a little rise nearby to watch us work. I realized then that we were in for a long hike since ewes and lambs don't hang out with the big rams at that season. It meant we would have to backpack to where the rams were.

Next morning as we made our way up along a ridge, we saw a wolf come loping down the valley directly toward our camp. I set up the spotting scope so we could study him, and at about that same time he saw the camp. He just dropped flat on his stomach and lay watching for a full five minutes. He was in easy rifle range, but we had no desire to shoot him. You don't learn much if you are always shooting. The wolf was undoubtedly seeing man's things for the first time, and he knew it was strange. At last he arose slowly and, with his tail tucked tight between his legs, he went off toward the opposite slope. A herd of some fifty caribou were grazing there and the wolf ran toward them. They watched him until he was about a hundred yards away. Then they ran up the slope. The wolf, seeing them run, angled off toward the valley and the caribou turned to watch him go.

We walked steadily all day; near evening we saw the first big rams on the skyline, but they were too far away for us to reach them that evening. We gathered together some dead willow brush and slept under the stars on a gravel bar. When you hunt sheep you don't often have a camp with you.

The next morning found us climbing the slope and soon we spotted the rams again. There were three and one was a really good head. The usual stalking and moving when the sheep fed out of sight followed, until at last we were in position from where Angus could shoot. A guide should prepare his hunter for the shot so he can make a clean kill. I moved rocks and made Angus a comfortable rest. The range was rather long, but since the ram was broadside and lying quietly, I figured Angus could make it. At the shot the ram's head just dropped. The other two rams never moved until the old ram made a few feeble kicks and rolled down the slope a few feet. They went over to see what was wrong. Even when we walked up close, they still stood about waiting for the old leader to give the orders. I have often seen this with sheep. An old ram teams up with a younger ram and they wander together. I believe the old ram is teaching the young one the ways of sheep survival, while the young one keeps guard for the old fellow. If the old ram is killed, the young one doesn't like to leave him.

Each hunt has been so different. That vast land of the pack ice is only accessible by air. You can only see the fringes without an airplane. I did much of the first exploration of the pack ice by airplane and it was a natural that I would take a few friends hunting there for sea game such as polar bear. Cleve La Fleur and his pretty wife, Bercy, have shared many Arctic adventures with our family. This trip we were after polar bear. Bercy had killed a beautiful big bear a few days before, so Cleve and I were hunting the pack ice on a bright sunny day alone.

The pack ice is a strange world crushed by wind and tide, frozen, wild, forbidding, and beautiful. The life of the Arctic Ocean is perfectly adapted to this environment. The environment is so different from that of the land that for centuries people spoke of it as lifeless simply because they couldn't understand it. A small ski airplane makes travel here easy, but you must know the land well or you can get into more trouble than you can get out of.

You can easily trail an animal from the air in soft snow, and when you know the game you can often fly direct to where the animal is most likely to be. I soon saw the trail of a large bear following a tide crack and so I knew he was hunting seals. I flew on to where seals would be most easily caught and there were the bear's tracks again. A moment later I saw him far ahead, sitting beside a seal's hole waiting. Polar bear wait beside a seal's hole like a cat waits for a mouse, and when the seal comes up to breathe, the bear hooks it out. The seal hole is often snow-covered and the bear depends upon smell to locate it. I saw the bear before it saw us and circled wide to land three miles away upon relatively smooth ice in the crushed pack. When the ice pack is crushing during a storm, some open water is left in the jumbled ice, and when it freezes solid again, this spot of open water makes a more or less smooth landing field, although ice buckles as it freezes and cracks and snowdrifts form.

We wrapped blankets around the engine so it wouldn't cool down while we were away, and then we started off toward the bear. Polar bears will often spend several hours at a seal hole just waiting. Cleve and I kept behind the pressure ridge that led to the bear, so that we would be out of sight and could have the softest snow to walk in, keeping sounds to a minimum. Cleve also stepped in my tracks to avoid as much snow crust crushing as possible. It is surprising how fast you can cover the pack ice when you are stalking a big bear.

As we crept forward those last few feet up to the top of the twenty-foot pressure ridge, I thought of how the old Eskimo hunters had turned their fur winter boots inside out so they would make less noise on the hard snow when stalking game. As I peeked over the ridge I could see the bear's long shadow and I knew he was still sitting beside the seal's breathing hole. I had my 16-mm. heavy movie camera and I set it up on the tripod and started taking a picture of the shadow. The slight whirr of the camera carried to the bear and the next moment he came into view to investigate the sound. Cautiously he advanced toward me with an inquiring look upon his face, wondering what could be making such a sound. A polar bear is so graceful in the ice. He just eased across the broken field and I kept the camera running. Cleve was behind me with the rifle. The bear had to climb up to where we were by moving from ice cake to ice cake. He was inquisitive but hesitant, as all animals are when investigating some new thing—cautious but ready to depart quickly. At last the bear stood only six feet away, uncertain as to just what was there. He was beautiful, all fourteen hundred pounds of him. Cleve was even more excited than I. He had waited years for a chance to hunt the Arctic ice pack, and here was the king of the ice six feet away. Cleve couldn't see a thing in the rifle's telescopic sight except white hair, so he had to guess what part of the bear he was aiming at as he fired. The bear rolled back down the ice ridge and Cleve shot again.

The polar bear is, of course, the supreme trophy of Alaska and many say of the world. He is big, powerful, and beautiful. He can hardly be classed as dangerous as he does not understand combat with people, and in my many, many years of association with polar bears I have never seen one offer to harm a man. But if you allow one to come as close as we had allowed this one to come without identifying yourself, you are creating a potentially dangerous situation. When you speak of the dangers involved in hunting polar bear, you then have a different story, for it is one of the most dangerous, if not the most dangerous, hunt on earth, not because of the bears—they are all but harmless—but because of the land you hunt in!

The future of the polar bear seems pretty well assured since his habitat will likely remain unchanged. He won't be crowded off his range. The lack of sportsmanship in hunting the polar bear with two airplanes is obvious, but the airplanes have spread hunting pressure far and wide, making the real problem a human one of upgrading sportsmanship and limiting the kill with a strict permit system.

On the pack ice you also meet the seal, which is the polar bear's main diet; he eats mostly just the seal blubber. This isn't the fur seal, for the fur seal isn't an Arctic animal; this is the common hair seal of which we have four varieties: the ringed, bearded (ugrug), spotted, and ribbon. They keep breathing holes open in the ice by scratching and gnawing out cigar-shaped holes under some deep drift or by just popping a hole in young ice with their heads. Where ice action is taking place they move about freely in the open leads as they do in the open water of summer, but when it freezes across they again take up the job of keeping breathing holes open. With the warmer days of spring and bright sun the seals enlarge their breathing holes and come up on top of the ice to sunbathe. They sink if shot in the summer, but when shot in the winter will float. We like to stalk them upon the ice when they are sunbathing. They are mighty elusive and must be killed instantly or they will slip into the water and be lost.

I have been in on many a seal hunt and each is fascinating in its own way. I like to fly out and land upon some flat area and hunt on foot from there. Emerson Hall and I made a little sled and dressed all in white so we could lie upon it and propel ourselves up close to a seal. However you hunt seals it's a grand sport, and the pelts make a beautiful coat for your wife, too. One of the blots on Alaska's history has been its senseless bounty upon seals, supposedly to help the salmon industry but forgetting that our highest salmon runs and greatest seal populations were at the same time!

The walrus is a sea animal that is also hunted in July or August. Walrus hunting is like hunting elephant in that it combines the challenge of the massive herds and the search for big ivory. You hunt them from a boat with an Eskimo crew, generally.

I took Mr. and Mrs. Sam Atkinson and Martha after walrus one summer. We flew into Barrow and used Tom Brower's boat. The walruses were up on pans of ice and larger floes in herds of from three to fifty and we went in and out among them looking for a big bull for Sam. After he had a chance at an enormous bull, it was Martha's turn. She had a new rifle that had been designed for her by Herb Klein and Roy Weatherby. It was a beautiful little rifle of .30–06 caliber. We saw a group of seven bulls resting upon an ice pan, and we put the boat into a position so that it would drift near the pan with the current and wind as many of the other cakes of ice were doing. The sea was rocking a bit and we drifted nicely until we were about fifty yards away; then the walruses started going off the ice. They reared up, looked our way, and began bellowing and slipped into the water. I don't know why the biggest bull decided to back off instead of diving, but he did.

"Where shall I shoot for?" Martha asked.

"The third wrinkle in his neck."

"What a shot," Kenny Brower, Tom's son, who was captain of our boat, shouted as he raced forward with a harpoon in hand to throw if the walrus should move. It wasn't necessary though, for the walrus had been killed instantly. Martha's fame as a marksman was well established in Barrow from that day on. A few years later when we finished a safari in Africa with Pat Hemingway and Martha had a record of one-shot kills on all her game, Pat Hemingway said it was the best shooting he had ever seen, so I began to think Martha really did know how to shoot her little rifle.

In the early days of the Arctic, walrus hunting for ivory all but wiped out the herds. A long closed season and the use of airplanes to check numbers and enforce regulations have brought back the herds again, and it is likely that the walrus population will be with us in goodly numbers from now on.

The bush pilots worked out a system of flying that enabled them to get to anywhere in the north from the ice pack, even up into the high mountains. It enabled them to take a few sportsmen who were willing to share the expenses and dangers into these areas to hunt. For the first time in history, man could go anywhere the animals could go and he could do so without the necessity of supporting himself or his dog team from the animals themselves. He could go and come as an observer, molesting and destroying nothing, while leaving all unchanged by his passing.

I was one of the lucky few who first crossed the Arctic by

dog team, canoe, and whaleboat while living the life of a native and exploring the land. I know how many hundred head of game it takes to support such travel and living—a big dog team will eat a whole caribou every other day, for instance. I also trapped the Arctic and got to know the animals firsthand. Then I learned to fly.

Flying was a wonderful experience for me because it enabled me to see the entire picture. I could easily follow a wolverine's trail from the air and see where it had been and what its range was. This was true of all the animals, even squirrels. I had followed them so long on the ground that one glance at the trail from the air told me the story. I could now spread my study of the game animals from my small trapping area across the entire Alaskan Arctic, and this I did. I was lucky again in being the first man ever to do this. In a few short years I was able to do what hadn't been possible before.

I came to a few surprising conclusions. The first was that the grazing animals were dependent upon the predators for their survival, the same as the predators were dependent upon the grazers for their survival. I was surprised to see in what close harmony the animals all lived. When I trapped and pushed along the ground, every time I saw an animal eaten by some predator like a wolf, I called it a "wolf kill," meaning of course an animal that would be happy and alive today if it hadn't been killed by a wolf.

When I kept track of a vast range by flying daily, I came to know the animals in the range and I was surprised at how many just died and often lay untouched for many days before some wolf, wolverine, bear, or fox came to feed upon the carcass. When I examined animals definitely killed by a wolf or wolves, I was surprised to find that in nearly every case the animal was injured or deceased.

In keeping a daily track of wolves I discovered another surprising fact. There are few wolf packs in Alaska, and these are of short duration. The wolf has very strong family ties and a strong sense of range ownership. Conservation is not a human monopoly but is practiced by almost every living thing. The wolf is a very strong conservationist—so much so that if the animals it depends upon aren't abundant, wolves will rear but one or two pups. Wolves live and travel as a family unit, and have a given family range. The group of wolves one sees is made up of mother, father, and young ones. Wolves are sociable animals and two families may visit for a romp, but this is about the size of it. Large "wolf packs" do not exist in northern Alaska. I discussed my findings with Fish and Wildlife officials and found them of the same opinion, so I feel it safe to say the wolf pack is mostly a myth. In all my years of flying the largest gathering of wolves I have ever seen was sixteen, and I knew each one in this group. They were the grays from the Itkillik Range romping with the browns of the Fish Creek Range. I knew the parents from the spring before and now they had come for a visit where the two ranges joined. Each had raised six fine children and the young ones were playing while the adults looked on. They had consumed a caribou between them for dinner, and the next day each family went its separate way.

We had a wonderful test in the Arctic of the wolves' value in game management. Under political pressure the Fish and Wildlife Department sent up a team of aerial gunners to kill off the wolves, and in their wake followed a disreputable lot of bounty hunters. They all but wiped out the wolves in the late 1950's. Bounties are paid by the politicians, not by the Fish and Wildlife Department, which is against the bounty system 100 per cent. Bounties are paid to please *voters*, not to protect any animal or resource. There is no connection between game management and the bounty system. The results were drastic though. The Dall sheep population fell to an all-time low. The caribou surged upward only to end with overgrazed areas and diseased animals, the first I had seen in all my years in the Arctic. "You don't find fat caribou any more," old Simon, an Eskimo who had spent his life as a caribou hunter, said.

The Fish and Wildlife Department knew from the beginning that the wolf bounty was a mistake, and they countered by closing the season on wolves in some areas and putting a limit on wolves killed in others. Fortunately, the wolf has the ability to recover and today sick caribou are once again becoming scarce. You can find a fat caribou and you can find a few wolves too.

Most all pilot-guides have worked closely with the Fish and Wildlife Department to better understand and protect our wildlife. Sam White taught Clarence J. Rhodes to fly when Sam was the only wildlife agent who flew, and Clarence joined the old Alaska Game Commission in 1935. Clarence went on to become head of the Alaska Game Commission. I often correspond with him, but since their office is in Juneau and I lived on the opposite side of Alaska, I rarely saw him. The commission's work was done primarily in southern and central Alaska, and, in fact, most of the reports on the early Arctic game that they had were those I sent in.

Stanley S. Frederickson was born on July 4, 1924, at West Yellowstone, Montana, and after serving in both World War II and the Korean War and working with the Idaho Fish and Game Department, he came to Alaska in 1953. I got to know Stan well upon his arrival in Alaska and we often talked about the Arctic.

On this particular occasion, snow was falling from a gray sky and slush ice was running in the Colville River as I walked over the river bar, throwing off the pieces of drift willow from the spring flood before I moved the airplane over for the early-winter wheel operation. Airplanes were still rare there in 1958 and when I heard the throbbing hum of an airplane I knew it was the remaining Fish and Wildlife Grumman Goose still searching for its mate N-720.

On August 20, 1958, Clarence J. Rhodes, his son Jack, and Stanley S. Frederickson left Fairbanks International Airport at twelve ten in the F.W.S. Grumman Goose N-720 on a flight into the Arctic. It was their first patrol into this section of the Arctic. They left the airport that warm August day and have never returned. Radio messages received at fourteen hundred after they had crossed the Brooks Range were the last contact with them. They reached Lake Peters where the Wiens's C-46 was pulled up on the shore after its bath in the lake. They were reported seen flying over Chandler Lake at thirteen hundred on the twenty-first by some hunters, but I was at Nelikpuk Lake hunting with Herb Klein and Toddy Wynn of Dallas, Texas, at that time and Stan had agreed to meet me there. He would have passed us first before Chandler Lake and yet we never saw him.

When N-720 didn't report in we all thought that they had motor trouble and would be on some big lake, but the radio silence worried us. We looked on every lake and big river for the amphibian. Stan knew of all my cabins and caches and I kept a check on these places. They were all superb woodsmen and as we began a systematic search we kept a close watch for campfire smoke or men walking. As the days passed we started looking for oil or pieces of the aircraft on the big lakes and we searched the rugged mountain canyons. The second-largest aerial search in America's history did not turn up a single trace of the twin-engined amphibian. The aircraft was equipped with the latest radio gear, carried full emergency gear, and had the best of pilots. What happened? Did man or machine fail? Why? Where are they? If we could answer one of the questions we could likely answer them all.

The years since have revealed no more clues. I hunt the area they were lost in every year and as I search the mountains and canyons for sheep, bear, or caribou with some friends from far away I also search for a bit of metal or a sign to show where N-720 vanished on The Last Patrol. The plane may be in some box canyon, or out on the open prairie, hidden in the timbered section, or on the bottom of a lake, but no matter where it is the men died working for the things they loved and believed in—the conservation and protection of our wildlife.

To those who would violate the game laws or sell our wildlife short for a dam, a promotion scheme, a new highway or personal gains, I would like to have them consider the price Stan, Clarence and Jack paid in passing on the unspoiled wilderness to us.

The pilot-guide is a most useful part of Alaska's economy today. Alaska's Arctic is a land where our *only* renewable natural resource is our game and fish and it is likely the only such resource we will ever have. The careful harvesting and conserving of this resource is of utmost importance to everyone.

There never was a more delightful piece of equipment for the fisherman than the small float airplane. They were just created to make fishermen's dreams come true. There was many a bush pilot who would have flown the North just for the fun of fishing alone. Almost everyone carried a fishing rod or fishnet as part of his emergency gear, for if you were forced down you could count upon living on fish in the summer. Southern Alaska has the heaviest fish concentration, but central and Arctic Alaska have fish in every pothole, lake, or stream.

One spring Sig Wien was on his way from Fairbanks to Barrow in the Bellanca when he ran into fog near Barrow. The lake ice was still six feet thick although it was full spring and the prairie was melted bare with water flowing; Sig landed upon the ice of a large prairie lake to wait for the Barrow weather to improve. It was lovely weather with continuous daylight, so Sig walked about the lake ice and soon realized that the grayling were migrating out of the lake into the little streams. The water was flowing through the grass and Sig found he could herd the grayling up into the shallow water until they literally swam up onto the dry prairie where he picked up quite a few of them. They were very fat since they had been living all winter upon fresh-water shrimp in the lake. Sig made a stringer from some ground willows and gathered up a stringful. Then he started up his plumber's fire pot, which many bush pilots carried to heat their engines in winter, and fried some fish in their own fat. That is as good-tasting a fish as you will ever get. I've fried fish like that across the entire American Arctic.

When the fog lifted in Barrow Sig took a couple of strings of grayling and flew on in. The people of Barrow were delighted to have the first fresh fish of the season.

No one ever needs to feel sorry for a fisherman, for it doesn't really matter whether he makes or loses money. He fishes because he likes to catch fish. Whenever I land upon some new lake the first question I ask is: Are there fish in it? I even peer through the seal holes on the Arctic Ocean looking for fish—and I have found them there. The main kind of Arctic fish are the Arctic char, shee fish, cisco, salmon, tom cod, and flounder, these all being ocean fish that run into fresh water. In the fresh water are whitefish, pike, lake trout, Arctic grayling, cod, and Arctic char. Except for the whitefish, all of these will strike a lure.

I was flying in the back-river country of northern Canada, having fun catching big lake trout at every landing. I had no reason to keep the fish so I released them carefully. I met two fish biologists there from Ottawa who were doing a study of lake trout and fish resources. Since I had caught fish easily everywhere I figured that fish were plentiful, and as far as I was concerned they were. The biologists explained that the carrying capacity of the Arctic waters was very low and that it took many years for a fish to grow to size. In fact, some of the trout I had been catching were older than I was! Each trout had its homestead, and if you caught and kept that fish, that area was barren of fish for many years. Their chief diet was snails, and no Arctic lake could stand any but the lightest and best-regulated fishing. The first time you fish an unknown lake it is the finest trout fishing imaginable, and if you keep every fish you catch, it is the last fishing in that lake for many years to come.

The biologists explained this was true particularly with

lake trout but to a lesser extent with Arctic char. That was a good many years ago, but I have found they were 100 per cent right, as I have seen one lake after another completely ruined by careless fishing.

Airplanes enabled the fisherman to spread out and crop the distant areas. They also enabled the Fish and Wildlife Department to check up on all the major lakes.

In 1963 we had one of the latest breakups I have seen. The ice just stayed in the Arctic lakes and it looked as if freeze-up would come before breakup was over! Martha and I flew into Fairbanks in mid-June to do some shopping before going on into our Walker Lake home. To our surprise we found that our friend Art Williams from Ithaca, Michigan, had flown up to Fairbanks to visit us. The ice moves out of Walker in early June, so since it was near July I felt sure it would be clear, but when we came in over the lake in the evening it was still white and solid with ice. Only at the far north end where the stream enters the lake was there a small patch of open water, and I landed in this. We have a trapping cabin here, but we didn't have any supplies. I hooked up the stove using some pieces of gas cans for pipes, set up the airplane emergency tent for Art, and we moved in. It was continuous daylight, and as soon as my family was comfortable, Art and I went fishing. In fishing from a float-plane you can paddle it about if it is dead calm, but a float airplane is mighty susceptible to wind. Or you can taxi about and troll. Art sat on a float and I paddled. It was quiet and smoke spiraled up from the cabin chimney. Loons called while a beaver swam back and forth eying us. Art fished and fished while I paddled, but without any luck, so finally I started up the motor and we trolled around the open water and soon Art hooked a ten-pound fish that gave him a good battle and we kept this one for the next day's eating.

There wasn't anything at the cabin so we improvised. We made plates out of cardboard and wrote our names on the bottom of each. We cooked out on an open fire in a skillet made of an empty gas can and drank from tin cans. We had some groceries from Fairbanks, and we enjoyed every minute of it. Fishing by taxiing an airplane takes lots of gasoline, so a couple of days later Art and I flew to Hughes to get some more gasoline and supplies. To my surprise Ed Cotie, from Bridgeport, Michigan, who had wanted to fish the Arctic with us, had arrived at Hughes that same day. Martha was doubly surprised when she saw three men return instead of two. I snapped the seats out of the airplane so Art could sleep in it. Ed Cotie got the little emergency tent and we cut another cardboard plate from the box and wrote Ed's name upon it. Art had the only raincoat, so when it rained he did the cooking outside. We paddled or taxied the airplane about and caught enough fish to feed us, and we all had a wonderful time.

It was July before we finally got into our home by landing the floatplane in across the ice, stopping in a small patch of open water beside the docks. Art had intended to stay but a couple of days and remained a week. Ed Cotie had meant to spend a few days seeing the Arctic this once-in-a-lifetime trip, but when he left ten days later, he left all his gear for next season. Ed had fished all across America and felt there just wasn't anything like fishing from a floatplane in the Arctic.

There is one thing you can count on from a floatplane fishing trip into the Arctic and that is the unexpected.

The Arctic grayling are fish for the dry-fly fisherman. They run up every stream in the Arctic, right up to the mountain peaks, and stay there until the freeze-up drives them down to the larger rivers or lakes for the winter. John Helphrey, Harvey Snook, and I were hunting sheep in the most remote part of the Brooks Range at a little lake we call Lake Martha.

It was late in the evening and we were coming down a small creek right from its source in the mountain peaks. It started as a trickle, but as soon as we came to a tiny wash-basin-sized pool there were two Arctic grayling. As the pools increased in size, so did the grayling, and by the time the pools reached the size of a bathtub we were finding grayling from fourteen to eighteen inches in length, which is about as large as these chunky little sailfish-like trout ever grow. We had been lucky in our sheep hunt and carried an entire ram divided up among our packs, so we rested often beside the pools and watched the fish. We were all ardent dry-fly fishermen, and as we followed the little crystal stream back to our camp in the valley below, it was clear to us that here where the brush grew only ankle-high and the clear water was exactly 32 degrees was a dry-fly fisherman's dream come true. The Arctic grayling is the dry-fly-"takenist" fish there is. It was pitch dark before we reached our camp and we left early next morning, so the little stream is still unfished, as are most of the creeks of our Arctic.

Wherever you land and tie up your floatplane, the grayling swim around under the floats, finding this an interesting place to explore, one offering shade and shelter. As I often washed the dishes from the bow of the floats, I discovered that the grayling would eat the crumbs and very soon eat from my hands. I always use a barbless hook in my fishing so I can release a fish easily, and they are just as easy to hold if you keep a tight line. So it was as our children grew up they all fished, and still do, from the bow of the floats, releasing each grayling. The grayling didn't seem to mind the contest of small boy and fish at all and just returned under the floats when released, ready to eat from your hand again when we washed dishes. In some of our favorite spots the grayling must have been landed many times. Needless to say we never ate any of these friendly fish. We caught "strangers" to eat.

You just can't beat flying about unknown lakes and fishing from a floatplane for adventure and the sheer joy of living.

Not too many bush pilots got into trouble fishing, but of course all the hazards of flying are involved and one of our saddest accidents occurred as the result of a fishing trip. It seems strange that people who are altogether unfamiliar with water will go out in a boat fishing or get themselves drowned in countless other ways. The bush pilots were not reckless and didn't get involved in these common "fool killers." Yet they did get caught in some bizarre accidents.

Some friends of Dick Morehead had gone fishing on a creek, using a wheel airplane, and landed upon a gravel bar. It was sort of a controlled crash, and they blew a tire. They radioed Dick to bring them out a new tire. Dick flew a Super Cub back with a wheel and dropped it to the fishermen. Apparently the radio in Dick's Cub wasn't working, for he flew around low to see if all was in order. Dick was a superb pilot and one of long experience, but of late in heavy aircraft. It may come as a surprise to most, but the skills required to fly a light aircraft and those required to fly a heavy aircraft aren't the same at all, and perhaps the most dangerous pilot of all in a light plane is an old airline or military pilot. Just because you can handle a big truck doesn't make you a racing car driver! It is also true that as you become more and more proficient in either type you lose proficiency in the other.

The Piper Cub was one of the easiest of all aircraft for the beginner to fly, but in the hands of an old pilot it is such a willing performer that it has one deadly flaw: when you roll out quickly from a steep turn it will—not often, but too often at that—stall out one wing at high speed, and the other wing that hasn't stalled acts like a powerful lever, spinning you so quickly you don't even know what happened, especially if you are at low altitude. The result is usually fatal. So it was for Dick that bright calm July day when he delivered the wheel to his friend. The Super Cub flipped and wrapped itself, as Jess Bachner put it, "three times around a spruce tree," bursting into flame at the same instant.

But some of my happiest moments have been in flying about the Arctic with some sportsmen who, too, shared my love of the wilderness. In this wonderful world of jet airliners that we old bush pilots understood long ago and pioneered, everyone has the freedom of travel we alone once knew. Anyone can reach the Arctic in a single day from wherever he may live and ride the modern Wien Consolidated jets on the routes laid out by Noel and Sig Wien. Flying has enabled us all to fully enjoy our vast land, to understand its intricate balance of animals and share our adventures with a few friends. I have always thought of our wilderness as a treasure passed on to us and for us to pass on to others in the same way we found it. This I have tried to do, along with a little better understanding of what I have seen there.

11

⟨∼⟩

STRANGE FREIGHT

To those who lived in north Alaska there was nothing strange about the freight the bush pilots hauled, regardless of what it was, because it was always a life necessity. The fact that it went by air in small airplanes was all that made it strange. The question asked before you purchased something was, Will it go into an airplane? With Noel Wien's Hamilton Standard that excluded everything from the size of a washing machine on up, but as the pilots became more familiar with their airplanes, they started tying things on the outside, so soon the range expanded to what you could tie on and fly with. This included some awful chunks of gear, such as big castings for mining machinery, pieces of caterpillar sleds, lumber, timbers, roofing, boats, bed springs, radio antenna masts, steel towers, fish traps. If you needed it and it ·was possible to tie it on and fly with it, the bush pilots would deliver it for you. Yet I can't recall a single instance where a pilot was killed handling this gear. Some of the later private pilots and air-taxi operators were killed, especially in southern Alaska, when they tried to do what pilot or machine wasn't capable of doing.

Then there was the odd gear, not because you couldn't get it into an airplane but because it usually didn't take to the air—such as a baby walrus for a zoo, a cow for some mining camp, reindeer, musk ox, moose calves, bears; in fact, every species of wild animal has been hauled. Then there were, of course, sled dogs and dog sleds and caribou or moose antlers that were too large to go inside.

One time Johnny James was flying the Wien Norseman near Kotzebue, hauling reindeer to replenish a herd. The deer had been tied and laid in the back. The day was gray and the Norseman is not an easy ship to fly. Johnny was busy up front when he felt a jab into the back of the seat. A hasty look showed one of the bulls had worked loose and the panicked deer was trying to get out and had butted the pilot's seat. Luckily, the seat saved Johnny from any injury, but he still had a loose, fear-crazed bull in the airplane, and if it tried to jump out the windshield or got tangled up in the controls, it would be most difficult to handle the Norseman. For the next half hour Johnny did a "toe dance" on the rudders as his knees shook and he cautiously eyed the loose deer, which of course was the most scared of all. The bull had meantime returned to the tied deer, and fortunately, aside from trying to jump out of a few windows, remained away from the pilot, and Johnny delivered his strange cargo unharmed. As Johnny told me later, "You don't know what a surprise is until you have been flying weather for a while and then get goosed by a loose reindeer."

Sam White hauled many an awkward load in his flying, but he said the hardest was a helicopter boom that he flew from Hughes across to Kobuk for Richard and Merrill Wien. The boom was too long to streamline with the airplane so it was tied on sort of angling on Sam's Stinson L-5. It took off with it all right, but it just couldn't get past minimum flying speed, and Sam had to maintain one notch of flaps to do even that. He had to go the long way around to get through the lowest passes.

A mean load doesn't have to be one that is so large that it has to be tied outside though, and Sam said his meanest was a load of iron rods and sheet iron that had been destined for Bettles by boat but got frozen in Tanana, where it was piled up on the beach and snowed under. In February the miners at Bettles asked Sam to haul it. Nothing could be cut or bent, and the iron rods were twenty-five feet long. In fact, they went from the tail to up under the instrument panel in the old Travelair, and they had to be loaded into the ship through the window and pushed away back into the tail. An airplane is mighty critical about its center of gravity (CG), and this load made the Travelair very tail-heavy. I should say there were four loads, and in the snow each load looked worse, and the last was the worst of all. It was four flights of steady terror, for it took full forward pressure on the controls just to keep the tail up, and any rough air or rough landing would shift the load about or drive it right forward through the airplane and pilot. Luckily, it was just the greatest flying weather ever.

Caterpillar tracks were Jim Freericks's burden, it seems, as were they everyone's who ever handled them in light aircraft. They were hard to load or unload, and the floor had to be padded with planks so they didn't break through. You unrolled the tracks from the drum and rolled them back up inside the airplane like putting in a heavy chain a few links at a time. Once inside, you had an overload in small area, and if you made a mistake landing, that solid chunk of metal would go through you like a cannonball.

Jim Robbins and a passenger were flying a Fairchild 24 with a bogie wheel for a D-8 cat in the back when they made a hard landing and went right up on their nose. The two pilots pretty well filled the cabin, so there was hardly room to put your hand between them, but in the crash that big chunk of cast iron bogie wheel went forward between the pilots and through the front of the airplane like a bullet and vanished. It didn't leave a mark on the pilots and to this day no one has ever found where that big cast iron wheel went! Sam White calls it one of the unsolved mysteries of the Arctic.

It didn't always take a piece of big gear or heavy gear to give a pilot a problem. In 1937, Pollack had a Hamilton Standard adjustable pitch propeller to deliver; they used a Stinson and it wouldn't fit inside, so they just tied it across the gear legs under the belly. You probably wouldn't notice it there, but the airplane surely did. It got off, but it could hardly fly, and the pilot went around the pattern and landed again, happy to be right back where he started from. They streamlined it with the fuselage and the next flight it handled fine.

The bush pilots always tried to help when they could, and this was all the time. I once asked Les James if I could bring back anything for him from Fairbanks since I had an empty ship coming back, and he said, "Yes—eight hundred pounds of cement." I loaded it in easily and headed for Hughes. It was a calm flight and a beautiful fall day. I was just passing Indian Mountain when zoop! just like an express elevator, I was dropping—and faster than the eight hundred pounds of cement, for it was floating around near the ceiling! I knew full well that such a downdraft could change into an equally violent updraft and that unless I caught my load gently before then, it might go right through the airplane. Luckily, I did manage to get the airplane back under its load gently. At Hughes I found the wind had kicked up to a gale, and I would have had an awful job handling an empty airplane, but that eight hundred pounds of cement held me tight on the field.

All the early pilots ran regular shopping services and most carried an order book. The people of the villages always had things they needed from town, and the pilot wrote it all down —baby bottle nipples, hair nets, "bone ache medicine," candy, "fresh things" (that meant apples, oranges, grapes, or whatever was on hand), parts for motors, radios, a dress, skin needles, ammunition. The list was limited only by the needs and desires of many people. There were messages to deliver, too. The people might have had a month since the last flight to write letters, but they would want the messages delivered verbally, and expected the pilot to do so—and the pilots usually did. Some of them spent a full day just filling the orders before the next flight. It was a free service, and the only pay was for the freight involved. Many an old-timer speaks kindly of some bush pilot who now is captain of some far-ranging jet airliner—or more likely has flown down that last stormy sky—and remembers the little order book he carried and the time he spent to help some isolated villager.

I often think the strangest sort of gear ever put into an airplane is when my family travels. It might be –40 degrees outside, but all the things dear to the heart of a growing family must go along. There is Jeffrey's blanket and cuddly toys; Mark's little bag of "emergency gear." Jim flies his own bush plane now, but he manages to have something for Dad's plane, such as his pet cat, while Ann has the things dear to the heart of a teen-age girl, and Martha has all the gear that no woman would possibly travel without. There is the emergency gear I won't fly without. I have not used some of it in a lifetime of flying, but I wouldn't taxi down the runway without it. The real payoff, though, is the pets. There are the houseplants and the bean Jeffrey started in a paper cup, the aquarium of goldfish that I once brought home in a gallon jug but that need a ten-gallon tank now, a tankful of tropical fish that can't stand too much temperature variation, twelve parakeets, two turtles, two pet cats, a cageful of hamsters, and a real live antfarm. There are also the necessary books for the correspondence courses for each child that Martha teaches. When I get all this into the airplane and tucked neatly away, I feel I have the most wonderful and strangest freight any bush pilot ever carried, and I also feel that one more houseplant, antfarm, or hamster and there won't be room for the pilot.

12

THE TRAPPERS' TAXI

The cash crop of all interior and Arctic Alaska in winter was furs. In summer it was mining chiefly for gold. The placer mines all shut down with freeze-up and trapping was about the only business until summer came again. The salmon industry is located along the southern and southwestern coast of Alaska and has little direct influence upon the economy of interior and Arctic Alaska.

In the winter the bush pilot found that most of his customers were trappers, traders, or fur buyers. Trapping grounds, or traplines as they are called, are the only real ownership of land in perhaps 98 per cent of Alaska. These rights to an area are pretty well respected by all and are passed on from father to son. Right from the beginning people have talked of registering the trapping areas, but no one has come up with a workable system of registration or, in short, of transferring legal ownership of the land to the people that use it. There is a system for acquiring title to small tracts of from an acre to eighty acres, but there is no legal way to own the vast tracts necessary for a sound fur- and game-ranching economy.

Of course, all the land around the villages was taken up for traplines long ago, but as you moved out past a fifty-mile limit, and especially back away from the big rivers, you came to areas where no one had ever trapped. These were all open areas and anyone could trap there. With the coming of airplanes many people feared it would make travel so easy that all the fur-bearing animals and game would be killed off. Some felt the sound of the airplanes would drive the game out of the area, while animals like lynx, fox, marten, or mink would kill their young when an airplane flew by.

Airplane usage did prove a problem for certain species of big game in some areas, and their use had to be regulated, but in the trapping field, and to a great extent in the hunting field, the airplane spread out the pressure, proving a blessing to all. The animals paid the airplanes no mind, and I have seen many never bother to look up as an airplane flew past. Right from the start the airplane became the trapper's taxi.

The life of the Arctic regions is ideally suited to trapping. During the summer when there is mining, freighting, or construction work to do, it is daylight all the time and people work long hard hours. The animals are working hard too raising their families and putting on new pelts for the winter. When the nights begin to turn dark in the fall, the bounty of the harvest is at hand as grasses, berries, and plant growth reach their peak, animals are fat, and the young are good-sized. It is time to gather the harvest and prepare for the winter ahead.

School was open in the summer in the village but closed in the winter. The families had been in the village all summer with the children in school while the men were away working. With the coming of fall they returned home and put up their grubstake for the winter. A grubstake consists of all the items you will need for the year. It is surprising how many items are needed for a season. There are all sorts of foods, candles, window glass for new trap cabins, nails, reading material, Christmas things, sewing kits, and medicines —the list is just about endless. The traders were experts in helping put up a grubstake so that you would have the right amount of things and nothing would be overlooked. They could also pack it so first-needed items were first and things wouldn't get broken.

When the last item was packed, and you couldn't think of anything else needed, into the riverboat or airplane it went. If it was past freeze-up, then into the dog sled or airplane it went, and today you can say it goes into the snow car or airplane, for the dog team has all but faded from the scene. No matter how you travel, though, the feeling of contentment, of the expectation of the winter fur harvest and the joy of living is always there. The old-timers had a good way of expressing this feeling in a few words when the grubstake was put up and all hauled in; they said, "I've got her made."

No people ever had it any better than the trappers with their year's supplies in and the whole season ahead of them to do as they pleased. The airplanes enabled a man to travel quickly to his trapping area and the bush pilots would come by each month with the mail. I have been fortunate to have used all the means of travel to and from my trapping camps and have trapped all across the top of Alaska. Each way has its good points and I have enjoyed them all.

Most people have a rather distorted picture of the fur business and the income that is derived from it, so I will set down a few facts before telling of the season's trapping. I have never found anyone who made a fortune trapping. I heard of a few, and I checked out the most prevalent stories. The first was told to me by an old trapper who should have known better. He related how a neighbor had taken three thousand mink from the Sand Hill country in one season. I was new in the country and on foot, so it all sounded logical to me. Later I flew all around the Sand Hill country and found it comprised a few square miles of rolling hills. It wasn't good mink country at all. Mink are creek and swamp animals and I doubt if there were more than sixty mink in the entire area. There just wasn't food nor shelter for more. After skinning and preparing a few mink pelts, I ran up against a second limiting factor. It takes me two hours to skin, clean, and stretch a mink pelt, and if that trapper would have only had to do this part of the work he would have had to average fifty minks a day! Even in the Sand Hill country the mink don't line up at the door to be skinned. I figure the trapper caught thirty mink that winter and paid for his grubstake, which led to the three-thousand-mink-catch story.

A story that still persists is of a man who made thirty thousand dollars shooting "rats" (muskrats) in the Mackenzie River Delta of the Yukon Territory. I just checked this one out using the time system; it was easy since muskrats brought a dollar apiece then. You hunt muskrats during breakup, which lasts about a month, and you shoot them in the head with a .22 rifle from a small muskrat canoe. This chap would have had to average a thousand a day. In reality, his yearly catch was more like three hundred, with an average of ten a day, and even this would have kept him busy hunting, skinning, stretching, and drying.

George K. Wood said that when he was a young man at Alatna the price of muskrats went from twenty-five cents to fifty cents apiece and George thought he would be a millionaire right away. Yet even when he didn't sleep much and had a partner to skin and stretch his catch, he had to really hustle to make two hundred dollars in a season.

One of the prettiest sights I ever saw was at Aklavik,

Yukon Territory, when the community-owned schooner came in from Banks Island with the year's catch of white fox pelts onboard. They had caught a shade over three thousand pure-white Arctic foxes that year and all were piled up for sale. The market price was twenty dollars average that year and the lot went for sixty thousand. It was the combined work of around a hundred people for an average of six hundred dollars per person. This is a realistic figure for the income of a good Arctic trapper.

The highest income I know of ever made by an Arctic trapper was made by Aivuk Tukle, with a catch of one hundred eighty Arctic white foxes in one season. The total value of his catch was thirty-six hundred dollars and his whole family helped him with the skinning and caring for the pelts.

The country around Huslia on the Koyukuk River is as fine a fur area as we have in Alaska. The people in that area are superb trappers who take care of their traplines as a rancher manages his range and trapping has been their chief source of income for generations. The income of these families from trapping ranges between two and three thousand dollars per year.

The price of pelts fluctuates a great deal and trappers made a better income at the turn of the century than they do today, while their dollar went further. It was clear right from the start that the income from trapping wouldn't support much bush flying, and yet the combined income from an area would and did support regular flights from the main cities to the villages and for taking trappers to or from traplines.

When the geese flew south and the berries were ripe, our busy season's bush flying was over and we used to retire to our trapline at Takahula or Walker Lake. Once a month we would heat up the airplane and fly to Hughes for the mail, to visit a little and pick up supplies. We didn't need much since we had all of our meat and fish along with butter kegs of blueberries and cranberries Martha had gathered in the fall. There weren't any electric generators to keep up nor any special problems. We needed only a little kerosene for the lamps and a few staples.

Before the snow fell we cut a pile of dry spruce logs and stacked them up behind the cabin. We gathered some birch-bark for starting fires and Martha picked the last low-bush cranberries; then we enjoyed the mystery of the first snowfall as it came sifting silently down through the spruce trees.

When the land was all white the trails of the animals were plain to see. The trapper is an optimist who dreams and spends his days unraveling the secrets of the wilderness about him. From the youngest trapper with a few rabbit snares in the brush about the cabin to the seasoned trapper venturing far up the river valley or into the mountain canyon, it is a fantastic world of wildlife adventure. What a wonderful world for a man and a boy to enter together!

Jim was just ten the winter we trapped at Takahula Lake. Our trapline wasn't a long one. It was just the distance a man and boy could walk easily in one day. As the snow fell Jim and I worked away making him a trap setter and a pack exactly like mine while Martha made him a caribou-skin parka. We read the stories of Ernest Thompson Seton's *Wild Animals I Have Known* and *The Lives of the Game Animals* in front of our fireplace.

We watched the grouse go mad with the moon of fall as the families broke up, and we watched Easy, our cabin weasel, turn from brown to white. It was Easy who caused us never to set a trap closer than a half mile to the cabin for fear of catching our friends. Of course, I wove a series of stories about the life of Easy Weasel and Mr. and Mrs. John, the other two weasels that lived in our woodpile. It was Mrs. John who next spring brought in her five tiny little weasels to show them to us!

The lake ice formed clear and hard while the lake boomed in its mountain fastness as the ice expanded or contracted with temperature changes. The ice was so clear that when we went sliding upon the lake it was as if we were walking upon water. When the shallows pitched off to the depths below, you would always be a little scared to venture there, for it seemed as if you would surely go through. If the lake just happened to boom or split beside you it gave you a start. The trout, whitefish, grayling, and pike would come up on the shelf to feed and you could skate right over the top of them and give them quite a fright.

Martha joined Jim and me on most of our excursions, for who could stay indoors and miss out on the fun? The trapping season opened November 15 and the soft snow was a foot deep by then. The sun had settled below the southern horizon, but it still shone upon the white mountain peaks at high noon as we laid out our trapline. The trail led across the hill and up the river valley, then back across the little neck of land to the lake and on home. I made a few sets with the big No. 114 toothed Newhouse double-spring traps for wolf, wolverine, and otter, anchoring the traps to log toggles. We set smaller traps for lynx, fox, marten (sable), or mink. Jim set his small traps for ermine and squirrels and set a few snares for snowshoe hares. We used fermented fish for bait, chopping it up in little pieces to sprinkle in the snow around the traps, and in the cold air it smelled strangely good.

Martha put us up a lunch and we would stop at noon to eat it. We would take off our snowshoes and sit down on a driftwood log along the river to eat our lunch and listen to the quiet world about us. A camp robber would light nearby to see if there wasn't a scrap left for it, or a raven would fly past with an inquiring tu-lo-wak.

Once the traps were set it was like waiting for Christmas to see what would be in them the next morning. Breakfast of caribou sausage, hot cakes with blueberry syrup by candlelight, and the friendly smell of burning spruce logs, chores done by kerosene lantern light, and then out on the trail by the dawn's early light. You hurried from trap to trap while reading the signs of the things that had passed in the snow. A moose had crossed our trail here and you could see how it had studied the strange snowshoe tracks before it ventured to cross them. During the coming months the moose became so used to the trail that they eventually used it for a road.

Jim learned all the tracks quickly and could soon identify them. He learned that a snowshoe hare puts its hind feet first as it runs, while mink, sable, and ermine leave two-by-two tracks and an otter slides, runs, and so travels on. Where the little creek stayed open all winter two water ouzels lived. These cheerful little birds would greet us each day with song. Here I set a trap back under the bank and we caught the first animal of the season. It was a lovely mink solidly caught and quite dead. I took the animal out of the trap, and Jim examined the beautifully furred animal as I reset the trap.

"May I carry it in my pack, Daddy?"

"You may, but I surely don't want to make your pack any heavier."

"It won't make my pack heavier. It will make it lighter."

There was no need for Martha to ask if we had any luck that day, for she could see success written all over Jim's face as he hurried toward the cabin. Each evening Martha would see us coming across the lake and try to guess what we had in our packs. It was always such fun to look in the packs and see what we had.

One by one we caught animals of every species and hung the pelts up on the cabin wall. Jim learned to skin his squirrels and ermine and not pull a "short tail." There is a trick to skinning out an animal's tail so as not to pull the tail off.

By midwinter the sun didn't even hit the mountain peaks at noon. It was twilight only a few hours at midday, and I often walked the trapline alone. I left in the dark of a morning and returned long after dark. During the coldest days the animals don't move about much, and I didn't catch a thing for days. A person burns up a lot of energy on the trapline and one's food tastes especially good. There aren't any diseases and you aren't plagued by colds or other minor problems that keep so many people operating below par. Even if I didn't catch an animal I had adventured into the quiet world and as I headed for home I felt I couldn't have had it any better. How lovely the lights of the cabin looked as I came across the lake.

I enjoyed the vacation from flying, and I liked to walk about in the storms without having to worry about icing up or flying into a mountain. We weren't making much money, but we weren't spending much either. The airplane sat tied upon the lake and I kept the snow swept off her, for deep snow can bend or break the wings and tail of an airplane.

We just let the problems of the world fade away. There weren't any newspapers or newscasts with the predictions of impending doom, nor stories of man's unkindness toward man. We looked at our traps, cut firewood, baked bread, roasted meat in the fireplace, and in this happy world where the joys of childhood are real again, Christmas came and went. We found a new meaning in time, and new dimensions in living.

Getting an airplane ready to fly in cold weather is a big job. First you must tramp a runway a quarter of a mile long and fifty feet wide a day or two before you are ready to leave so it will have time to freeze solid and hold up the airplane. When you are ready to depart, you clean all the snow and frost off the airplane, heat the engine and instruments, put the battery in, pour in hot oil, and start up the engine. The skis have been blocked up on chunks of wood and you pour five gallons of hot water over each ski to clean off all the frost and smooth up the bottom of the skis so they will slide on the granular cold snow. All this has to be done before daylight, as the days of midwinter are short at best.

With everything ready off we would fly to Hughes to pick up the monthly mail and purchase a few supplies. We would hurry back home again to put the airplane up on blocks and tie it for another month. That night we would light a big fire in the fireplace and sit nearby and read all the mail.

You get into a routine of living in the land and you are carried quietly along by it. The birds and animals were always about us. Martha loves all the wild creatures and their intricate lives fascinate her. Their lives are more fascinating than those of many people, as each in its own way protects itself and its family while making a living and providing for the future. We spent much of our time observing them and never a day passed that we didn't learn something new about them. The chickadees fed on our window ledge and one day four moose came up the path by our cabin, walked by the house, and faded into the spruce forest. One morning there was two inches of fresh unmarked snow when we awoke. After breakfast we saw the tracks of a moose right by the window not ten feet from where we had eaten breakfast; yet we hadn't seen it pass! Caribou moved about us all winter long.

I had promised Jim that when he could put three consecutive shots in a three-inch circle at one hundred yards, and when he had read all the stories on caribou we had at the cabin and could tell the age, sex, and physical condition of a caribou by its antler formation, then he would have passed his caribou test and could shoot a caribou on my license. In Alaska a boy is allowed to hunt on his father's license until he is sixteen, provided his father accompanies him for big game. I am grateful to Alaska for its sensible laws. The Alaskan citizen enjoys the greatest freedom of any person on earth, and with all the modern devices we now have I feel safe in saying that the Alaskan citizen of today enjoys the greatest freedom any man has ever known.

Jim passed his shooting test for caribou by hitting the three-inch bull's-eye three times straight at one hundred yards with my .30 carbine. The next day a band of caribou came around the lake and Jim was ready. We needed meat and Jim was to be the provider this time. Martha and I watched him make his stalk and he slid the last fifty yards downhill in a sitting position, keeping out of sight. The snow worked up under the back of his parka until we expected to see it come out around his hood!

He made it into position, though, without the caribou seeing him, and we could see him squatted down in the snow waiting as the caribou began to pass a hundred yards away. We saw him aim and fire while the old cow he had selected moved away from the herd and lay down and the rest of the herd moved quietly on, unaware that a boy had just shot his first big game. Jim had made a good shot, too, hitting the animal exactly where he had been taught. There is a pride in sharing, doing a job well, and in being together. All these were present as we gathered on the lake ice to congratulate our young hunter and dress out the new meat supply.

Beaver trapping starts in February and the season is open for two months. You cut holes down through the two- or three-foot ice near the beaver houses and set traps or snares on poles. It is a slow process but a rewarding one, for beavers aren't hard to catch and their pelts bring a good stable price year after year. Beavers are the only fur-bearing animal there is a limit on. (Polar bear used to be classed as a fur-bearing animal.) The limit runs from five to twenty per trapper, depending upon the area and the year, and a trapper's children and wife are each allowed a limit if they work in the trapping.

Beavers are very local animals, and if a trapper takes good care of his trapline he has a steady cash crop each spring. The available water and food supply in an area limits the number of beavers your area will support. If your area will support a hundred beavers, you may as well catch fifty each year, for if you do you will have still a hundred beavers; but if you never trap you won't have any more than a hundred either. Beavers are a stable crop and today in most all the villages they are the only animal of any consequence that the trappers go after. The pelts average thirty-five dollars apiece and they rank as the world's finest beaver pelts.

An interesting shift in the lives of the native people has taken place over the last twenty years. The old-timer who prospected in the summer and trapped in the winter, as was so popular at the start of the bush-pilot era, is gone. Gone too are the natives who once made their living hunting and trapping. The desires of the people for more worldly goods couldn't be supplied by their old hunting and trapping life and they concentrated in the villages or moved away to the cities. Two things caused this change to be permanent.

First of these was the social security program. A man who worked all summer in the seasonal occupations was eligible for unemployment when the summer work all closed down. Previously he had gone on to trapping as a normal part of his life. Now if he went to trapping he lost his unemployment checks, and he was sure of the unemployment checks while trapping was hard work and a gamble. A few of the older generation realized that this was direct relief-charity and wouldn't take it, knowing those who did forfeit human rights and dignity. The younger generation feels relief is its just due and today almost no one traps until his unemployment has run out. This usually happens by the time the beaver-trapping season begins, so beaver trapping is still popular.

The second factor that contributed to the end of the old system of trapping was the new school system. There are excellent schools in every village today, but they run the regular fall, winter, and spring terms. The people want their children to have as good an education as possible, so instead of moving to the traplines each fall to enjoy family life there, the family now lives in the village the year-round, where the children can go to school. At first the men would go to their trapline homes and trap alone, leaving the family in the village, but it was no life at all. They had been away working all summer, but being away most of the winter too was unbearable. They could draw unemployment and that is what they did.

Today many of the young people know little or nothing of the land and the life their fathers knew. This prompted the bishop of the Northwest Territories to say that modern education has produced a generation of educated fools who have no place to go and can't live in their own homeland any more and who have as well problems with drunkenness and juvenile delinquency. He is unfortunately correct about Alaska as well as northern Canada. Yet modern transportation and communication has brought change, and progress moves in many directions.

Perhaps a block system similar to the one British Columbia uses is the answer to most of the land usage of future Alaska, a system whereby a fur, fish, and game rancher has control of a very large area that is capable of supporting him and his family by trapping and the sale of game through guiding and hunting or fishing leases. This seems the best solution to returning the land to the people and the people to the land. It would also serve as a basis for a tax structure and help develop Alaska's major industry, which is recreation.

Martha, Jim, and I didn't trap many beavers, for we live right at the northern limit of their range and food isn't too plentiful. Thus that season we caught five and quit. There is a lot of work involved in cleaning a beaver pelt and we spent nearly half a day in skinning, cleaning, and tacking the pelts in a circle. A beaver pelt—a "plew" as the old mountain men called it—makes a perfect circle. The muskrat season follows the beaver season, but there are very few muskrats in our area and we didn't bother the few there were.

Our trapping season was over and the spring breakup was starting. We flew to Hughes on our monthly trip and we talked fur prices with Les and Patty.

I was a little puzzled by our beavers' size, though, for beavers sell by measure, with a 72-inch skin bringing so much and an 84-inch skin being about tops. Since beavers are stretched round I thought it would be the distance across as did Martha.

"Our beavers must be babies," Martha said.

"I'm sure they are full grown, but the largest is just 42 inches across," I told her.

Les heard us talking and burst out laughing.

"Bud, you know a beaver is graded by adding the length plus the width or some people would stretch them longer. Your 42-inch beavers are 84 inches and really big ones."

Les offered us more for our pelts than we could get anywhere. Our season's work would bring a little over the five hundred dollars we estimated. Back home again we looked at our collection. There was the mink that was our first catch and had made Jim's pack "lighter." Old Grandpa, the sable, with a bent tail that was so old he was turning gray; the big gray wolf I shot on the river bar in the moonlight; the lynx cat that we had hoped so to catch and finally did; the lovely wolverine we had so hated to kill—they were all beautiful pelts now, but beyond that were personalities and memories to us. Jim looked over his string of squirrels and ermines remembering each fondly. We spread them out and took pictures of them and then stood admiring them.

"Do we have to sell them?" Martha asked.

"No, we don't have to sell them," I said, feeling rather bold and independent, "but we are trappers, and after all trappers do sell their catch."

"Let's keep them all. Let's not sell any. I want the lynx mounted to go above the fireplace."

Jim and I hated to sell any of the pelts too, but a man has to be practical, set a good example, and teach his son to be practical too. We kept them all—and it set a pattern for the years that followed. The lynx cat hangs above the fireplace, old Grandpa, the graying sable, and the other sables make up a sable stole for Martha, the mink that lightened Jim's pack is a collar for one of Martha's suits, the big gray wolf is sometimes used for a throw rug, and all the rest are tanned up and looked at from time to time. One of Jim's ermine hangs on a peg above my desk as a memento of the beautiful animals of our land, a small boy who needed lunch on the trail to make it on home, mountain peaks pink in the low midday sun, and the soft light from the cabin window as we crossed the lake on snowshoes thinking of dinner.

Trapping is for men and small boys. It is a fast-growing sport in our land where you make your stake in the summer and enjoy it in the winter. Almost all the children who live beyond the towns make their first money trapping. It is their first business venture. Through trapping they acquire an understanding of the land, its wildlife, and their own ability, which they can learn in no other way. It is the best father-and-son sport of all.

The light economical snow machines we now have make it easy to travel to and from or about your trapline. It is possible for anyone to enjoy this winter sport. The old dog teams were hard to handle, expensive in time and food while a big drain upon the land, for they were fed from the fish and game of the land. One old trapper told me it took a hundred caribou a year to feed his dog team.

The furs of the Arctic are rare luxuries and should be used to bring beauty and joy to women and men. The furs are a very perishable crop that must be harvested carefully and regularly or else they are wasted.

The first bush pilots were the original trappers' taxi and they opened up a new era of living for us all. They made it easy to harvest the precious furs from all the Arctic, but above this they made it possible for us all to become wealthier by sharing the understanding, freedom, and love of our wilderness. It is up to us to pursue it, use it wisely, and pass it on to our children.

13

BARROW AND POINTS SOUTH

When Captain Beechey's sailing sloop *Blossom* made its voyage of discovery in 1826, it was blocked by ice near the Seahorse Islands, and the mate, Mr. Smythe, in the ship's long boat went on north with a crew of twelve men to explore. At a spot they called Cape Smythe they found the largest settlement of "Esquimox" they had ever encountered; there were between four and five hundred people. They had almost reached the tip of North America and had found the largest Eskimo settlement in the world. The Eskimos called the spot Utkeavik, which means "Place of Retreat," and it is the Eskimo name for Barrow Village of today. It is the present site of the twin towns of Barrow and Browerville.

There is no settlement at the sandspit top of the continent that changes with any big storm and is called Point Barrow. This true Point Barrow has no settlements at all, although a few hunters did camp there until 1940, and the town of Barrow is some ten miles away to the southwest. The idea that people and some mapmakers have that there is such a settlement as Point Barrow may have been responsible for Wiley Post's crash, for some believed he found Point Barrow and then when there was no settlement there he felt he had made a mistake in navigation and flew past Barrow searching for it, only to run low on fuel and crash on beyond his destination. Colonel Charles A. Lindbergh had the same problem when he flew north to the Orient, but he had better weather and luckily located the village.

The location of Barrow made it useful, first to the Eskimo people, for the ocean current running north met the ocean current running west and created the worst ice conditions in the American Arctic. It created an open lead right near shore where a sea-hunting people could catch seals all year round and where the bowhead whales passed in their migrations

136

each spring and were killed by the people using jade-tipped harpoons, jade lances and skinboats.

Here took place the battles of the giants. The Eskimo whaling crews camped on the edge of the leads waiting for the whales' return each May. A bowhead whale weighs up to eighty tons and would supply food to the entire village for a long, long time. Despite its size, a bowhead is not a fighting whale, even when wounded, but you can get hurt by its dying struggles; and then, too, killing an animal of this size with stone-tipped tools from a skinboat in the ice is no small chore. The Eskimos harpooned them using seal skin floats attached by walrus- or ugrug-hide lines. The bravest and most ambitious men were the whalers, and since the entire village shared in the whale, the best whalemen were the leaders and heroes of the village.

Pursuit of the bowhead whales for baleen brought hordes of whalers following in Captain Beechey's wake, and the village of Barrow became the stopping-off point because ice conditions pinned down and crushed many vessels at Barrow. As a consequence the toughest and mangiest lot of humanity ever assembled poured into Barrow as the whalers of the seven seas descended upon the friendly hospitable Eskimo village. So many shipwrecks took place there that the government built a survival station at Barrow under the direction of Lieutenant Ray. The impact of this nineteenth-century whaling fleet upon the Stone Age people would have been disastrous had it not been for the Arctic winters. The Eskimos understood the Arctic and the whalers did not, so this horde of men were like small children in the grip of Arctic winters, and the Eskimos showed them the way. The Eskimos also felt that the "Tunick"—as they called the white man—was not a very intelligent person and couldn't even survive without special help.

The Presbyterian Church established a mission at Barrow and a few years later the government built a schoolhouse. The price of whalebone fell from five dollars a pound to thirty cents with the invention of spring steel, all the whaling crews left the Arctic in one year, and the Eskimos went back to leading a quiet life. The whale run had been pretty well depleted, but there were still enough for the villagers, and life flowed on easily.

The exploration of the Arctic was on, though, and the air age was bringing Barrow into the picture as our most northern point of land. In 1926 Roald Amundsen's dirigible

Norge flew across the North Pole, and in 1928 when Ben Eielson and Sir Hubert Wilkins flew across the Arctic they started from Barrow. They, of course, stayed with the hospitable Charlie Brower and plotted their course in his dining room.

Wiley Post tried to reach Barrow. Lindbergh landed there on his way to the Orient. Joe Crosson, Sig Wien, Noel Wien, and John Cross flew in and out of Barrow. Charlie Brower had developed a unique system for talking in pilots that we use even today. People living a quiet life have extremely acute sense of hearing and can detect the sound of an airplane many miles away. Charlie Brower used this facility, and he would send a person out in each direction from the station to listen for the airplane, and when they heard it, report its position. Then Charlie would tell the pilot how to turn to come in over Barrow. The method worked well, and Martha still uses it to bring me in or any other airplane groping its way through the fog.

Barrow was becoming a magic word if for no other reason than that it was our most northern settlement. The Navy decided to build a base there in the early 1940's and the second big push was on, and this one was for the exploration of oil and the resources of the Arctic.

Until then all who ventured into the Arctic were a friendly lot, like the Eskimos themselves, and they shared in what they had, were willing to lend a hand, and were dependent upon one another. Stealing as such was all but unknown, and anything you left in a cache was safe. Yet the people owned all the land and its resources.

The Barrow naval program came in in ships, and a group of quonset tin shacks went up six miles north of Barrow out toward the point, with all the security, red tape, and high-handed governmental policy that is necessary to the establishment of a naval base on foreign soil—for the Arctic section of our nation was considered foreign soil! The naval program's main purpose was to partially explore Petroleum Reserve No. 4, which covered all of northwestern Arctic Alaska from the Colville River on west. There were known oil seeps in the area, and in 1924 this vast tract of land was set aside. The coming of the Navy and the vast network of government agencies and bureaus was the beginning of the end of the good old days. Before then the people who had gone north or lived there did so because they either loved the land or wanted to learn from it. The whalers had been strictly motivated by profit, but they stayed to the seas and didn't change the land. However, the newcomers now began to change Arctic Alaska, and the people's lives changed quickly with it. The oil-exploration camp of Umiat was built on the Colville River, and the Arctic contractors began hauling in heavy machinery from Barrow by caterpillar trains—a combination of big tractors pulling boxcar-sized sleds across the frozen prairie. The machines used much fuel, and fuel came in 55-gallon drums that were cast aside whenever empty until the Arctic prairie was littered with empty oil drums and trash of every description from beer cans to complete abandoned camps. In summer their tractors tore up the prairie, leaving scars that are clearly visible twenty years later.

They found oil, and just about six miles from the village an excellent gas well. This was piped past the village to the naval base, but although fuel was Barrow's biggest problem, no one in Barrow was allowed to use any of the natural gas; nor were the people allowed to drill for their own fuel upon their own land—the blanket withdrawal of all the land for a petroleum reserve had taken them all in! The permission to keep warm in Barrow was argued out in the U.S. Senate until, in 1964, permission to use their own natural gas to keep warm was granted the people at Barrow.

In 1884, Charlie Brower came to Barrow. Born in New York of Dutch parents, Charlie Brower became a guiding force in the development of the Arctic. Everyone loved Charlie Brower, and he was called "King of the Arctic" because he knew and understood the people and the land. Every expedition and every new project in the Arctic sought Charlie Brower's help. Because of his work in exploration and his scientific achievements he was elected a member of the Explorers' Club. Charlie Brower guided his adopted people from the Stone Age and dog teams through the beginning of the age of the air. In his excellent book, *Fifty Years Below Zero,* Charlie tells of those years.

It isn't often that the son of a famous man takes up where his father left off, but this was what Charlie Brower's son Tom did, and yet Tom made his own way right from the start. As a boy he sailed on whalers and spent much time in California. From his father and the whaling captains he learned to understand the Arctic Ocean. From his trapping and dog-team driving he learned about the land, and from his work with the air expeditions—like the Wilkins-Eielson flight across the Arctic Ocean—he learned about airplanes and the air. Tom Brower was Sig Wien's closest friend in the Arctic and taught Sig much of his Arctic lore.

The winter Tom turned eighteen, the sailing ship *Arctic* was making its way to Barrow when the pack ice came pushing and shoving in. Tom was hunting down the shore near where the Post-Rogers monument now stands, and he realized the captain was going to lose his ship, so he paddled out to the ship in his skinboat.

"Captain Bertencenee, you had better take your ship out into the sea and round the point to anchor behind the hook or she won't survive," Tom told the captain.

The distraught captain said he didn't dare attempt such a bold move because his insurance wouldn't protect the vessel if it rounded the point.

"You're caught if you stay here," Tom said. I suppose the warning of an eighteen-year-old boy didn't carry much weight to the old captain for he decided to play it safe and sit in the path of the oncoming pack under the shelter of his insurance policy.

Tom just stayed aboard and watched. The ice closed in. The small pans first shoved in until the ship was blocked off, then the big floes came knifing in like ice breakers and punctured the ship. She was doomed.

"I'd take a thousand dollars for the lot and a safe passage ashore," the captain told Tom.

"You have yourself a deal, captain," said Tom.

Tom ferried the crew ashore in his skinboat. Then Tom figured out the best-looking ice floe and tied the *Arctic* alongside it by running the anchor lines up onto the ice and making them fast. The ship was taking in water rapidly, but she was steady and wouldn't roll and trap the men working to salvage cargo. The ice had carried the ship within sight of the village, and as the ship's crew made their way to Charlie Brower's home, a group of Eskimos gathered to watch the ship go down.

"Lend a hand here," Tom called, and through the cold night they worked, sloshing through ice water, piling things upon the ice and relaying them to shore.

"It's our winter supplies, so don't overlook a thing."

Tom went through the ship that now hung by the lines only, for it had been crushed in by the ice. Every box on board was vital for the winter ahead. At the same time Tom kept even a more careful eye upon the ice and current, knowing full well the pack would swing soon, taking all out into the moving pack and crushing it.

By the afternoon of the fourth day Tom knew that all the supplies really needed were ashore. The time had come to abandon ship. The men were all dead tired by now, but some still wanted to go back for more.

"We better quit," Tom warned. "Our luck has held this far. Let's don't push it."

All went ashore. As if to verify Tom's warning, the ice began to move and the ship, loosed from its berth, slid into the sea.

Tom made his way back to the village and into the living room where his father sat talking with Captain Bertencenee.

"Here is your thousand dollars," Tom said.

"Is this your son, Charlie?" the captain asked in surprise. I'm sure the idea that he had sold a hundred-thousand-dollar cargo for a thousand now seemed odd as he stood in a warm safe home instead of upon the deck of a sinking ship in the crushing ice pack.

"Yes, that's Tom. He's old enough to make a deal and wise enough to handle it, too."

In reality, according to the laws of the sea, Tom had salvaged an abandoned ship and wouldn't have had to pay a nickel for it, yet without Tom's timely know-how, the winter supplies would have been lost.

Tom married Kate and they moved east and south of Barrow into a land where Tom had trapped. Here they built up Half Moon Three reindeer ranch. They ran a little trading post there and here their children were born. The reindeer business grew and their business prospered. Tom and Kate are very hard-working people and are happy to be useful. In addition to the business, Tom collected all the birds of the Arctic for various museums and worked with each agency that arrived in the Arctic.

Then Charlie Brower died and soon the things he had built were up for public sale. Tom and Kate were wanted in Barrow to fill the void left by Tom's father. They were needed to supply the village's needs. They left their much-loved ranch and bought all his dad's things. It was no small job to provide the necessities of a village for a year, to anticipate its needs and have things ready to last the entire community until the *North Star* arrived next year—for Barrow is ice-locked ten months out of the year, and the ice pack can drive in at any time to virtually stop shipping the year through. As Tom at eighteen had carefully selected the essentials from a sinking ship, he now ordered a year in advance the supplies from the South Forty-eight.

I am sure the little store with its big warehouses run by Tom and Kate handled more of a variety and a greater volume of goods than any store of its size in the world. Tom also changed business methods. In the past it took a 100 per cent markup to handle goods on the once-a-year supply schedule. Tom figured it would be better to turn over the merchandise more often at a smaller markup.

Tom's friendship with Sig Wien and his supplying the even more remote trading area at Half Moon Three had quickly taught him the use of airplanes, so Tom set out to order the lighter necessities by air, and the Wiens hauled them in at thirty-five cents a pound from Fairbanks. In Charlie Brower's day mail went out by dog team along the coast every couple of weeks. Now it came by air on Wien Airways. As the volume of goods ordered increased, so did the size of the airplanes, and the cost of shipping dropped to fifteen cents a pound. The government decided to send all Arctic mail via air at the regular rates. The things Tom and Kate ordered now by air included everything that would fit into the new airliners, and Wien began to provide daily and often twice-daily flights. Tom and Kate Brower were always Wien's largest customers. They led the country step by step. No village in America ever had more problems to solve than did Barrow as a Stone Age culture bridged the gap to the Atomic Age in one generation.

The guiding influence in Barrow's change from a Stone Age culture to modern life was the Presbyterian mission there. Tom Brower is one of its strongest supporters, and when the people in Anaktuvuk Pass wanted to build a church there, Tom sent his check for one thousand dollars to help.

Life has not been easy for Tom and Kate. They have made a success through hard work and faith in themselves, their land, and their Creator. They have lost four of their children in accidents. Many of the jobs they have undertaken have been thankless ones. They have gone ahead building a better life for all about them. Tom once built a small apartment house that was beautifully constructed to house the shifting population of Barrow. The rent was reasonable and accommodations excellent. It was only up a season when some careless tenants burned it down. The fire was beyond control, and everyone was standing around watching it burn; then someone noticed Tom walking along the beach whistling. "Listen to that guy whistling away while his house burns." Yes, Tom was whistling while his hard work burned down, for he knew well that there was no use crying over spilt milk and the carelessness of others.

The fall of 1963 was the roughest in Barrow. The ice pack protects our coast from storms by holding the wave action down. This time the friendly pack was far away when the storm swept in from the west, raising the water, and the big waves driven by gale-force winds swept across the village. The houses near the beach were washed away. Big cakes of ice as large as the houses came in like battering rams. It looked as if the whole village were doomed. Tom had made a museum and restaurant out of the old whaling station that had been built by the U.S. government as the first building in Barrow, then purchased by Charlie Brower for his home, and all Arctic travelers and expeditions had made their headquarters here in Charlie's time. Here were on display all the treasures of Barrow's past, and on the wall facing the sea hung the framed numbers of Wiley Post's airplane. During the fury of the storm Tom and Kate were busy trying to save the irreplaceable things, but the pounding waves beat out the wall, took it out to sea—the airplane numbers with it. Tom and Kate still worked on between waves and grabbed a hold of something solid each time a wave receded so that they wouldn't be carried out to sea.

It was Barrow's worst disaster and half the buildings in town were washed away, but not a single life was lost. Barrow people are among the world's most resourceful and took the worst storm in their stride. The relief workers sent to help were surprised to find help really wasn't needed. The people had helped themselves and began rebuilding as soon as the storm let up. Tom and Kate put up a makeshift wall to replace the one carried away by the sea and shored up the sagging buildings until permanent repairs could be made next summer. The numerals off the Wiley Post plane were gone, though, and no search turned them up.

A year later no trace of the storm remained, and someone had even found the Wiley Post airplane numerals and they were back upon the wall in their old place for all to see. This is all that is left of the historic airplane that carried Wiley Post and Will Rogers as far as the monument near Barrow. A collector once offered Tom ten thousand dollars for the numerals, but Tom declined, saying he felt they should remain in Barrow for all who venture there to see.

It isn't often that the son of a famous man takes up the work his father started and is even more successful at it than his father was, but this has been the case of Tom Brower. The Explorers' Club recognized this several years ago and elected him to membership, as it had his father before him, because of his work in the Arctic, his exploration into the unknown, and his service to mankind.

Barrow is the top of our American world—the farthest north. It is the largest Eskimo settlement in the world. Here the eastern pack ice meets the southwestern pack and goes crushing north. Here every extremity of the government bureaus can be seen amidst the Eskimo culture that has in one generation bridged the gap from the Stone Age. There is a good landing field at Barrow now, completed in 1965, where the Wien jets now land twice a day. Barrow is the glamour girl of the Arctic, and you haven't seen America until you have seen Barrow.

There are other towns in the Arctic, too. If you follow the Arctic coast east of Barrow for about 180 miles, you will find Colville where the Colville River flows quietly into the Arctic Ocean. Here once the inland Indians and Eskimos met with the coastal Eskimos to trade jade, birchwood, furs, pitch, and trinkets of the inland for the seal oil, walrus-hide rope, ugrug skins, whalebone, ivory, and trinkets of the seacoast. There once were quite a few people living in this area, but now only our home is there. Going on east another 180 miles you come to Barter Island where the people of our Alaskan coast met the Canadian people to trade for oil lamps from the magnetic North Pole area or for things from Greenland and the Hudson Bay area. There were well-established trade routes all across the Arctic from Greenland across into Siberia that functioned long before America was discovered. They are gone now, as are the people. Going on east you come to the Demarcation Point where Canada and Alaska join. There isn't anything there and you will have to read your map closely to find it. Of course, you will have to "clear customs" to cross that point to either Fairbanks or Inivuk, Canada! That covers the Arctic except for the little village in Anaktuvuk Pass to the south where the Brooks Range opens up to let the inland people into the Arctic prairie.

As we go southwest of Barrow we pass the small concrete marker where Wiley Post and Will Rogers were killed and travel on to Wainright, Point Lay (now abandoned), Point Hope, Kivalina, Noatak, and Kotzebue. All are little Eskimo villages, aside from Kotzebue, and they sit beside the Arctic Sea, still served by small airplanes and using a few dog teams—but fewer each year.

The day of the dog sled is over. The first airplane started its decline and the power snow sled that runs on an endless track driven by a small gasoline engine sealed the sled dog's fate. Almost no one has a dog team any more. Dog teams are a thing of the past, along with covered wagons and the pony express. Picturesque and faithful, I hated to see my own dogs go. Yet few can afford the cost and time needed to keep up a dog team, and fewer still want to take the time and patience to train one. A select number keep them for racing and sport, but aside from these the dog team has gone down the last long snowy trail and will be seen no more as a mode of transportation.

14

THE WIRELESS, CHART, AND BEAM

When Noel Wien made his first flight from Anchorage to Fairbanks he followed the railroad north, making his way through the sky by what he saw upon the ground, but navigation by railroads ended at Fairbanks and so did highways. From Fairbanks on the only reliable guides were the rivers. The maps were topographical ones that showed the river systems and mountains, but even on these much was dotted in or marked unexplored. As for radios and air charts, they didn't exist as yet.

Every pilot was grateful for the river systems because they provided landing areas on their bars for the wheel planes, on their frozen surfaces for skis, or upon the rivers themselves for floats, but best of all, rivers led somewhere. No matter how they twisted and turned they led you safely through the bad weather and were guides in an unknown land. Andy Anderson's remarkable flying records out of Bettles were due in a great part to the Koyukuk River, for Andy could make his way up and down this river when "even the birds were walking." The rivers still remain the small operator's best guides across Alaska. When I pushed north into the Arctic prairie to the ocean, I followed the rivers because all of them flow north from the Brooks Range to the Arctic Ocean. In winter when the land is white and all other features vanish in a whiteout, the willows along those Arctic streams have guided me across many, many times. I learned the rivers from a canoe and the willow-bordered frozen streams from a dog sled. It was natural that I would feel at home flying along them. Sam White was a river-flying man, as was Archie Ferguson. In fact, Archie was a river-barge pilot before he learned to fly, and he

Carl Ben Eielson characteristically garbed for action north of the Circle. The helmet and goggles are modern, but the caribou calf parka is as ancient as the Eskimos themselves. *Noel Wien*

Each November the Helmerickses haul supplies to their home for the winter. Here Bud used the Wiens' C-46 as a charter plane. *Harmon Helmericks*

The Wien-Alaska "airport" at Bettles in 1952; Andy Anderson in the doorway, another bush pilot making flight reports at the window. *Angus Cameron*

Bud Helmericks at work on their house which he built in the summer of 1958. *Martha Helmericks*

The Helmerickses' house on the Colville River Delta in the spring. *Harmon Helmericks*

A guide's work often begins after the game is down. Here the author is "caping out" a Dall ram. *Angus Cameron*

Bud loosening the snow from the skis of the *Arctic Tern* with boiling water. *Martha Helmericks*

A winter view of the Helmerickses' summer lodge at Walker Lake. *Harmon Helmericks*

Jim Helmericks, also a pilot and hunting guide, and his *Golden Plover* on her oversize tires. *Martha Helmericks*

Kisik and Oineak (Mr. and Mrs. George Wood). *Harmon Helmericks*

A Brooks Range fishing camp. *Harmon Helmericks*

A bull caribou still "in the velvet." *Harmon Helmericks*

The dog team on the Arctic prairie is now rarely seen and has been replaced by the diesel oil-transporting truck. *Harmon Helmericks*

used the rivers as much by air as he ever did when he piloted barges. So it was that all us bush pilots used the rivers for our maps and the seat of our pants for instruments—but, as Sam White put it, "they had serious drawbacks." The rivers didn't always go where you wanted to. And in bad weather you put in some terrifying moments trying to follow them and hoping you made the right turn and were really headed through the pass instead of into the box canyon. It takes a lifetime to learn all Alaska's rivers.

The seat of your pants was a wonderful instrument and by its use you could handle an airplane as easily as a gull flies, being conscious of its every whim and movement. This was flying, and none ever loved flying more or handled an airplane better than those who flew by the seat of their pants. But such flying had one fatal drawback that cost the lives of those who tried to fly by that instrument in a whiteout or when they lost all reference points—the seat of your pants won't register if the airplane is perfectly coordinated. Thus, if an airplane is in a perfectly coordinated maneuver, the seat of the pants says all is well. If you have a reference point such as a patch of prairie grass only feet below or a dim line in the sky or a single star or lantern, you are all right. But if all reference points are gone, you are in serious trouble. The airplane plows straight ahead and as long as the forces of gravity—the seat of the pants is a gravity-sensitive instrument—are exactly balanced, you believe all is well. With your directional sense gone, though, you begin a perfectly coordinated turn and then begin a dive either right or left. Like a man lost you go in a circle but you also have the up-and-down dimension and begin to dive as you turn, and all the while you feel you are flying straight and level. As the speed builds up you know by the sound of your airplane that you are going too fast, but if you pull back to climb you only tighten your spiral. At this point it isn't just a spiral any more; it is the graveyard spiral that few ever walk away from. Whatever the pilot does at that point is the wrong thing, and unless he breaks into the clear in his screaming dive for the earth, he will plunge straight into it. The artificial horizon and directional gyros today eliminate this hazard. But these instruments can fail or be eliminated by some element of chance and so the graveyard spiral still claims the unfortunate pilot who loses his reference points.

Very few people have ever seen a graveyard spiral because

of its very nature. It must happen under conditions of no visibility. Some few have seen the last frantic moment as an airplane broke out of low overcast and dove into the earth. A few, a very, very few, have seen a graveyard spiral from beginning to end. I saw my son Jim caught in one.

We had been delayed in leaving our Arctic home a little over a month by Wien Airlines. They had agreed to haul our supplies a month earlier and then hadn't done so. As the days passed the airplanes were tied on the runway and the seeds of disaster took root as frost formed inside the heater ducts.

Jim's plane was a Piper Pacer 99K. It was a pretty little ship that he loved and flew well, like the many pilots before him had flown. The sun had set for the year in our Arctic land by the time all our freight was hauled. The job had proved impossible for Wien Airlines and Interior had to do it. Martha and the smaller children went in on the last C-46, leaving Jim and me to bring the two airplanes into Fairbanks, a flight of about five hundred miles. There is quite a bit of good work to closing down an operation for the winter, with pipes to drain and shutters to close. It took us a day to get it all done, and as the faint light of a second day dawned we were ready.

It was a gray day of no shadows and only a faint horizon all around. It was nearly noon by the time we had the airplanes ready to go. Jim had just put his airplane on skis and wanted to fly it around a few times before he loaded it up, so I gave him a push to break his frosted skis loose to start him and he taxied out on the runway. I went back to working with my airplane and watched Jim take off at the same time. You couldn't see his airplane very well because of the cloud of powdery snow it threw up, but when it broke ground I could see it plainly. The airplane climbed about two hundred feet and Jim started turning to the right. I turned to look at my airplane when I noted a change in the pitch of sound from Jim's ship and looking I saw the ship, instead of straightening up from the right turn, go right on turning and as the turn tightened, the ship rolled into a graveyard spiral and plunged earthward. I knew in that awful moment that there wasn't a chance for Jim to recover; he was too low. The engine wound up in a thin screeching drive that was all but lost in the snowy world. The ship started to spin as it dove and then it struck. The engine and right wing hit first. It was like slow motion, partly hidden by the snow that flew up, yet I saw pieces sailing through the air. A ski and landing gear sailed up and out. Pieces of fabric and then a silence—louder than the impact.

It had all happened in the center of the frozen river about a half mile from where I stood. I started to run to the spot but realized I could go faster on our Ski-doo (a power sled), so I hurriedly started it up. Should I get a hacksaw and ax to cut Jim free if he were pinned? A shovel to fight fire? No. Just get out there. So I raced full speed across the snow, scared, praying, hoping fire wouldn't break out, and straining my eyes to see signs of life through the tears. I had been to airplane wrecks before. I knew what they were like. There is an old saying among pilots that if you can hit with the nose up you can walk away from it. Jim had plunged right into the ice.

I was about halfway to the airplane when I thought I saw something move in the plane. A cloud of steam from snow and gasoline upon the hot motor partially obscured my view; then I was certain I saw a movement and I realized Jim was busy throwing out his emergency gear and dragging it back away from the airplane in case it caught fire. Jim didn't see me until I was close and then he came stumbling toward me, his face and hands a mask of blood. Blood covered his clothes, but I could see no arms or legs were broken.

"I've failed, Dad . . . The *Plover* will never fly again."

These were Jim's first words. We went to the house and I looked Jim over for injuries, but I could find none except for the cuts on his nose and lips where his head had hit the instrument panel. We packed snow on these and soon had the bleeding stopped. Then Jim wanted to go back and look at his airplane. So we did.

Jim hadn't known he was in trouble. He thought he was climbing out straight ahead and the first indication of trouble he had was when he hit the ice! What had happened was that the frost in the heater ducts had melted as he took off, water ran down into the hot heaters and came back as steam that settled on the windows. It came softly in a white land covering all. The frozen instruments read normal.

I have had this happen to me twice but luckily each time I had had a window open so I could see a little horizon and hold the ship straight until engine heat had melted a small peephole in the frost and the cold sluggish instruments warmed up enough to record accurately.

Jim's airplane lay nose down, tail up in the air. Both wings were ripped and torn halfway back, while the fuselage was half twisted. The propeller was wrapped around the engine, which was driven back into the cabin halfway. Every window was broken and the gasoline tanks were split wide open. Jim's face had stamped its imprint in the instrument panel! The *Golden Plover* was dead. She had torn herself apart saving her pilot. When the plane struck the ice, it had luckily slid and torn apart as it did so. The pieces of airplane were scattered over a two-hundred-foot area, but the young pilot had crawled out to save his emergency gear and walked away. An airplane is a graceful thing that is built light and strong and it comes to life with power. In a wreck, given half a chance, it will tear itself apart slowly so that the people inside are spared.

One of Wien's pilots, flying the Arctic coast with a De-Havilland Beaver in midwinter, nearly "bought the farm" a few weeks later. He had unloaded some gear at an oil-well drilling site, leaving the engine idle as he worked; but with the cabin doors open, the instruments froze up and frost formed all over the windows. It was a white featureless day and when he took off he switched to instruments at once. All read normal as the ship climbed away in the −50-degree air but the pilot had left a little crack in the window and suddenly he realized that either the oil-well derrick was in the sky or he was on his side going into a graveyard spiral. His gyros had frozen and read straight and level regardless. With eyes locked upon the oil-well derrick, he righted the ship and in a little while cabin heat had the sluggish instruments working. But for that lucky glimpse of the oil-well derrick a routine instrument flight would have been his last.

When the CAA began its work just before World War II, it set up radio ranges across Alaska. A radio range consists of four separate towers that each send out a signal. The letters are A and N in Morse code because the − — of the A and the — − of the N when they are synchronized go together to make a steady hum in the thin line where they overlap. This creates a "beam" that radiates from the station in four directions. By your compass heading you can tell when you are flying toward the station and also by the increasing or decreasing strength of the signal if you are completely lost. If you wander into the A side, the A signal becomes predominant, and of course the same happens if you wander into the N side. It all sounds simple and in truth it is. In practice you must fly instruments steadily to be proficient in their use and this adds another tremendous variable to flying because beams can swing due to things still unknown and the beam that brought one pilot through a mountain pass may lead another right into the mountain.

Radios were always undependable when you really needed them. Snow static blocked out your beam in storms and so the old bush pilots never quite trusted all these electronic marvels, but as air transportation grew they had to use them. You couldn't wait day after day for clear weather on a scheduled run. The people they served were changing their attitudes.

"It used to be when you flew into the village a week late with the mail on the once-a-month run the people all gathered around and were happy as can be that you got there at all," Sam White once told me. "Now with mail flights four times a week, if you are a few hours late a couple of them will come down to the field to grumble and the rest will write a complaint to the Post Office Department."

The age of instrument flying was here and those who would fly the routes would have to be instrument operators. The many marvelous electronic navigation aids of today make flying by any other way obsolete, except, of course, for those of us who still love flying for flying's sake. Man has mastered distance pretty well and by his ingenuity can now circle the planets, but there still remain the unknown and the human element of error. When the two combine the results are disastrous.

Ice fog hung in the air as I finished my chores and stepped into our snug home on the Arctic coast. It was near −50 degrees. Martha was preparing our dinner and I dumped a sack of wood into the bin for the fireplace.

"I'm glad I'm not looking for the lights of home in this stuff," I told Martha.

The radio had been crackling and humming as there wasn't much airline traffic, but it suddenly came to life as a pilot somewhere out in the night pressed his microphone button, and then a voice cut through the frosty air. "Wien Barter Island Beachcraft C-18 landing Barter Island two minutes." It was Tommy Thompson on the chartered flight along the Arctic coast returning after a long day. We know the pilots' voices and mannerisms in using their radios.

"Roger, Beachcraft C-18 landing Barter Island two minutes . . .". and the Barter Island operator went on to give the weather conditions. They were identical with ours, but of course Tommy Thompson was on instruments and the radio would help him in until those first lights of the runway appeared.

Martha went on cooking. I picked up Mark and the clock ticked away. The next sound from the radio would be Tommy Thompson's report that he was on the runway.

"Beachcraft C-18, what is your position?" we heard the Barter Island operator ask. No answer. Martha and I looked at one another. We knew. Tommy Thompson was dead. Somewhere out in the ice-fog-choked darkness where −50 degrees held the land in an unrelenting grip, two lines had met and crossed, X marked the spot.

The voice on the radio was insisting now. "Beach C-18, what is your position? . . . What is your position?" Then silence; there was no use calling now. It was time for listening and waiting.

They found the ship in the Arctic winter's midday twilight. It lay a few miles from the end of runway and all were dead except for one passenger who had survived the crash and the −50 degree cold. He had been piled under the rest and lived.

The story was plain to read in the snow. Tommy Thompson had made a long flight that day and was now nearing home, letting down to land. The altimeter setting changes with the air pressure and it is affected by the local barometric pressure and by the altitude of the airplane. Somehow Tommy's altitude had read perhaps five hundred feet when he really was at ground level. In that white world he couldn't see a thing and his first hint of trouble was when the propellers nicked the ground. Instinctively he had come back on the wheel to climb away from there and came on with fuel power. The ship had shot up away from the ground and the engine responded with a roar. That was the right thing to do but for one factor. The tick of the propellers on the ground had bent the blades back and their usefulness was gone. They were powerless to pull and so the ship shot upward; instead of climbing as it should have with engines at full throttle, it stalled and plunged nose-first into the frozen beach. Had Tommy been flying a ski airplane he would have had no problems for the skis would have touched first. The retractable-wheeled Beach had allowed the propellers to hit first.

The radio has eliminated isolation, as, of course, has the airplane. Isolation exists only in the mind today. Radios aren't pieces of equipment that can be repaired or installed by anyone, though, contrary to popular belief. We in the Arctic really owe our excellent radio communication and teletype operation to one man—Ed Parsons.

I first saw Ed Parsons at Hughes back in the early 1950's. He flew in with a Stinson Voyager to talk with the Jameses. We fell to talking flying and radios ànd he gave my faithful Lear T30 a check for me. Ed soon went to work for Wien Airlines and the next thing we all knew there was a regular reliable radio network across all ninety of Wien's stations.

When Ed meets a problem he doesn't put it aside, nor go around it; he solves it, and not tomorrow but right now. His Stinson was soon traded in on a Cessna and the night was never too black for Ed, nor the hour too early.

Ed and his wife, Grace, built their own home in Fairbanks and into it went every kind of electronic device. Where the bush pilots distrusted electronics, Ed put unlimited faith into them because they are his life and he understands them. If the electricity falters in Ed's home a standby generator comes on automatically, and when city power is restored the generator cuts off. His hot-water system was worked by "stack robbers" that used waste heat from his stove pipes. A recording system records everything said on the air all day so Ed can keep track of how his radio system is working.

When the Alaska Centennial Committee wanted a device to start the countdown second by second for the Centennial still a couple of years away, they looked far south and found one like they wanted at nearly a million dollars. This was many, many times over their budget. Someone thought to ask Ed Parsons. Ed made a trip to Seattle for a few extra parts, made his own cabinet, and for a few hundred dollars had the device operating perfectly—not at some long-off delivery date but that week.

Martha and I had built up our Arctic coast home piece by piece from the tent camp to a modern home and, as Ed put it, we were ready for a modern radio. We made arrangements to tie in with the Wien Air Alaska radio system and I put in the antenna poles. Ed had told us he would be there on a Thursday. It was October and not too good weather, but Ed appeared on time. I had expected it would take him a couple of days to hook up a new radio station. He asked Martha where she wanted the radio, made a few measurements, cut some antennas, took the big radio senders apart, fastened the radio cabinet to the wall, put the senders back in, tuned up the set, and we were on the air. Ed called several stations, made a few adjustments, and called for the Barrow weather. After lunch Ed was on his way to Barrow to work on its radio, and that evening as the dark and fog moved in, we heard Ed file his instrument flight plan for Fairbanks. That was the way Ed's day went. From time to time he would call in to see how our radio was working. It never gave us a moment's trouble. When Ed did a job it was done right and didn't need a second checking over. "The Great White Father of Communication" is what Ed became known as, and in truth he is the father of Arctic communications.

When Jim Freericks and Al Mosley were trying to make a go of charter flying with the Fairchild C-82 Flying Box Car they had the right landing gear refuse to retract. The Anchorage mechanics couldn't make it retract. It was illegal to fly that way, and dangerous, as well as nerve-racking, but pilots with bills to pay and work to do kept on. In Fairbanks the mechanics couldn't make the wheel retract either. "Ask Ed Parsons" someone said. Ed took a look at the wheel and made a few minor adjustments.

"Try it now."

The wheel retracted perfectly.

When the job was done Ed lost interest in it. Things that worked perfectly were no challenge. In his white shirt and tie Ed looked like a regular bank vice-president, but there the resemblance ended. Ed looked beyond the horizon of the known into the future and he didn't stay still long just looking. It was inevitable that in ten years Ed would have all the problems of Arctic communications solved to his liking. Wien had the finest radio hook-up possible. All the stations worked like a vast party line, aircraft were in touch with all stations, and the teletype clicked away. There were more pressing jobs to do elsewhere. There was need for modern connections with Vietnam, and the last time I saw Ed he was working on that problem. We miss Ed in the Arctic. We miss his sure, confident radio messages regardless of time or weather—like the night we heard Ed call for Fairbanks weather and then Bettles weather. He was on his way from Barrow to Fairbanks up over the Brooks Range in a black sky. Fairbanks weather was impossible and so was Bettles. Ed then called Patty James at Hughes.

"It's not very good here, Ed," Patty said, "but it looks like the best you have."

"Hughes hasn't a lighted runway. We will have Abraham put out some lanterns for you, Ed."

"Thanks, Patty. I'll be in at 9:55" was Ed's confident reply.

We heard a little further talk and a little while later we heard Ed call Patty and say he was on the field and would remain overnight—as if there was a question of going on in that storm; but with Ed there really was.

"That's fine, Ed. I put you down at 9:55," Patty replied.

Ed is a superb pilot. He used to fly in many of the airplanes that needed repairs until Grace* made him stop that. She didn't like to see him fly in a craft that others wouldn't.

The year Ed left the Arctic vibration broke a wire on our light plant and ran 220 volts through our 110-volt radio, blowing some tubes—a really minor problem that Ed would have had fixed the next day. It took the airline seven months to get it repaired. Funny what a big hole one man can leave in a vast land.

---

*EDITOR'S NOTE: Grace Parsons was later killed in an auto accident in Seattle, Washington, in 1966.

15

SAM WHITE

"'Sam O. White' was what was painted on the side of his pick-up truck," Andy Bachner told me as we worked away on the airplane engine at two A.M., getting it ready for Eldred Quam to repair the next day.

"I remember it well; I've lived right across the road from Sam, and he was always hauling gas boxes or people back and forth from his airplane in that old pick-up—he was always helping somebody do something. I guess I grew up thinking Sam was the best pilot in the world."

He was right. There weren't any better than Sam.

I like Andy's father, Jess, who operates the Bachner Aircraft Service. Jess has the ability to see right through the fanfare and red tape to the simple truth. Talking about Sam White, Jess summed it up: "He's still here, isn't he? He flew longer than any bush pilot and still flies. Lots of them fancy Dans tailed in because they couldn't fly. Of the bush pilots Sam's the best."

Thus Jess in his direct manner eliminated all the list of great pilots who had tried and failed, who had used bush flying to go on into the airline business as had Noel Wien (who Sam says is the best), and the list of men who went on to fly the airlines or into other business. Like in any other elimination contest—and bush flying surely was an elimination contest in more ways than one—only those who finish the race can stand and be counted. Thus if for no other reason than because he was the only one who stayed the course from the first conception of bush flying until the end of that era, Sam O. White will be chosen by the historians of the future as the greatest bush pilot of them all.

Sam O. White was born in a log cabin on a homestead just six miles from a wide spot in the road called Eustis, Maine. Their homestead was the last farm before the Canadian border. It was a two-and-a-haf-mile walk to the log school that his father had helped to build, and school lasted but two and a half months each year. There were ten children in the family, and at fourteen young Sam went to work in the woods lumbering. At sixteen he was guiding each fall for deer and black bear.

From here he went to work with the International Boundary Survey and became a foreman. This job finished, he went to scaling in the lumber mills, measuring the board feet in the logs. Already Sam was dreaming of how he could get to Alaska, but World War I started and Sam enlisted.

They sent Sam to Fort Slocum, where special skilled men were being gathered to make up Company C of the Rangers. Two and a half months later Sam was in Europe. In Fort Slocum Sam had met Jack Allman from Fairbanks, Alaska. Jack was a physically tough man and just the kind Sam liked. He was a real soldier, Sam recalls fondly. Jack told Sam all he could of Alaska. They landed in Brest, France, together and fought through the entire war in the trenches.

In the spring of 1919 Sam was again working for the company surveying in the summer and scaling logs in winter. In 1921 Sam went with the U.S. Coast and Geodetic Survey level party to Green River, Utah, where they surveyed the Colorado River as far as Lees Ferry, Arizona. In 1922 with the Colorado River survey over, Sam was back scaling logs again, and he took the Civil Service exam for U.S. Geodetic Survey Reconnaissance man for work in Alaska.

Sam and his youngest brother sailed for Alaska on the steamship *Northwestern,* landed at Seward, and went on to Anchorage where they worked. The young brother stayed a year and a half and returned to Maine. Sam and his outfit moved on up to Fairbanks.

It was a horse outfit with some thirty-odd horses and six mules and about forty men. They would pack all summer and fall surveying and each winter sell all the horses for from seventy-five cents to seventy-five dollars a head and buy a new set next spring. It was difficult but satisfying work for Sam, and he learned the terrain of Alaska well. He walked, rode horseback, and canoed all across interior Alaska and up the border line between the Yukon Territory and Alaska.

In 1924 Noel Wien began flying from the ball park at Fairbanks that was later to become Weeks Field. Sam saw his first airplane in Alaska when Noel Wien flew a mining man named Ingram and his secretary from Nenana to a river bar on the Kantishna River. It was the first meeting of the two great Alaskans that were to usher in the new era of travel.

By 1926 the U.S. Coast and Geodetic work was finished, and the outfit left Alaska. On their way south, Sam stopped in Juneau and gave Mr. E. P. Walker, head of the new Alaska Game Commission, founded in 1925, a record of the game distribution he had kept during his survey work. It was the first report of game conditions ever made in those areas. Sam went on with his outfit to Minnesota and Louisiana, but Alaska was where he wanted to be. It was in Louisiana that Sam received a telegram from Mr. E. P. Walker asking if he would join the Alaska Game Commission. Sam was on his way. He stopped in Juneau to become familiar with the outfit, and in July 1927 he arrived in Fairbanks and went on to Fort Yukon to his first assignment. Sam hasn't left Alaska since.

Sam was the first game warden in Fort Yukon, and it was the first time game regulations had ever existed in the North. Being a game warden is not an easy job in the frontierland, but Sam's love of the land, its animals, and peoples made him liked wherever he went, and in the many years I have known Sam I have yet to hear anyone say a word against him. Sam always knew right from wrong and had the courage necessary to stand behind his convictions so that even those he arrested admired him and were his lifelong friends. I never tire of talking with Sam about his Alaskan adventures, for there is an honesty and reality in every one—like the spring Sam made a patrol up the Novie River to check over the trappers and game conditions. It was spring flood and everything was underwater on the low ground and ice was so piled up along the higher ground you couldn't land easily. They were about forty miles upriver when they came to an old cabin with water right up to the eaves. The sod-roofed cabin was just like a small island, and upon its roof were gathered the field mice of the area. Sam landed on the cabin roof and the mice just moved over. Soon they lost their fright and wanted to look in the grub box and sleeping bag. Sam let them look about. At seven A.M. and three P.M. they would all leave the roof en masse—as if they had received an order—and swim away in to the willows. They would be gone about one hour feeding, and then they would come back in groups of twelve to fifteen and climb back up on the roof. Sam spent three days camping upon the rooftop, and although there were mice all over and underfoot he never injured a single mouse.

When the floodwaters dropped a little, Sam proceeded on upriver, where he soon met the traffic coming downriver and checked over their catches. A few had an illegal piece of fur that Sam confiscated and the trap or firearm used to take it. One Indian had an illegal beaver he had shot. He also had several .22 rifles all beat up and one brand-new one that he obviously loved and kept neat.

"Which rifle did you shoot the beaver with?" Sam asked.

"I use this one," and the Indian pointed out the new rifle.

Sam was a little taken aback by this superhonesty since all Sam wanted to do was educate and regulate a little and not really work any hardship on anyone. He asked again, thinking the man would change his story now that he had a chance. Sam picked up the oldest, most worthless .22, saying, "You meant this one," to take along with the beaver.

"No, I use this rifle." And the Indian took back the old rifle and gave Sam the new one. There wasn't anything Sam could do but take the new rifle, of course.

The trappers heading into town from the winter spent on traplines were out of most everything, and Sam shared his provisions here and there. An old trapper had half of a fresh-killed moose in his boat, and he thought Sam had come to arrest him. He said he had killed it because he was out of all food, and Sam's examination showed it was true. He hadn't wanted to waste any so he had brought every bit along, sharing it with others short on food, too. Sam said the man had been within his rights and gave him a little grub to go with it.

The patrol work was all by dog team or canoe. In 1929 Sam transferred to Fairbanks. He had been thinking about using airplanes in his work, so he set about pestering Noel and Raph Wien to teach him to fly. They were busy with other flying but every spare moment they would take Sam up. The rate was thirty-five dollars an hour with Sam furnishing the gasoline. All Sam could afford was one drum a month on his salary—twenty-eight hundred a year—and the flights were mostly of an evening with a crowd of spectators looking on.

Then Sam bought his own airplane. It was a Boeing Golden Eagle parasol monoplane, open cockpit, of course, and two-passenger. It was powered by a Leblond 90 h.p. radial seven-cylinder engine and cost Sam thirty-five hundred dollars.

Ralph Wien finished Sam's flying instructions in the Golden Eagle.

It was a lovely evening and about half the town was gathered at the ball park, watching the airplane as Ralph Wien put his student through his lesson. As they landed, Ralph remarked, "If you hadn't made that one mistake I would have soloed you—I've half a mind to anyway."

"Well, go ahead."

Ralph hopped right out and walked away. Sam thought he would take off and just fly around for an hour, but once up alone he couldn't get back to the field fast enough. Sam wanted to rest then after one solo trip, but Ralph made him take off and land five more times. At the end of this Sam taxied up to where the other plane was tied, and Helen Junas, "about the prettiest girl in town," came over and shook hands, congratulating Sam.

Sam flew then of a morning and evening until his drum of gasoline was gone, and then he had to wait until next month when he could afford another drum. Sam always did his business on a cash basis. By fall he was using his airplane regularly in Game Commission work, and the Game Commission was furnishing the gasoline.

Thus by personal initiative and at his own expense Sam White became the first man to use an airplane for conservation work in Alaska, and from all I can gather this holds true in all America and likely for all the world. The year was 1929, and young Sam White, after years of pack horse, dog team, and canoe, at last had a way to cross Alaska's vastness in hours. All he had to do was furnish the airplane, maintain it, repair it, do all the work, and the Game Commission would furnish him the gasoline while paying him twenty-eight hundred a year. A man just couldn't have had it any better, Sam felt, and as usual he was right. He was doing an old job a new way. Sam had also met Mary Burgess, the pretty nurse who had come to the hospital at Fort Yukon, and the airplane provided a happy way to get over there. In both Game Commission work and courting the airplane proved very successful and soon pretty Miss Burgess was Mrs. Sam O. White.

The Golden Eagle hadn't proved too successful, so Sam sold it for five hundred dollars after thirty hours of flying and purchased a Swallow biplane for another thirty-five hundred dollars. It, too, was an open-cockpit two-place airplane. The Swallow had a three-hour–twenty-minute range, and at

—40 degrees, no matter how many clothes Sam wore, three hours were about all he could take in the open cockpit, so the Swallow's cruising range was just right.

The airplane now enabled Sam to cover his whole territory in a few days, a thing he hadn't been able to do in a year before. At first Sam was disappointed in the amount he could see from the air. He was so busy just flying the airplane he wasn't able to look about much, but a little experience and a little more training in reading the things he saw from the air enabled Sam to even track a marten or rabbit from the air. It was possible to check on traplines and visit most of the trappers as well as the towns. It surely put a damper upon game violations, for no one could tell when an airplane might appear.

Out at Lake Minchumina one cold day Sam stopped to visit an old Swedish trapper. He welcomed Sam and fed him well, but Sam knew that the man didn't have a license. Since all Sam wanted was for the people to comply with the laws, he didn't say anything when the old trapper "couldn't find his license." The nearest licensing officer was eighteen miles away, and Sam knew the trapper would head for there and purchase his license just as soon as Sam left, which, of course, was Sam's reason for stopping in the first place. Sam heated his Swallow, and after many preparations, he was on his way. The old trapper had harnessed his dog team, and after just as many preparations he was on his way too "to look at some traps." Sam made a few circles looking things over, and when he was sure the trapper was on his way for a license, Sam decided to just head on across to the town— sort of a race between the airpane and the dog team, but the dog team got there first!

Sam was about halfway there, sitting up all nice and happy in the open-cockpit Swallow, flying along at eighty miles per hour in the −30-degree air when he saw the oil pressure falling, and he landed as fast as he could in a small slough. It was about seven hundred feet long and there wasn't any room to spare. An oil line had broken, leaving a stream of frozen oil across the snow and a pile of it where he stopped. Sam got busy and gathered up his oil off the snow, for it was all he had. He melted it in a pot, separated the water from the oil, and after repairing the broken line he poured the oil back in and flew on. The trapper was already in town and duly licensed, although, of course, Sam didn't mention it.

Broken oil lines were and still are a constant cold-weather

problem, and one equally as bad is the frozen-up crank-case breather. The moisture that should run out freezes and cuts off the escape of gases from inside the hot engine. Pressure builds up then, until something has to let go. The oil seal around the propeller hub often is it, and you get a bath of oil right in the face, so it seems, as oil blows out and plasters the ship. You land fast then, or it may blow off an oil line or blow out the dip stick and squirt the oil out through that hole.

Fred McCoy of Kansas City, Missouri, and I were hunting polar bear in the pack ice on a thirty-below-zero day, and after many hours of flying I headed home. I noted the oil-pressure gauge wavering as I taxied in for the landing. After we landed I saw that the whole belly of the ship was coated with oil and frost. The breather had frozen, and the last oil in the engine had blown out the dip stick hole as I landed. Luckily no damage was done and I was home. Most of us carried extra oil just in case this happened. Later in Fairbanks I asked Jess Bachner about this and how to lessen the danger. I thought that an electric breather might be the answer.

"Simple, just fix it with a hacksaw." Jess just sawed a cut, partway through the line up near the engine. "Now when it freezes at the bottom, it can blow out the top."

I haven't had any trouble since. Jim purchased a new Super Cub all fixed up for the *Arctic* to replace his first *Golden Plover*. On our second flight together we were coming in home in −31-degree air when I missed Jim. I circled and couldn't see him so I started back and there he stood beside his airplane with oil all over its belly. The breather had frozen up and luckily blew an oil hose loose. Jim had seen the pressure go up on his oil gauge and just landed. Luckily no damage was done, and next day in −40-degree air Jim took the Ski-doo and returned with canvas, made a little tent, repaired the airplane, and flew it the fifteen miles on in home. You learn again and again what the first bush pilots learned so often: don't trust anything until you have checked it out, and then be a little scared and suspicious all the time. When a Stateside manufacturer says "made for the Arctic," he means northern Illinois apparently.

Heating oil, broken oil lines, blown-out oil, and draining oil took up much of Sam's early flying. One evening Sam saw the oil-pressure gauge drop, and he landed in a narrow swamp. It was pretty small, and the skis left two deep ruts in the soft snow. During the night it first warmed up and rained, then turned cold and hailed the size of marbles, and the wind blew, filling the ski ruts with the icy marbles. "It was just like being on ball bearings," Sam remarked, and he had to tie the tail of his Swallow before he dared prop it (start it by hand). The Swallow came up out of there, off that icy ball-bearing runway like a helicopter, and, "It was the only time I ever saw such a condition in Alaska."

Hugo Stromberg had a place up on Dry Creek, and Sam knew he was violating the game laws, so Sam saved up his gasoline until he could make a trip there. He couldn't land there with the airplane so he landed eighteen miles away. From here he walked in on snowshoes. As Sam came close, Hugo's dogs began barking, and Hugo came out of the cabin. He picked up a .30–06 rifle and took the ammunition from it and stood it back against the cabin. Sam was unarmed but walked right on up. It is an interesting thing about a land like Alaska where we all have many firearms and use them all the time. The idea of using a firearm for shooting another person is competely foreign, and crimes involving the use of firearms for such a purpose are rare indeed.

As Sam reached the porch, Hugo came out again, and Sam said, "I've come to arrest you, Hugo."

Hugo stood erect and saluted. Parts of two cow moose and a dozen rams lay scattered about the front yard. Sam found evidence of the killing of over fifty sheep and eight moose since September. While they were talking the dogs began to bark and Sam realized they hadn't been fed. "Just go ahead and feed your dogs as if I weren't here. It won't be used against you," Sam told him. At this Hugo took a big ram from off the cabin roof, chopped it up and fed it to the dogs. They visited the cabins on Hugo's trapline and found a set gun on the door of each that would have fired had anyone opened the door. It was all done to protect the cabins from "bears"—in midwinter? They spent the night at his main cabin, and in the morning Sam started Hugo off with his sled and the evidence to leave his dogs with a friend twenty miles away on the road while Sam walked back to his airplane. Hugo was waiting for Sam at the highway with all the evidence just as Sam had directed him to. The judge gave him a stiff sentence for his depredations.

"Hugo was really an honest man though and knew he

was doing wrong, so he took his punishment and bore no hard feelings," Sam remembered.

All weren't like him though, for many, after killing off vast numbers of animals, then fought it out in the courts, claiming they needed them all to prospect and open up the country, which is the polite term used when anyone wants to destroy a land and change it. "By and far the real prospectors lived in peace with the game and would eat bacon and beans all season rather than kill any of it," Sam recalled. "The game was their neighbors."

From 1929 until 1936 Sam furnished his own airplane and worked with the Game Commission. They were happy days working in the land he loved with his own airplane and working with people and animals. These were the things that made Sam the happiest. For above everything Sam has his entire life been proud of his country and counted it a privilege to serve all in it.

In 1936 the Alaska Game Commission purchased its first airplane, a Lambert monocoupe. Then in 1938 they purchased two Fairfield 24's, and Sam went to Hagerstown, Maryland, to pick one up. One went to Interior Alaska and the other to Southeastern. In the years between 1936 when Sam quit furnishing his airplane and 1938 when they purchased their first one, they chartered aircraft.

Fairbanks was a pleasant town in those early days. There were but fifteen hundred people in all, and mostly older folks with names like Hard Luck Louis, Moose John, Snowshoe Kid, Malemute Kid, and so on. Big dog teams were the rule, and they didn't bother with snow removal in winter. People worked in the summer and coasted through the winter. There were a few bush pilots, and life had an easy pace in a vast quiet land.

Sam had almost everyone buying a license, and game violations were at a minimum. There was much game in the interior, and the Arctic was still an unknown quantity. Then World War II broke across the horizon, and all Alaska awoke to the bustle. Sam had thoroughly indoctrinated the Game Commission in airplane usage and taught young Clarence Rhodes to fly. The previous commissioner had been pretty much against aircraft, but Clarence Rhodes was all for them when he became the head of the Alaska Game Commission.

It was the beginning of the end of game work for Sam, though. The military started arriving in vast numbers, and,

"They wanted special concessions to violate the game laws. The generals and commanders were the worst, and it went right on down through the ranks."

Sam brought in a few and saw them turned loose. Next Sam was told to overlook these violations. Sam took a dim, dim view of the use of helicopters to kill moose and bears and the wanton killing, and so brave, honest Sam spoke up.

One pilot refused to take his commander on a moose hunt from a helicopter and hid in his tent. "I hadn't thought much of the guy," Sam recalls, "but I had to change my mind. When the commander located the pilot and told him to take him moose hunting, the pilot said: 'Sir, you are setting an awfully bad example for your men, and I will not fly you for this purpose.' Well, of course, that pilot didn't stay, but I sure had to admire him for it."

The pressure on Sam began building up, and he got the word that he would have to go along with the trend. The military set the pattern and you went along with it or else. When I think of Sam White, I always remember a painting by Norman Rockwell that shows one man standing in a crowd while all the seated audience is apparently going along with the popular trend, and you can tell by the look on the fellow's face that he is right.

Low wages, furnishing his own equipment, dangerous, cold work, and endless hours hadn't dampened Sam's spirit. When he had to submit to popular pressure and go along the easy path that he knew was not right, he resigned. Maybe it was the honest Indian trapper who had insisted he broke the law with the brand-new favorite .22, maybe it was a trapper floating down on the spring flood feeling guilty because he had to kill a moose out of season to survive that made Sam protest by resigning. I believe it was due to a combination of all these, plus Sam's understanding of the rights of wild creatures to their wilderness and the dignity of man in his relationship with them.

Sam resigned in Anchorage and went to work for his old friend Noel Wien, with an increase of salary of from thirty-two hundred dollars to seventy-two hundred, flying the Gull-wing Stinson, Fairchild 71, Travelair, Bellanca CH-300, and Model 33 Stinson. The cargo was mail and passengers.

Up until then Sam had never had a serious air accident. This was true of all the early flying. They made many, many forced landings but had very few serious accidents.

The pilots were pretty much their own mechanics, maintained their own airplanes, and knew them inside out.

It was in the winter of 1942 that Sam set out with a load of cased gasoline in a Gull-wing Stinson SR10 that had some old ski harness on it. New ones could not be had even with priority. He was going from Fairbanks to Circle and was over the Yukon when the right ski harness let go and the ski hung down. It threw the ship into a spin that the left rudder couldn't counteract. It happened at twenty-five hundred feet, and the spin was so violent it snapped the left ski harness, and now with both skis hanging down the ship quit spinning at last, and Sam had control at nine hundred feet. Air speed was down to 85 and stalling speed at 80! It was still eight miles to Circle, and Sam couldn't quite hold his altitude. If only he could find a patch of glare ice. But it had been a snowy winter, and he couldn't find any. Now Sam had a big decision to make: should he head straight for Circle and if he couldn't make it crash in the trees, or should he follow the winding river where he had a landing but a much longer route. He took the route across the trees. As he neared Circle with full power, he was just clipping the trees, and there wasn't a question of reducing power; he just flew onto the field and the hanging-down skis stubbed their toes. The loading gear came off in one-foot sections. The skis weren't broken but flew off, and so did the motor. The cabin and wings stayed together upright. It hadn't been possible to cut any switches. There were eleven cases of gasoline in the cargo net, and three burst wide open, spraying gasoline over all. Sam sat in the pilot's seat, his right hip broken. He was dazed but conscious, and the airplane had stopped in forty feet. Eddie Moore pulled Sam from the wreck. There was a wide black-and-blue welt across his stomach where the safety belt had held. Eddie propped Sam against the airplane, and there he sat. The Indians had been keeping well back, thinking Sam was dead and a ghost, but when Eddie began talking with him, they came forward, from the oldest to the youngest, to shake Sam's hand and pay their respects.

In some 11,500 recorded, and hard telling how many unrecorded, hours of flying, Sam had perhaps eleven forced landings and only two accidents. The other was when he flipped a Stinson 35 straight wing on its back, landing upon a gravel bar near Ruby. Sam's flying wasn't the routine run of the mill; he was always breaking new trails.

In 1944 Sam's old outfit of Coast and Geodetic Survey came back to map Alaska, and Sam fitted out his L-5 Stinson, which he flies to this day, for Arctic work, and began flying with them. The work was moving camps, directing and pushing into unknown areas. Sometimes he had men scattered all over, and he alone knew where they were. If anything had happened to Sam those crews would have been in a spot.

This was the kind of work Sam loved. It had only one drawback, and this was the wanton killing of big game that the newcomer is so likely to indulge in. Almost everyone who arrived had a rifle, and Sam knew it was up to him to hold back "the kiling and burning" that followed in the newcomers' wake. When the oil camp of Umiat was starting up, I talked with a worker there who said that there wasn't a moose or caribou got by that area that half a dozen weren't shooting at it. A man committed suicide right in camp near Hughes by shooting himself. He wasn't discovered for several hours. When the police questioned the rest of the camp as to why they hadn't investigated a high-powered rifle shot in their midst, they answered that people were always shooting at moose or ducks about camp. A shot was so common that no one paid it any mind. This was in July when no seasons are open.

The piles of illegally, wantonly killed animals always saddened Sam, and he didn't hesitate to enforce his own punishment by telling the offenders. One worker he had taken out to a site killed two caribou. When Sam came after him he was all ready to leave and abandon the animals. "You will pack out both of those animals so I can fly them to where they will be used, or I'm taking you direct to the game commissioner." The chap packed out the caribou.

In the early horse and mule days it had taken days or weeks to move from one area to another. In Sam's L-5 it was but minutes to the next camp; and that was Sam's job—camp mover, guide, manager, pilot, cook sometimes—and when camp was up he moved separate survey parties here and there. At times there would be two airplanes or even a helicopter to help Sam take care of his brood.

One day at Port Hiden Sam set out his survey parties in the morning and at noon when he went to change them he realized a whopper of a storm was brewing, so he hurried everyone back to camp and had all battened down for the blow, as dark descended. Rain swept in on fifty-mile-an-hour winds and four-foot-high waves sloshed up on the beach, but the second floatplane didn't come home. Sam knew they were in trouble and took off into the storm to search for them. You can nearly always see water during a storm, even in the dimmest light, so Sam followed the beach until he could find the lake the party was on. In the center of the shallow lake was a yellow-and-silver blob. The airplane was upside down in the water. After circling the lake in the near-darkness a few times, he saw a flash of light and located the three men on the downwind side of the lake where the waves were the worst. He made a landing in the storm and picked up two of the men first as this was all he could safely take off with from the wild water. The pilot remained. He had been a B-29 pilot, and after the glamour of the big planes and government money, he was quite disdainful of the lowly bush pilots and their small patched-up self-maintained airplanes.

"You won't be back," he told Sam as Sam said to wait there for him.

An hour later in the black of night Sam picked up the pilot. "I don't see how you do it. You have eyes that see in the dark like a cat's . . . I never would have believed it were possible to fly in such a storm, but in the dark besides . . ."

The accident had been caused by the pilot's trying to turn into the wind with power, and the high winds had just flipped him over on his back. No one had been hurt, and in the shallow lake all had waded to shore. When all were safe at camp, Sam's day was finished and his faithful bush plane anchored while the storm shook the tents.

Each winter the survey parties quit until open water the next year, and Sam then would change his L-5 Stinson from floats to skis and fly for the Air Corps Geodetic Survey. They were mapping all of Alaska from the air, making up the excellent aerial maps we now have. In summer they took photographs of the country from high-flying airplanes on clear days. In winter they had to tie in the exact locations on the ground by locating prominent landmarks exactly by triangulation on the stars. "Star gazers," we called them, and Sam flew them about to gaze at the stars through their instruments from first one location and then another. It was done in the dark and cold of winter when temperature could sink to the −60- and −70-degree levels.

This meant Sam had to take care of a crew of men in

this cold, using tents and carrying all the necessities of life along in the airplane while ranging across the entire Alaskan Arctic. You were dealing with the "experts" too, men who could locate any point on earth within a fraction of an inch from the stars but who, as Sam soon found out, couldn't tell a big lake's location from the air when they saw it! On one mapping trip near the Canadian border, Sam flew to the lake indicated, but the men disagreed with him since this lake wasn't where it should be on the map, and they told Sam to fly on. After all, hadn't their superiors made the map? But Sam's Superior had made the lake, and Sam knew where it was. After flying fifty miles into Canada, they finally asked Sam to find the lake for them; he turned around and flew back to the lake he had wanted to land on in the first place.

Sam had a knack of getting along with men under trying conditions. He kept the crews happy and always had some trick up his sleeve. Sam could pull off some of the most amazing feats of flying and come out slick as you please, so the crews never knew if Sam was just lucky or really had abilities beyond their ken—and of course it was a little of both. But the main ingredients were hard work and common sense. This last was something all frontiersmen had in abundance but seems to be dying out in the city men of today. Sam also has a joy for living never surpassed.

When the temperature dropped below −40 degrees, none of the bush pilots liked to fly unless it was a real emergency. So they just stayed camped when this happened. Sam had a new crew fresh from the States and all "goosey" about wild animals. They were camped on a lake shore and there were snowshoe rabbits all about.

"Wolf tracks," Sam would say with finality, or "lynx tracks," when asked about the many trails. There isn't much daylight in midwinter and it was 60 below out. Sam had a comfortable tent camp and a big pile of wood cut. Inside the warm tent Sam told stories of wolves just converging on such a tent camp and eating up all the people. In the yellow lantern glow the new crew listened open-mouthed. The dumbest savage isn't as ignorant about the animals of our wilderness as some "civilized man" when he wanders away from the asphalt jungle. So Sam built up the story, and then, taking his flashlight, he went out to "look at his airplane." In reality he went out to catch a rabbit. He shined the flashlight in the eyes of a couple before he managed to grab one, and its terrified screams rent the air. The next moment Sam slipped the rabbit into the tent flap and an awful commotion broke loose inside with people coming out under the tent or out the door. The rabbit of course made its way out the first crack. Sam had to hurry and save the tent from the hot stove. The crew didn't stay out in the 60-below air long, and Sam told them the true facts of the wild: that no man in the history of America has been harmed by a wolf or lynx cat, that your main danger is from yourself in the wilderness. It was a few days before they forgave Sam for his buildup and loose rabbit.

Sam's cooking, and his stews in particular, were always a mystery. The stews were excellent, but what went into them Sam was only too quick to relate. In reality it was plain good food, but Sam had to tell them the ingredients were all sorts of things from polar-bear paws to ravens.

Sam always had an answer for everything—like the time the ladies at Ruby couldn't get the gravy to thicken up at Christmastime. "Did you use snow water to make it?" Of course they had; we all use snow or ice water in winter, and in fact all of our Alaskan water is from snow or ice at some time. Sam let them think snow water wouldn't make thick gravy for six months, until they figured it out and cornered him on it. I once read, though, in a learned work on mountain climbing where you couldn't quench your thirst on snow water. This old boy was worse off than the ladies and their thin gravy, for you can't get finer drinking water nor purer drinking water than from melted snow.

Making the flying pay was always a next-to-impossible task. Everything cost so much and it was hard to break even. Then there was always the chance to lose it all in one moment's carelessness. Sam was the common man't pilot, hardworking at any job that had to be done and always mindful of the needs of others. Alaskans depended upon their pilots and rarely took advantage of them, knowing full well that a pilot's income and his life were both precarious. The thousand dollars he worked all summer to save could be lost in a rough landing when gear folded.

One time Sam had broken a landing gear at Point Hope on an unmarked prairie landing, and there were no repair facilities there. Sam made temporary repairs and flew on into Kotzebue on his way to Fairbanks to have the gear fixed. There were three planes there all going to Fairbanks, and since a storm was making up they all left. Sam was about ready to follow in his crippled ship when the Bureau of Indian Affairs doctor came down and said there was an emergency. Some natives at Barrow were ill and had been for several days. The doctor wanted to go to Barrow by way of Fairbanks and had just decided there was an emergency.

"I wish you would take that emergency back off," Sam said when he heard the nature of it. "This ship is crippled and can't pack a load. I'm already heavy."

The doctor wanted to get to Barrow, and now that he had been a Johnny-come-lately and already let the three good ships leave, he held Sam.

"Well, you got me, then, so let's get going," said Sam.

The doctor wasn't ready.

"The storm's moving in fast, and I can't take any extra load, so hurry."

An hour and a half later the doctor arrived with two enormous suitcases of heavy gear.

"It's way more than we can pack," Sam protested.

"I have to have it."

It was late, and the storm was pressing in. They made it as far as the Koyukuk River, and where the Kutheel joins it they hit a solid front of snow and ice. Snow, darkness, and icing with a crippled ship overloaded. The mechanic was peering out the right side. "Pull up." They missed a spruce-covered point by feet, wallowing along in the gloom following a river just feet above the trees. Sam knew where there was a lake a little way past Johnny Dayton's trapping cabin, and he made a blind shot for it and landed there. They unloaded and made camp for the night, happy to be safe and alive.

The next morning it was 45 below and Sam didn't want to fly, but the doctor was in a hurry. Sam heated the airplane and they loaded up. As Sam taxied out to take off, the right gear let go and the plane fell heavily on the right wing. They were stuck. That evening Johnny Dayton came up with his dog team to give Sam a hand. He knew Sam was in trouble when he heard him go by the cabin. Sam managed to get a message through on the radio, and in three days Alden Williams, flying for Dodson, came from Fairbanks and to Sam's relief took the doctor back with him.

It just hung in the −35- to −45-degree bracket as they worked repairing and getting Sam's plane back out. In the end it cost Sam ten thousand dollars before the airplane was flying again. The natives named the lake Sam White Lake and later the U.S. Geodetic Survey officially put the name on the maps. Yet this wasn't the end of Sam's experiences, for a few years later an earthquake shook that area and opened up a crack so Sam's Lake drained away and isn't even there any more!

Then came the day when the bush flying in Alaska was done. The CAB had already eliminated the title "bush pilot" in favor of "air-taxi operator," and Alaska wasn't a territory any longer. It was always hard to make bush flying pay; now it was impossible. The Coast and Geodetic work was finished. Airlines and helicopters were everywhere. Sam and his old L-5 Stinson were passed by in the rush as turboprop airlines and jets ruled the skies. He had opened the trail, made the maps, shown the way, and progress went roaring past.

People remember, though. It was a sunny day at Hughes in early September. I had flown down from the Arctic coast to pick up a hunting party and Sam's L-5 was tied up at a little float landing he had made beside the trading post.

"Sam is flying for Wien out of here now," Patty James told me. "He is stationed here."

I hurried down to the field, just an extension of the street, and there was Sam fixing up a freight shed. The Wien 180 Cessna was parked nearby. Sam's friendly bulk with a mosquito bar thrown up on his hat was working about tidying up.

"Nice landing, Bud. It does my heart good to see you handle a floatplane." That was Sam, kind and complimentary.

"Awfully good to see you, Sam, and nice to have you here with us for a while."

We both chatted a bit. Sam said there was space in his deep freeze if I needed some for meat and to use his gas cans if I liked. He didn't expect to fly his L-5 much but wanted it near him.

Then we were silent for a while, and at last Sam spoke, "I can just hear Noel: 'We can't have Sam at loose ends, better put him to flying out of Hughes,' and so I'm back with Wien again."

By the late 1950's the big airlines serviced all the main stations. They based in Fairbanks, kept constant radio contact, and didn't even change altitude en route without permission from the Fairbanks control center. They hauled tons and tons of freight, hundreds of passengers, kept exact schedules, and returned to Fairbanks. Noel Wien had quit bush flying years before and so had every other old-time bush pilot. Sam was the last left flying, and the bush run out of Hughes was the last one left, too. It consisted of delivering the passengers and freight on past Hughes to Utopia Creek, one of the meanest landings in Alaska, and to the mines at Hog River, as well as flying to Huslia and Alatna or any charter work in the area.

Sam took over and without incident, accident, or fanfare he filled the job nicely. In his late sixties, Sam was not only the oldest bush pilot but the oldest commercial pilot left flying in Alaska. Sam knew every Indian and Eskimo in the area and their fathers and grandfathers often. They all thought of Sam as the patron saint of aviation and several named their children after him. One cute little girl at Alatna is called Sam White, and the little rascal has the independence of her namesake, too.

One evening in midsummer I flew into Hughes about a year later and loaded up groceries and gear for the family. We were then living at our Walker Lake home. Sam came out to the riverbank to watch me take off. It was a warm evening when a floatplane doesn't like to fly, but I made it into the air all right and climbed out heading for home when I saw the oil temperature go on into the red and at the same time a whistling sound came from the engine as power fell off. I turned for the river again and managed to land about ten miles upstream. It is wonderful to land upstream, for then you can float back down. So it was a couple of hours later when I paddled the airplane to shore in front of Hughes and Sam was there to help me. We checked it over and found a piston had come apart. Sam got his tools and I dug out mine. We made a tripod of Les James's four-by-fours and while the Arctic sun swung around the north we took the motor off the *Arctic Tern* and crated it for shipment to Fairbanks. We both knew how lucky I had been to have made it back to the river. By breakfast-time the engine was ready to load on the Wien airline flight, and Sam took off in his L-5 Stinson to tell Martha I was delayed while I went on in to Fairbanks with the engine to get it repaired. So it was that at two A.M. the next morning as Andy Bachner and I worked taking apart the engine that we fell to talking about Sam, and

Andy said he had grown up thinking Sam was the greatest of them all.

It took five days to repair the engine, and then, Jess Bachner's mechanic (Marvin Jones), Sam, and I put the engine back in.

"What do I owe you for flying in to tell Martha, Sam?"

"You don't owe me nuthin'."

"How about gas then? You used up quite a bit on that flight."

"No. You don't owe me nuthin'. I've known you ever since you came to Alaska and you have taken good care of the country. Made it right pleasant. I've always wanted to have a place like that pretty one you have at Walker Lake. You have taken good care of the game too and you have a wonderful little family . . . just glad I could help."

That was Sam's pay. He loves the land, its game and people, and if you take good care of them you are on his side.

"Sam is more interested in the people, moose, and bears than the paper work," Patty explained one day as she tried to straighten out his flight manifests. "He is too independent."

I thought about one of the mechanics complaining about Sig Wien, saying he never makes an entry in a logbook, and then Jess Bachner telling about Archie Ferguson when he had an airplane worked on and the mechanic asked about his logbooks. Archie looked blank and said, "What logbooks?"

They were all too independent. Too busy living and doing things to get caught in paper and red tape, and Sam never did bow to the dictatorship of paper work. But what went on in the world about Sam he sure understood, and without asking a lot of questions he got in and did his part—like the time Patty James picked up a few words of a radio message. Radio signals often fade in and out or completely go away so you are left to fill in the gaps. This one went, ". . . half-drowned . . . usla [that would be Huslia] . . . Sam." Patty figured someone was half-drowned at Huslia, send Sam, and she called him. He was en route to somewhere, but he altered his course right then for Huslia.

When Sam landed upon the small dirt strip, they showed up with a twenty-two-year-old Indian man in as dirty a sleeping bag as Sam had ever seen.

"Can he sit up?" Sam asked.

"No!"

Sam laid him down in the back of the airplane, and they were on their way for the hospital at Tanana just that quick. Of course, Sam wondered how anyone could be half-drowned, but he didn't cloud the issue with a lot of questions; he just did his part. No one told him what had happened—Sam hadn't asked.

At Tanana Sam landed and the doctor and nurse met the airplane.

"Can you walk?" the doctor asked the patient in the sleeping bag.

"No."

"Why can't you walk?"

"I got no pants."

They used the stretcher and carried him away.

"Sam, you might as well stick around. I will X-ray his lungs, and if there isn't any water in them, you might as well take him back with you," the doctor said.

Sam drank a couple of cups of coffee, and the doctor came back.

"I X-rayed his lungs first, but I was too high. I finally found a .22 bullet in his ass!"

It was the first any of them knew the chap had been shot. At Huslia a few days later Sam learned the full story. Some of the men had been hunting muskrats and were walking single file along a trail. One had an old .22 Winchester automatic rifle with the trigger guard broken off. The trigger had caught in some willow brush and shot the man ahead of him right in the britches. He luckily had had a pack on his back so it went through the bottom of the pack first and hadn't done much harm to the recipient. Sam never did figure out how the half-drowned part fit in.

Sam did a wonderful job flying out of Hughes. He flew the routes, skillfully and consistently, and he handled the airplane with that skill and love of flying that the old bush pilots knew. When he moved a control he knew exactly what went on in each part of the airplane and why as only those who bought, saved, rebuilt, repaired, maintained, and flew their own airplanes ever will know them.

It was the closing of an era, and Sam closed it with the same efficiency, safety, and dignity that Noel Wien and he had opened it with some forty years before. It was the number of years, not lack of skill nor enthusiasm for the land, that caught up with Sam. Seventy was the CAB's deadline for commercial pilots, and as Sam reached seventy he retired from bush flying, and with his retirement came the end of an era. Sam was the people's bush pilot. He never made the headlines in the big papers outside because while he was often confused he was never lost. He never injured a passenger in all his years of flying. He didn't try to become a big-time operator, he liked the land, its people and his flying, and he flew steadily. Any old-timer will tell you that Sam never forgot the little orders nor that we all often needed a helping hand. He and Mary still live in a little log cabin home not far from where Weeks Field used to be. They have lived there longer than this generation can remember. It is a gathering place for all. If someone is down on his luck, they go to stay with Sam, or if they are in from the "bush," they look up Sam. If you get stuck in the snow or have car trouble near Sam's house he will be out shortly with his jeep to pull you out and help.

When some other form of travel has erased the contrails of the big jets from the skies and the scheduled airlines are replaced as easily as they replaced the bush planes, someone will sift through history and pick their favorite bush pilot from the facts at hand, as each Alaskan once did when bush flying was the new means of travel, and I'm sure the bush pilot will be Sam White. He was there with the first, he flew it all the way, he not only helped open the area but he closed it as well. He flew longer than any. In that steeple-chase that was bush flying, Sam White was the only starter who finished the course.

16

GAS-BOX-WIRE MECHANICS

They almost broke up Arctic housekeeping as well as put the mechanics out of business when some misguided individual decided to put the five-gallon gasoline cans up in cardboard boxes. It didn't last, though, for while paper cartons replaced the milk bottles, I'm happy to say they didn't replace the wooden gas boxes.

Gasoline, "gas," went north in cases. Two neat, square five-gallon cans were packed in a really handsome wooden box with two bands of galvanized wire around each case. The pilots needed the gasoline and everyone needed the empty cans and gas boxes. In fact, you couldn't set up housekeeping without empty gas boxes for cupboards, shelves, tables, or chairs. The empty cans made water buckets, dishpans (when cut in half lengthwise), berry-picking pails, and even dog-feeding pans. The uses of the five-gallon cans are endless even today and it did my heart good to see that the modern Honolulu Airport in Hawaii still depends upon the empty five-gallon can, for the clean-up men there use them cut in half diagonally for super dustpans to keep that beautiful airport clean.

In a couple of seasons the gas cans would rust through and then they became useful for the metal. You could flatten them out and roof a cabin, put them around the cache poles to keep squirrels and mice from climbing up, or even make Christmas tree ornaments from them. Sam White and I still carry small wood-burning stoves made from a five-gallon gasoline can.

The case gas was always higher-priced than drum gas, so we refilled the cans from drums for easy handling. They packed well in an airplane and were easy to handle in "gassing up the airplane." If the gas ran out of the pouring spout a little slowly, one could punch a hole in the upturned bottom to make it run out faster, or later when they put plastic pour spouts on the cans one could cut the spout out with a knife instead of opening the spout. This practice, which would save a minute of time, was never indulged in by the old-time bush pilot, because it ruined the can that someone needed and a man who did so was not to be trusted by honest men. If you didn't need the cans yourself, someone else did, and you took them along to the next village where all were happy to have them.

When our son Mark had just learned to walk he used to drag an empty gas can around calling it "Old train nine nine," and so they made good toys, too.

The mechanics found plenty of uses for the empty cans and boxes, but it was the wire that came around the cases that they really needed and they never would have kept the early airplanes in the sky without it. Gas-box wire was to those first mechanics what baling wire was to the early prairie farmers.

The first airplane mechanics were interested people who were willing to work under the toughest conditions just to be around airplanes. They were mostly farmboys who had tinkered about farm workshops from childhood and were handy with their hands. There were about a dozen such mechanics that made possible the bush pilot's operation. Each pilot had his favorite mechanic. Those of us who flew and still fly put our airplanes, our faith, and our lives in the hands of our mechanics. The airplane mechanic was the bush pilot's best friend. A bush pilot would fight for his mechanic and even pay him as often as he could. An airplane just won't operate without T.L.C.—tender, loving care.

The success of Wien Air Alaska would never have come about except for the existence of the fourth Wien child— Fritz—who was destined by the Fates to be the mechanic of the family, although, he did fly a little and each of the Wien brothers were excellent mechanics. It was Fritz, though, who did the dirty work, furnished the tender, loving care, and kept the airplanes flying to build the business from a single bush airplane into a modern airline.

Fritz recalls the early days: the Wien family lived at Lake Nebagmon, Wisconsin, where Fritz was born the fourth child to John and Mary Wien. Ralph, Noel, and Edith preceded him, while Sig and Harold were to follow. In 1904 the family moved to northern Minnesota where the children grew up in a log cabin on a homestead. They went to a log schoolhouse and tinkered about in the farm toolshop, learning those skills with their hands that are so necessary in a well-educated man and absolutely essential in a bush pilot.

It was while Noel was studying electrical engineering at Dunwoody Institute that he met Major Ray Miller, who gave him a ride in an airplane and sealed the fate of four of the Wien brothers. Harold alone never became interested in airplanes. Noel went right on into flying and on up to Alaska as did Ralph. It was in 1927 when he returned home that he found Fritz out of a job and ready to go to Alaska; broke, too, as so often happened in those days, but he borrowed the money and they headed north. Noel and Fritz landed in Seward with tickets paid for to Fairbanks and but one dollar between them. I did the same thing thirteen years later, but I was ten times as wealthy when I landed in Seward!

The train from Seward to Fairbanks stopped at every village, mine, or cabin and in between, too, if someone wanted off. It took two days to make the trip that today's airliners make in thirty-five minutes.

When the train stopped at Healy, Noel and Fritz were hungry, so Noel went uptown and purchased doughnuts with their last dollar. On the way back to the train he passed so many big-eyed native children that a doughnut each soon emptied the sack. They had met a miner on the train by the name of Joe Dalton. He parted with them at Healy and before he swung down from the train he shook hands with them. Noel noted as he stepped down that he had left something in his hand. As the train rolled away Fritz and Noel examined the "something." It was a ten-dollar bill. Joe Dalton had noted they hadn't eaten on the way up, and with a true Alaskan's insight he knew the reason and the remedy. They never were able to repay Joe Dalton, for he wouldn't take the money. Finally he said to buy him some chances on the Nenana Ice Pool, which Noel and Fritz did, but they weren't the lucky numbers.

Ralph met them at the train that frosty March 5 in 1927, and introduced Fritz to Charlie Fowler of the F.E. Co. (Fairbanks Exploration Company).

"Can you play ball?" Charlie asked.

"I sure can. I would have played most anything," Fritz confided, "for I needed a job badly."

Fritz went to work for the F.E. Co. and they issued him an employment card that he still carries. The job was running a compressor in the vault tunnel where the ditch went through a hill. He held this job until June 1928, when he went to work for Noel and Ralph, taking care of airplanes.

One of his first jobs was to repair an airplane out in the bush. A group of miners had purchased a Steerman and cracked it up on the south end of Walker Lake back a few hundred yards in the brush. The Wien brothers bought the wreck from the miners.

Ralph Wien and Earl Borland made a wing for the broken Steerman in Fairbanks and then took it all apart. Earl Borland was to die in a crash off North Cape, Siberia, with Ben Eielson just a few months later and Ralph Wien to die very soon, too, in a crash near Kotzebue, but that spring as they worked away making an airplane wing so it could be flown out in pieces and assembled in the bush, tragedy seemed far away.

Noel then flew Ralph, Fritz, and Earl into Walker Lake, using the Hamilton Standard to haul in them, the taken-down wing, tents, fire pots, food, and other necessary parts. Luckily, there was the old miner's cabin nearby to live in. It was early spring, snow six feet deep, and the nearest village, Hughes, almost a hundred miles away. The Steerman was buried clear out of sight in the snow and they dug it out using snowshoes for shovels. They then pitched a tent over the airplane and went to work. Noel flew in a welding outfit and Ralph went to work welding up the broken parts. It is a tribute to Ralph's ability that, although he hadn't welded before, the job was entirely satisfactory. In the continuous daylight they worked: walking the half mile from the old cabin to the airplane on snowshoes, while chickadees and red poles sang their spring songs and the snow melted. The Steerman's wreckage gradually emerged as an airplane. They fitted together the wing and used fire-pot heat to dry the fabric dope, all the while being cautious lest the whole thing go up in a blaze.

Since the airplane was pretty well wrecked, they weren't quite sure how all the parts fitted back together. The push rods that worked the ailerons they put in straight up—they should have been crossed! Noel soon found this out on the test flight. They had cleared a strip as the snow melted. All was ready.

The J-4 engine started easily and turned up beautifully. Noel taxied it about a little on the small airstrip and then opened the throttle. As quickly as he was in the air he tried to correct for a low wing, but it dropped even lower. Things were just backwards! Noel cut the throttle and landed, narrowly avoiding a crash. Few pilots could have sensed disaster so quickly and avoided it as Noel did. In recalling Sam White's remark about Noel—"He was the best"—one has to agree. Soft-spoken, quiet, and kind in all things, in an airplane Noel's reaction was instant, exact, and correct.

Fritz, Ralph, and Earl went to work again and crossed the push rods so all worked normally. Since those days it is just standard procedure to check the controls before flying an airplane that has been worked on, for even in the best shops they still can and do cross controls! When you are doing things all alone in the bush you don't always get everything right the first time, but those Alaskans who went way beyond the towns were a breed of men who wouldn't be stopped. "You couldn't stick them," Sam White said. "They died trying but they didn't stop."

Ralph then took Earl Borland and the tools in the repaired Steerman and flew on into Fairbanks. Noel and Fritz followed in the Hamilton with the rest of the gear.

One of the first jobs for the repaired Steerman was when Noel and Fritz flew Miss Kay and Miss Hill to Alatna, where they landed upon a river bar. For over twenty years they were the missionaries there.

Fritz had decided to become a pilot, too, and that fall he went out to Minneapolis to learn to fly at the Universal Flying School. Here he found each instructor had a different system of landing, but he finally mastered one of his own and soloed.

Back in Alaska, though, Ralph and Noel kept Fritz busy packing airplanes with freight, gassing them up, and repairing them, so that it was just hard to find a free airplane or time to practice flying. Fritz did keep up his flying, though, and put in more than fifty hours in the air, but each time there was an airplane available the inspector wasn't, so Fritz never did get his pilot's license.

The Wien flying business grew so fast that Fritz just couldn't be spared from the shop any more and then the final blow to his pilot's career came when he got married. His wife didn't want him to fly at all, so Fritz settled into the life of the mechanic. From the Hamilton Standards, Steermans, Wacos, Cessnas, Martins, Douglases, turboprop planes, and finally intercontinental jets; through skis, floats, and wheels to the big multi-wheeled gear; from fabric, wood, tubing, and aluminum to stainless steel; from a tent in six-foot-deep snow and fire pots for heat, where Ralph did his first welding at Walker Lake, even saving a C-46 that had gone through the ice, to the modern Wien hangar where the sleek jets are now repaired, Fritz guided and repaired the Wien aircraft. Wien's fantastic safety record in this frontier land is due to the fact that Fritz was the man behind the wrenches.

Fritz can't be cited as the typical bush pilot's mechanic. He started out that way, but like his brothers he drifted into the airline business and left the solitary bush pilots along the way.

Hutch was the dean of the bush mechanics and took care of the bush ships for first one pilot and another all through the bush pilot's era.

My association with the mechanics revolves mostly around the Fairbanks Aircraft Service—finally renamed Bachners' Aircraft Service—which it, of course, always was, and its owners Jess and Ann Bachner. "Bachners' Aircraft Service" it says on the letterhead and underneath it, "We have everything but sometimes we can't find it." When the town fathers sold Weeks Field for a building development Jess and Ann moved out into the country and opened up a new airport right from the brush called Phillips Field and built a small airplane hangar. Here the bush ships congregated and the little crew of mechanics, Eldred Quam, Marv Jones, Dave Phillips, Bill Ackerman, and Ernie Hubbard, still take wonderful care of the bush airplanes there.

Jess and Ann are both native-born Alaskans. This is something you don't find very often among the flyers. Ann was born at Valdez, while Jess was born in Fairbanks just across the street from where he now lives, right back of Sam White's home. Jess, short, solid-built, good-natured, gruff, bald, and with the ability to see right through the fanfare to the center of things and the courage to tell you what he thinks, was driving a truck between Valdez and Fairbanks in the summer. It was long before World War II and in those quiet days they just let it snow in the winter and work stopped. As a boy Jess worked for V. F. Jacobs, who was past sixty then and ran Birch Tree Gardens. He was an old Barnum & Bailey trumpet player and used to play the trumpet for the-kids while they worked in the garden. The pay was twenty-five cents an hour. Then as a young man Jess began driving the truck to Valdez, where he met Ann.

It was in early October when the road closed and Jess was making his last trip of the season that Jess decided Ann was the woman he wanted to spend his life with, and he persuaded her to marry him. It was a wonderful combination for bush flying, and the world just never would have been as pleasant a place without them, their children, and now grandchildren.

"Anything that can happen to anyone has happened to me," Jess said one day shortly after I had landed and taxied up to the hangar. Jess was looking at an airplane that looked as if someone had kicked it.

His teen-age son, Andy, whom I have spoken of before, was ever helpful about the hangar and quite a handy boy, having grown up around airplanes. Jess uses a small caterpillar to keep the field in shape and move airplanes about. It was parked near the hangar when Andy needed it for something; he jumped on the seat, started it up, and away he went out through the parked airplanes. Someone had left a long rope hitched to it and still tied to the tail of an airplane a hundred feet away. The first thing Andy knew there was a big crash behind him and he saw pieces of airplane flying while people came running.

"I thought there had been a wreck and someone had missed the runway and landed in the parking area," Andy told me later. "So I hurried to get out there."

In the meantime he was dragging an airplane backwards right through the parking lot! About the time the running people got to Andy he looked back and realized he was the cause of it all. It took a lot of gas-box wire to put all those airplanes together again and Andy is still suspicious of ropes or chains tied to a tractor. The passing years have made the story even sound funny to Jess.

There is a friendly smell to an airplane hangar. The smell of fabric dope, cleaning solvent, wax, paint, grease, and planes. Here and there sits a bush plane in stages of repair from a complete dismantling and overhaul to a gear change or a twenty-five-hour check-up. They have ranged the far Alaskan skies but have gathered here at the airplane hospital for a check-up and here, too, the pilots meet.

In the evening when only the dim night lights are on and you wander among the worn, time-scarred airplanes sitting silent and snug in the hangar, you can almost see the ghosts of long-departed airplanes and their pilots who traveled the skies as you do now, and think of those who will come after you. There sits your airplane all apart and silent in the dim light and while the history of the other planes about you is a mystery only partly understood, this airplane you know for it is a part of you and you are a part of it.

Morning brings the hangar to life. The rattle of rivet guns, the sound of hammers and electric tools with people moving about. You pass from the hangar area where Marv Jones or Dave Phillips is working on your airplane to the engine-repair section where Eldred Quam works. Here he carefully dismantles the engines and repairs them step by step. It is the "major surgery department."

Eldred Quam came to Alaska in the spring of 1935. Garfield Anderson, a friend of his, had a cousin in Anchorage, Ingvold Thomasson, and they wrote him about work there. He answered, "Sure, come on up."

It was the dustbowl era of North Dakota and all were starved out, so north Quam and Anderson came and are still here. Quam—as we all call him—had put in four years in the Navy as an aircraft mechanic, so he tried to get work in that field; finding none, he went to work braking on the railroad. He and Anderson saved up their money to go mining and worked prospecting two summers at Manley Hot Springs. After two seasons they had enough money to pay their grub bill and a hundred and twenty-five dollars left, so they headed for Fairbanks, where Quam went to work for the old Pacific Air Motive Shop. Ted Hauffman was shop foreman and the work was on radial engines, Pratt & Whitney, Wright, Warner, and Jacobs. The shop was at the end of Barnett Street and you couldn't get an airplane inside, so you worked on them out in the cold, or made a nose hangar of canvas. When an airplane went down in the brush, you took your camp gear and went out and fixed it. In such mishaps it was usually pilot error that caused them, or it could have been a mechanic's error, or it could have been a combination of events that no one was really responsible for alone, but all had a hand in, and if it had a happy ending it was funny.

Quam had majored a Wright J-6 engine for Lon Brennan's Travelair. There was a bulletin out (the engine manufacturers or the FAA put out these bulletins that state when this or that part of equipment has proved faulty and a change should or must be made) on the cam timing gear. It was a serrated gear that backed out a half turn and slipped, allowing you to adjust and time the engine. Quam ordered the new part and left the cotter key out. The engine wasn't needed for a year and when the new part came he would just replace the old one, key it tight, and all would be in order. He left a note on the engine to this effect and went moose hunting. While he was away Lon Brennan needed a new engine and they put the one Quam was waiting to finish into his Travelair and away Lon went. Quam of course didn't know the engine was back in service.

Things ran fine until early December when Lon was flying a woman and small baby from Minto to Fairbanks and the engine quit cold. He made a safe landing and snug camp for them and radioed in. The next morning they flew Quam out. It was the first he knew of that engine being in service, so he knew its problem at once, and he timed the engine by the valves, started it up, and they flew back to Fairbanks.

"What was the trouble?" Lon asked.

"The cotter key wasn't there."

"Where did it go?"

"Well . . . I don't think it ever was there to start with!"

George Oswald's Bellanca had low fuel pressure at Barrow, so Quam started north. There weren't any airline connections there then and he flew to Kotzebue and Lloyd Peterson flew him on north in a Gull-wing Stinson, picking up whatever cargo he could en route to make the trip pay, and the last lap he had a load of sled dogs. As is often the case at Barrow, a wind of 30 knots was blowing and drifting snow. The problem was slush ice in the fuel strainer. It took but a moment to fix and then the long trip back. It was a hard flight for Lloyd Peterson. Some months later he was killed in a crash back in the mountains.

In 1941 Quam went to work for Wien Alaska Airlines. Airplanes were increasing in size and Wien had some twin-engined airliners, but they, too, need to be repaired and brought in from the brush at times.

In 1947 Cliff Everts and Bill Smith were going from Nome to Fairbanks in the Boeing 247. It had two-geared H. Wasp engines for power and was a real good airplane. They had plenty of altitude when they lost an engine, due to faulty maintenance, near Galena. Cliff missed on his approach—of all times when a pilot would have liked to have landed just right—and when he saw they were too high he tried to start the dead engine but the unfeathered blade swung them around. They couldn't hold altitude, and there wasn't enough left to get them back to the field. They landed her wheels up in the niggerheads about eight miles from the field on the opposite side of the Yukon River.

Jess Bachner and Quam flew out in a Cessna 140 to repair it in the snows of winter. It was a large airplane and needed a dragged runway to get out from, so Clarence Zazer took his D-8 caterpillar across the Yukon River ice pulling a big sled on a long cable behind him. The river ice was but 30 inches thick and they spent two days drilling holes across the river testing the ice for any thinner spots, for even 30 inches of ice at its best isn't really enough to bear the weight of a D-8 cat!

Clarence Zazer was really the hero of that operation, Quam recalls, for it that heavy cat had gone through the ice, his chances of getting out alive would have been a little less than zero.

Jess and Quam jacked up the Boeing airliner and put on new propellers and fixed the faulty engine. It had a broken governor control cable that had let the propeller go into full pitch, which was more than the engine could turn and of course it was impossible to feather the blade. They then heated the engines with fire pots, started them up and Cliff Everts and Quam took it off from the improvised strip and flew back to Fairbanks.

A few years later a Boeing Strato-Cruiser gave Martha and me a few anxious moments as passengers on the run between Seattle and Fairbanks with a similar problem. We were sitting right up beside the number 3 engine, and I was enjoying the view and ease of letting someone else handle the problems, and besides, the stewardess had fed us all well. We were way up in the blue above a solid overcast, when Martha said, "Isn't that engine throwing a lot of oil?"

At about that time the ship gave a surge and oil swept back across the wing of the big plane. We started losing altitude fast and the passengers looked a bit alarmed. We soon heard the captain telling us they were having a little trouble with the number 3 engine, but all was in order. The big blade kept on turning and oil kept flowing back across the wing.

"Isn't there something really wrong?" Martha asked, knowing all wasn't under control.

"Yes, there is. He can't feather that engine and we will have a runaway engine shortly that will either throw its propeller or burn when the last of the oil is gone," I told her while feeling for our life jackets under the seat for we were above the North Pacific.

We were coming down fast in the overcast by then and a moment later the ship flared out as we saw treetops flash by the wing tip and we landed at the little strip of Gustavus. The pilot later told me he had used up the last of his oil reserve just as we landed. There was a caretaker's house there and some of the passengers stayed in it and the rest of us slept in the airplane. A mechanic flew in the next day, fixed the broken oil seal, and we were on our way.

The bush planes often needed anything from a minor adjustment to a major overhaul in the field—and even a little work done on the co-pilot as well, or at least Gordon Mackenzie felt it was the case. They were flying a new twin-engined Lockheed Loadstar out of Kotzebue and had a load of tourists aboard. Gordon was trying to break in Norman Weaver as pilot and he told Norman to go up front into the pilot's seat (pilot sits on the left, co-pilot on the right), but Norman went up and sat down in the co-pilot's seat. It was a fast airplane and Norman felt he wasn't ready to handle it yet. Gordon wasn't one to have his orders not followed, he just walked up the aisle, grabbed Norman out of the seat, dragged him down the aisle, between the seated tourists, took him out the door, gave him a good thrashing, hauled him back up the aisle, plunked him into the pilot's seat and said, "Now you fly this airplane."

Caught between the hot airplane and the tough pilot, Norman decided he had better fly the airplane, and he did. Gordon Mackenzie was a man of action, he flew for many years, and finally died of old age. Norman Weaver flew eight more years and vanished into the sea on a flight between Kotzebue and Candle.

It always took a lot of ingenuity to keep an airplane flying, to change the gear, repair engines, and keep things going. Many times you had to do it alone. An airplane is a lot larger than most people think and it is hard to manhandle. There weren't always jacks nor even planks to lift it with when you wanted to change from skis to wheels, to floats, or any of the combinations. I learned that if you can't lift an airplane, you can taxi it up on a snowdrift. Then you can block it up and dig out from under it! You change your gear and then dig out from under the blocking to let the airplane back down again. To this end and to help in making camp or clearing a runway, I always carry a shovel in the airplane.

I also carry a smal tool kit in a little metal fishing-tackle box so I can make repairs in the field. I have used it to repair most every kind of equipment wherever I have gone, and of course, work upon the airplane at times. In all my years of flying I have been most fortunate in not having a single accident of any sort, but I have had two minor mishaps that could have been serious if I hadn't had my tool kit along, both took place in the pack ice.

The first happened when I was hunting polar bear with Dr. Edison French and Ken Glick of San Luis Obispo, California. Ken was riding with Jim Freericks in a Cessna 180 and I was hunting with Edison, flying our Cessa 170-B, the *Arctic Tern*. It was 35 below and far too cold for landing upon rough ice, but the day was clear and time running short. The heaters couldn't keep the frost off the windows or windshield. We spotted a bear and I selected the smoothest landing area in its path and landed. It was rough but usable and we were just losing flying speed when the right ski axle sheared off clean. I felt it go and held the airplane on the left ski for a few yards but as the wing lost flying speed we came down in the stump of gear and it dug into the ice. Luckily that tough Cessna spring gear held, and although it bent it kept the wing from striking the ice. We made a tight circle but little was hurt. Only Edison's sunglasses flew off and were broken.

As soon as we saw the *Arctic Tern* wasn't badly hurt we went after the bear, and Edison made a really surprising long shot on it running at near 650 yards. Jim Freericks landed then, and after we had skinned the bear we decided it would be best to go get a new gear rather than try to repair this one. Jim ferried us all back home and then he and Ken left for Fairbanks to get the new gear and bring back our Super Cub, the *Golden Plover*, on her enormous tires. It was Ken's first trip into this part of the Arctic, but he is a pilot, too, and we decided to let him fly the Cub back.

In Fairbanks Jim's plane had propeller trouble and he was held up for a day. Ken had already started for our Colville Delta home in the Cub and he just kept on going, making the five-hundred-mile flight alone. In the pink of evening we saw the Cub coming across the white open prairie and Ken made a beautiful landing on the big tires right across the snowdrifts. He was mighty glad to see home in the gathering dusk and we were surely happy to see him. Jim flew in at breakfast next day and we all went out to the *Arctic Tern* together.

I had cut some two-by-six planks to use in blocking up the airplane and together we lifted her up, blocked the wing, and put on the new gear. As we worked we had the fire pot heating the engine and when the gear was ready the engine was warm. It was −25 degrees and cold working. The day had turned gray and a wind swept along the ice from the east sending snow drifting. On the way out I had noted the ice was going into motion as cracks and leads opened, which is a sure warning of a coming storm.

I taxied about on the ice, feeling out the plane, and then took off. Ken followed in the Cub and Jim in his Cessna; as we headed toward land the leads were opening wide. Black fog, like the smoke from forest fires, came from the now-big open leads and the ice swung slowly as it moved westward. The sky was gray as we flew in V formation heading for home a hundred miles away. The storm increased and visibility lessened. Jim led the way following the radio range toward our home until we were near, then I took over and we dropped down low so I could follow the familiar riverbanks right up to the house. Visibility went down to a few hundred feet, and when I caught sight of the familiar markers that lead to our runway I let down my landing flaps. Ken and Jim, knowing I was landing, fell in right behind and we came in, "like three ducks," Martha said later—one, two, three as we touched the runway and taxied to our tie-downs while ice fog and drifting snow went swirling past.

I hadn't needed any gas-box wire that trip, for the ultra-modern Cessna gear locks in place with a single bolt, but I surely needed plenty of gas-box wire on my second mishap.

Leon Kelly and I were hunting polar bear and all we had seen were small bears, one really large bear that Leon had photographed at a few yards, and females with cubs. It had been a wonderful trip. Leon's partner, Carl Swanson, had taken a very large walrus and a polar bear, but Leon still needed a bear and finally we found the one. The ice had broken up and tracking was hard. This big bear had eaten a seal and then headed out across the drifting ice.

We were going so slow that the plane only made a half-turn and stopped, facing the bear.

It all came as quite a surprise to Leon and me. An airplane with one wing on the ice and the other pointing skyward at a 45-degree angle gives you quite a different perspective. Leon climbed out while the surprised bear stood looking at him a minute and then departed. Leon and I looked at the airplane and then took stock of our situation.

I could call in on the radio and Bobbie Fisher would come after us or the Search and Rescue would, or we could fix up our airplane and fly home again. A landing-gear strut had snapped, letting the left gear swing out. The propeller wasn't bent and the wing tip, while beat up a little, would still hold. All else was fine. But how could we hold up the airplane while we patched the gear, for we had no blocks at all. Just a six-foot piece of plank was all we needed, but there wasn't any!

If you can't block up you can pull down. The right gear was fine and so we dug an ice toggle under the right wing by chipping two holes into the ice sixteen inches deep and a foot apart and joined them at the bottom. Then we ran a rope through this and tied it to the high wing. Here I pulled down and, with Leon lifting on the left wing, I pulled the right wing down and tied it. Thus the *Golden Plover* was balanced on her right ski. I ran a tie-down rope around and around both skis, then at the axle, and lashed the gear together solidly. We made a splint from a hammer handle and splinted the broken tubing, using gas-box wire to wire it in place. Then we twisted the rope between the skis and wired it tight. It was a snug job and the *Golden Pover* sat bravely upon its wired-up, roped-up skis. It had taken us about two hours to make the repairs. Leon and I checked over the landing field, taxied into position, and headed for home. The *Golden Plover* handled beautifully and I set her down at home as if landing on eggs, for with the gear wired solidly there wasn't any spring in it.

The landing was uneventful. I had a replacement piece of gear that we put in and we wired up the wing tip and taped it tight; it worked fine and we continued the hunt without further incident.

An airplane can take quite a lot of damage and still be flyable with a little straightening out of parts bent and a little gas-box wire plus a little tape to hold broken parts in place. I have helped to turn airplanes right-side up, to straighten out the bent parts, and even to take the curl out of the metal propellers. It isn't difficult to straighten a metal propeller by bending it with a piece of two-by-four plank or similar leverage lashed to the blade.

Today you can call on the radio for repairs and even get a mechanic to fix an airplane. There are landing fields at every village and help is near at hand. This wasn't true just a few years ago, and when the pilot left home base he always carried a coil of gas-box wire along just in case. Many's the airplane that limped back held together by that thin little line of steel. Some of the repairs were marvels to behold. It is even against the law for the modern-day airline pilot to do any mechanical work on his airplane, and so the modern-day mechanic shuttles about keeping all in top shape. In those early days not so long ago there was a law that brought us all back, too. It was the law of self-preservation and survival. In spite of all the new laws that have been passed, that old law still holds true, as I found out when the gear let go on the *Golden Plover*. It is a simple and really not a bad one to live by, and so to that end as long as I fly and wherever I fly I will carry my tool kit and in it there will be a little roll of gas-box wire—just in case . . .

17

THE MISSIONARY PILOT

The original Eskimo settlements were out on the sandy peninsula called Point Barrow, some ten miles from Cape Smythe and at the present sight of Barrow Village.

When the first Europeans arrived they realized the impossibility of permanent buildings on that low sandy point, often washed over by high storms of late summer; so they built their permanent buildings at Cape Smythe. Charlie Brower built his first trading post there in 1886 and the people moved from the old hunting site, where it was easier to get the seals, whales, and eider ducks to the Cape Smythe site, where it was easier to get the flour, tobacco, and white man's *Tunick's,* things.

The first Presbyterian mission school was started at the present site of the Shooting Station, a spot near the point where eider ducks fly low over the sandspit and are easily shot. The new mission was formally organized in 1898 and moved from near Point Barrow to the Cape Smythe site of today. Unfortunately, the Europeans also moved the name Point Barrow as well, irrespective of geography, and Cape Smythe in the general public's vernacular became Point Barrow. It didn't confuse the local people, for they called it Utkeavik Presbyterian Church. This little oversight of moving a name and calling a straight piece of shoreline a point that really existed some ten miles away didn't trouble too many people. The local dog drivers knew the difference, but to a new pilot looking for the village in bad weather it could be fatal and was probably the main factor that led to the death of Wiley Post and Will Rogers on that foggy day. They likely found Point Barrow but, not finding a village there, felt they were lost, never realizing that the village they searched for didn't exist at Point Barrow. They turned southwest and landed at the first place that resembled a point where a big salt-water lagoon enters the ocean. Here they had seen tents pitched. They received instructions for finding Barrow Village and were killed in the crash on take-off. This spot is called the Monument today in their honor, and the real reason why they missed Barrow died with them.

The first mission work in North Alaska was instigated by Dr. Sheldon Jackson. A group of Protestant churches had met to divide up the mission work in Alaska, to better serve the people and prevent duplication of service. The Episcopal Church took western and portions of interior Alaska as far north as Point Lay. Dr. Jackson realized the whole Arctic area from Point Lay north and east to the Canadian boundary was being neglected because of its remoteness and sparse population and he took it for the Presbyterian mission. This area is a vast prairie land called the North Slope today and comprises the real home of the original American Eskimos.

Mr. L. M. Stevenson was the first missionary from 1890 to 1897. He was not ordained, but a teacher, and he laid the ground work for education in the Arctic. In 1897 the Reverend H. R. Marsh arrived and the church was organized in 1898. He also taught school as well as carried out the teachings of Christianity. In 1899 the Reverend S. R. Spriggs arrived to teach in the new government school as well as work with the church, and in 1904 he became the minister when Reverend Marsh was away, until 1908, when Reverend Marsh returned to serve until 1912. Reverend Marsh served until Reverend Cram arrived in 1914. After this date he stayed on as a teacher and T. L. Richardson came to head the mission until Dr. Frank H. Spence, the first medical missionary, arrived in 1915 to bring the first permanent medical help to that outer region. Dr. Henry W. Griest arrived in 1921 to carry on the medical missionary work until 1925 when Dr. A. W. Newhall came up to relieve him. Dr. Griest returned in 1929 to continue the work until 1936, when the hospital work was turned over to the Alaska Department of Health and under the U.S. Department of the Interior. In 1955 the U.S. Public Health Department took over the hospital work. In the meantime the Reverend Fred G. Klerekoper served the mission field from 1936 until 1945, when the Reverend Samuel Lee arrived to carry on the work until 1951.

This, then, is the past history in brief. It is so brief that the names of the wives and children who went to that distant isolated land to help are not even mentioned.

Many of the oldest Eskimos remembered each missionary and even the years before they arrived. They knew no better calendar than to fix dates as being during the time of this or that missionary. During those years the Barrow people went through more changes than any other race of man has ever faced in so short a span of time, for they went from the Stone Age to the Atomic Age in one lifetime.

The Eskimos saw the peaceful occupation of the Arctic by the whalers first and then the military and government agencies. These thousands of men didn't bring their wives and families, or try to teach the Eskimo people the long road to civilization and Christianity. They were interested in plunder, and the Eskimo women were often stolen, traded for or bribed with whiskey. Theirs was the play for goods in the field and promotion in the home office; as one Eskimo man said when his friend kidded him because a newcomer had run off with his wife: "Too much calico, too much flour, too much coffee shop, and Cok-sook don't got no chance."

Translated into simple English it means: "Against the dresses, the fancy food and entertainment that the European men could furnish the Eskimo women, the Eskimo man with his dog team and old culture had no chance of establishing or maintaining his home."

The work of the mission had changed from one of teaching the ABC's and simple fundamentals of Christianity to a nomadic hunting people to one of dealing with every possible complication of a modern civilization, since every last Eskimo had moved from the country into the villages, excepting the Wood family, some of whom still live on the Colville River Delta not far from our home.

The old nomadic hunting culture of the people was gone. The era of the wage-earning Eskimo culture was at hand. There were five villages that the Barrow Mission now served: Barrow Village, Wainwright, Meade River, Anaktuvuk Pass, where the inland Eskimos had gathered, and Barter Island.

Reverend Samuel Lee realized that an airplane was needed to adequately serve all those farflung villages and backed by his old congregation in Haddonfield, New Jersey, and the minister there, the Reverend Brian Kirkland, along with the Piper dealer, raised the money to purchase a Piper Clipper equipped with floats, skis, and wheels.

Sig Wien, the old Arctic bush pilot, flew the Piper Clipper, christened the *Arctic Messenger,* from Fairbanks to Barrow. Reverend Samuel Lee had the vision of using an airplane in the Arctic mission field, but he didn't have the training. He knew his failing and after orientation flights he tied down the airplane and left it for the next missionary, praying a qualified pilot would be found.

The next missionary was the Reverend William C. Wartes and family. Bill was a veteran pilot of World War II with many hours in flying the B-24 Liberators. There was also his lovely wife, Bonnie, and their children, Merrily, eight; Mark, five; and Teena, three. The story of the Warteses' work in the Arctic is typical of the lives of all missionaries who have left the comforts and safety of home to share in the lives of those of distant lands and to help in whatever way seems best. Their lives are dedicated lives and I have developed a deep respect for them all.

It was July 2, 1951, when the Warteses arrived at Barrow. They came by steamship to Seward, railroad to Fairbanks, and then flew on the Wien weekly DC-3 trip to Barrow, where they landed at the military base out near the Point. Barrow didn't have a regular landing field until fourteen years later (but wheels were used on the sand strip along the beach by small aircraft). From there to Barrow Village it was a six-mile ride over a flat pea-gravel beach that only a four-wheel-drive vehicle or a caterpillar tractor could traverse. The year's supplies and groceries were following on the steamship *North Star,* which makes a yearly trip to Barrow. George Burdick was waiting for them at the metal mat airstrip with the mission caterpillar tractor and a big sled. Max Adams and the Wien station manager, Forrest Soloman, were out at the airport too, and together they all rode the big sled along the sandy, wind-whipped beach to the old green-stained, shingle-covered manse that was to be their home in Barrow beside the Arctic Ocean for the next seven years. Bonnie was to see the mission plane engulfed in a flaming crash before her kitchen window, to light up the snow with the colors of a sunset in the dark of winter, and three children were to be born—one in the kitchen with only Bill and Eskimo midwives to help—but these things were for the future. At present the manse seemed a little small in the light of the low, never-setting sun that gave the land a feeling of perpetual morning or evening.

The entire Wartes family fit right into the fabric of Barrow and all worked together. There was an enormous amount of new work to do as well as the regular work of daily living. Bill had been selected for this post because of his knowledge of carpentry as well as flying because a new church was badly needed, and thousands of dollars' worth of materials were in piles around the mission grounds, awaiting new hands and inspirational leadership.

The *Arctic Messenger* had stood nearly a year unused, so it needed checking over. Children had played inside it, the wind had whipped it, and the skis were sunk in the soft prairie sod of full summer. In between his other work Bill got the airplane in flying shape. He checked it all over, replaced the skis with wheels, and charged up the battery. There were no landing fields where Bill needed to go, so his first trip would be into Fairbanks to have Jess Bachner put floats on the *Arctic Messenger*.

For three days it rained softly and softened up the prairie. There is no underground drainage in the perma-frost land, and this was a feature Bill wasn't aware of. When he decided to test-fly the airplane before the long trip into Fairbanks, Bill's take-off was on the best-looking stretch of prairie. The Piper Clipper wouldn't gain flying speed on the soft sod, and when the plane's wheels dropped into a cater-pillar rut cut into the prairie and hidden by the grass, the *Messenger* flipped neatly over on its back. Bill wasn't injured, but the *Messenger* was pretty well twisted and required new struts and propeller and bent parts straightened. The two local Wien pilots (that he would outlive in Arctic flying) had been telling Bill the do's and don't's of Arctic flying and they felt they had let him down. Mission flying hadn't got off to a very fast start. New parts for the *Messenger* were ordered and flown up from Fairbanks on the weekly mail plane, and when the airplane was flyable, Sig Wien arranged the flight back to Fairbanks for repairs.

Sig left the *Arctic Messenger* with Jess Bachner at the Fairbanks Aircraft Service and it was early winter before the airplane was repaired and Bill could pick it up again. In the meantime the Wartes family was picking up daily knowledge of what it takes to live in the Arctic.

By early fall, the mission's yearly supplies were in. There were shortages of some things and doubling up on others. It was schooltime again, but as Merrily and Mark prepared to enter school there was a surprise in store for them. They wouldn't be allowed to go to the government school; it was for natives only. The missionaries had founded the school system a little over half a century before, but now they were not allowed to send their children to the same schools! So it fell to Bonnie's lot to teach the children by correspondence courses as it has always been Martha's lot to teach ours. Sadie Neakook and Kate Brower helped modify clothing and made fur parkas, boots, and mittens for all the family, and the excitement of a first Arctic winter settled over them.

Bill took the Wien Alaska Airlines' DC-3 into Fairbanks, where he picked up the *Arctic Messenger*. It was on wheels, although the land was white and frozen farther north— Fairbanks had no snow, but with the sun moving farther south each day, making flying more and more difficult, soon winter would grip all Alaska.

Some local person nearly always traveled with Bill, for there was always someone wanting to go somewhere, and Bill welcomed their company as well as help.

Bill flew on many search missions when dog teams came back without their drivers, a boat was missing, or an airplane was overdue. The embarrassed dog-team driver would usually be found walking toward home because his dog team had gone off without him; the boat would be located where hunting had been a little better than expected, or there had been a breakdown, or they were out of gasoline; and the pilot was usually found with his plane out of gasoline or with some broken part, waiting for help. That these happy endings weren't routine came close to home when George Harrington, bringing Samuel Simmonds's wife, Martha, and their little son to Barrow, flew a Cessna 170-A head-on into the prairie a few miles out of Barrow. George and Martha died instantly in the crash and were thrown yards from the spot while the airplane just disintegrated. Several hours later the searchers found them and to their surprise the little baby Arnold was alive, snug and warm in the pouch in the back of Martha's parka, although one protruding arm was broken in six places.

For three years Bill flew the *Arctic Messenger* and after his bang-up beginning he had no further trouble. Bill and I flew together on many flights and I taught him a little about Arctic flying. The D.E.W. (Distant Early Warning) sites were constructed and Bill served as a chaplain at several of them. The increased use of the airplane made it clear that the Piper Clipper was too small to carry on the work and the *Arctic Messenger II* was purchased in 1954. It was a Cessna 170-B like our *Arctic Tern* and it was all fitted up for the northern flying. Bill flew it up from Seattle, where Washington Aircraft had fitted it all out. *Arctic Messenger II* was a beautiful airplane and ideal for the mission work.

During those years the new Barrow church had been built. Bill started it the year they arrived, and with the aid of a few men and the women they completed it in three years. A new member had come to join the Wartes family. Martha LeNore had been almost born en route to Fairbanks aboard the Wien DC-3 airliner when lack of oxygen at high altitude over the Brooks Range had brought on labor. From then on it was a race between the workhorse of the skies and the stork with the DC-3 winning by eight hours.

The life span of *Arctic Messenger II* was a short one through no fault of her own nor her pilot's. Bill flew her until that cold, dark morning of January 31, 1956. The sun had just returned to the Arctic to shine from the south for a few minutes at high noon when a woman came to the manse and said her husband's dogs had come in one by one and she was afraid her husband was in trouble. Bill, Bill Zeiger, the missionary intern, and Roxy Oyagak went down to heat the airplane in the way-below-zero frosty air and semidarkness of early morning. They had the *Arctic Messenger II*'s engine all wrapped up and were using a Herman-Nelson gasoline heater to warm up the engine. The men were working away, cleaning off frost and getting the airplane ready to fly after being tied down since early December and subsequently well drifted in snow. Bill had left the engine oil on the kitchen stove to heat, Bonnie was keeping an eye on the airplane from the kitchen window, for we all fear fire in the Arctic and especially when airplanes are being heated and we watch them as a matter of course.

The Wien crew had just heated the Wien Norseman with the Herman-Nelson heater and then turned the heater over to Bill's crew when they finished and the Norseman taxied off down the lagoon in dim light and mild ice fog to its take-off position. Bill Zeiger (most often called Bill Z.) was under the airplane hooking up the heater ducts; Bill had been cleaning the frost from the left wing but had decided to go check on the oil heating on the kitchen stove, while Roxy was busy shoveling out and sweeping frost from the tail section. Bonnie, at the kitchen window, hadn't noticed Bill come in to check the oil, nor did Bill Z. or Roxy know he had left. The Herman-Nelson heater was making quite a little noise so that, wrapped in their heavy parkas, no one heard the Norseman coming until it was upon them. Heavily loaded with no wind blowing, and covered with frost, it came out of the ice fog on a collision course, but in those last desperate seconds, the pilot couldn't make it fly. With the screaming roar of a flat-pitched propeller at full throttle it crashed into the *Arctic Messenger II*. Bill Zeiger looked up to see the purple exhaust flame of the Norseman right by his face as the world erupted in flames. The Norseman's propeller had cut through the gasoline tank of the Herman-Nelson heater spraying gasoline like a Fourth of July spin wheel; the exhaust flames instantly ignited it wherever it flew, and the Norseman burst into flames. The impact sheared the left wing from the *Arctic Messenger II*, driving her back and to the side while crumpling her body, but she didn't catch fire. The Norseman came to a stop a few yards away and lay there burning fiercely. Bonnie watching from the kitchen window where she was kneading bread dough had heard the Norseman coming; she could faintly see the figures of the men working about the *Arctic Messenger II* and then all vanished in a ball of flame that lit up the world brighter than day. It seemed impossible that anyone could have escaped alive. Bill Zeiger just knew Bill Wartes was dead and Roxy felt sure both Bills were killed. The Norseman's pilot knew Bill Zeiger was dead for he had seen Bill's face through the propeller blades just before the crash. All raced for the burning Norseman, for surely no one could have survived in that flaming wreckage. What a wonderful reunion to meet the Norseman's passenger and pilot coming to help them! No one could figure what happened to Bill. Then he came running with a large fire extinguisher from the house. The Norseman's crew had hurried from the burning plane protected by their heavy winter clothing and no one had been hurt, although faces were cut and ruffs singed. The *Arctic Messenger II* appeared also to be on fire, but it was rather gas-saturated snow all around it and the canvas heating ducts of the plane.

Luckily both airplanes were insured and in a few days the order was in for *Arctic Messenger III*. It was another Cessna 170-B, exactly like *Arctic Messenger II*, and with her Bill continued the mission flying.

By 1955 the people of Anaktuvuk Pass were dreaming of their own church. There isn't any timber near the Pass so all the logs would have to be hauled by dog sled nearly forty miles from the Hunt Fork area to build the little log church. It was slow work of hauling a log at a time. The people brought in the logs with the dog teams and Bill brought in the rest of the material with the *Arctic Messenger*. The church would have oil heat, glass windows, and be insulated. Bill brought in a chain saw to help with the log work, a portable light plant, and table saw, windows, nails, and the work began. It would be a long slow process, as are all building programs in a land where material is so scarce.

At Barter Island the Air Force had completely changed the lives of the people and even moved them from their old home sites. It took them quite a while to get a town site of their own and then they too wanted a church. So it was that the people changed from a nomadic life to permanent residents, built homes, churches, and settled tighter into a wage-earning society with, of course, the problems of a wage-earning society.

It is far easier to accept the benefits of a wage-earning society than it is to accept its responsibilities. It was the mission's job to teach responsibility. This was a tough assignment at best, especially when all the advantages appeared to be on the other side, as in the case of marriage. In early times the husband was absolutely indispensable, for without him to hunt and provide for the family in the nomadic hunting life all would perish. In times of starvation, the food was wisely given to the best hunters who needed the strength to search for more food. In hard times the young, old, and weak were left to die. If a woman lost her husband, she would have to live with another family unit giving a good hunter even two wives to support. There was no place at all for the lazy, and a woman with children and no husband to claim them was in serious straits.

In the new wage-earning society there was often unemployment. A hunting life could no longer support the desire for all the luxuries that the wage-earning society had provided and there was no way of returning to the old culture. It didn't take long to figure out that the government would pay a bonus for illegitimate children and the women with several drew a steady income. The more fatherless children, the bigger the income. The mission made strong statements against such thinking actions! Husbands became an expensive burden, and the man, already hard put to fit into the new society's competition, fell from the top of the list in his old culture to the very bottom in the new with his new government paying a steady subsidy for all children he didn't support and would at times pay him too, providing he was absolutely useless. It is small wonder that alcohol became the crutch for many.

There were many irresponsible people in Barrow, but there were more responsible ones, fortunately, and the village council that governs refused to allow the sale of liquor there. This was a big help and kept the damage from alcohol to a minimum, but there is always the renegade who gravitates to an area where two cultures overlap and Barrow had its share of them to handle, bootlegging liquor or dope. Then, too, there was always a steady source of supply from the military bases, D.E.W. Line sites, or package liquor stores in Fairbanks. The village councils in the villages could prevent the open sale of liquor, but they couldn't prevent folks from ordering it from other areas to be shipped in air freight (it is illegal to send liquor through the mail), and a few stores in Fairbanks profited from a traffic in liquor to the villages regardless of the cost in human life. Liquor was and is the biggest problem in all villages.

Seven years pass quickly when you are usefully employed, as was Bill Wartes. The new church at Barrow was completed while those at Anaktuvuk Pass and Barter Island were in the hope and prayer stage. The Wartes family had grown to six children as Eldon Lloyd made his appearance: this time born in Barrow Hospital. Things were moving forward toward equality for all. There was even a dim hope that the people might eventually get to use the natural gas as our able Senators Gruening and Bartlett carried the fight to the U.S. Senate. Alaska passed from a territory to become the forty-ninth State. News of special importance to our family was the birth of our little son, Mark Harmon. Martha and Bonnie each had a little baby boy to carry in the parka pouches on their backs. It is a wonderful way to carry a baby, giving the child a sense of security that children dearly love. When a mother picks up the parka the child heads for the nest like a little kangaroo heading for its pouch.

In church on Sunday morning the women with small babies in their parkas would stand in a group in the back of the church, and in a loving mother's way they would sway back and forth to rock the babies. They would all be swaying in unison and Bill standing in the front of the church watching this swaying group would subconsciously start swaying too.

It was 1958 and full summer on the Arctic prairie. The seven years of mission service were over and all had passed so fast. The *Arctic Messengers* had united the people and begun the close of the mission field. The purpose of the missionary is to prepare the people to handle their own problems. Bill took Bonnie and baby Eldon and they flew to all the villages for a last visit. The new church was up in Anaktuvuk Pass and Barter Island had a temporary building; and a sense of solidarity had come to the Arctic. On their way back to Barrow, Bill and Bonnie stopped to spend a day with us at our fish camp. Our house there is nine feet by eleven inside and yet we were all comfortable in that small place. Often we recall the happy times we spent in that tiny house, as we enjoy the larger house now. (The Warteses visited us there in 1961.) The Arctic has taught us that it isn't the size of the home that dictates if there is room enough for the traveler but the hospitality of the occupants.

It is harder to leave a place than to arrive, for you have roots there and a place where you are needed. The younger children knew no other home than Barrow. Those born there had Eskimo as well as English names and spoke the Eskimo language as well as English. Happy, the pet dog, had grown old there and the trip with the heat of the south would be too hard on him. A lot of ties and things must be broken, destroyed, or left behind and Happy was one of them. The children were growing up and needed to move on where there was a high school. The Arctic chapter of mission work was closing for the Warteses.

We flew into Barrow for the last church service Bill held there. The new church he had built was packed. Brave, confident, happy, Bill with the help of his family had led the people a long way. His presence brought faith, courage, and hope to all. He often sang a solo for the people wherever they were gathered and that day at the close of his sermon he held infant Eldon Lloyd in his arms and sang "Mighty Like a Rose."

The family flew to Fairbanks on a Wien airline while Bill flew the *Arctic Messenger III* to Fairbanks. From there they all took the regular airline to Seattle. During their seven-year stay at Barrow the airlines had completely taken over the passenger travel to and from Alaska.

John and Barbara Chambers with their little daughter Sarah Lynn, just one day older than our Mark, were the next missionaries. I flew with John on some of his first flights and helped him in every way I could, especially with his emergency gear and its use. John has the wonderful ability to listen and learn without question; so I taught him all I knew. Each time we met I had a list of things to do or to avoid in flying. It is amazing how many do's and don't's there are in Arctic flying when you try to tell them all to someone.

The Arctic changed fast, though, with a new airport being built at Barrow, and natural gas for the village use was approved, so the people could build and heat modern homes. John helped build a new manse while daily or even twice-daily airline service came into Barrow. Dial telephone service linked Barrow with all the world and isolation became a memory. There were regular flights into Barter Island, Anaktuvuk Pass, and Wainwright. Meade River ceased to exist as natural gas replaced coal and the coal mine shut down. The village of Point Lay was abandoned as all the people moved to larger towns.

The Reverend Samuel Simmonds became our ordained minister and the early mission field work in the Arctic was really coming to a close. It would be a church and minister relation from here on. So it was that the Chamberses brought to a close the mission flying era in the Arctic that the Warteses had opened. John, like Bill, did a wonderful job for us all. We put in many happy hours with them and when the Chamberses' years of Arctic service were up, the mission sold the *Arctic Messenger IV* and the job of Arctic mission flying was over. The present pastor—the Reverend Charles V. Clark—was the first minister to be routinely called by the vote of the Barrow congregation.

In telling the story of mission flying in Alaska there were many missionaries who used light planes in their own work with success, especially in central and southern Alaska. Several were killed, as was Ralph Wien, the oldest of the Wien brothers, in the first mission flying at Kotzebue. Many ministers still use the light aircraft in serving their churches in central, southern, and western Alaska and likely will for many years to come, but its history in the Far North was brief.

The missionary pilots have carried on the Lord's work in what was once a most distant land. They had the same traits as their contemporary bush pilot friends; these were ones of faith, courage, the will to work hard, confidence in the people and in the land they served.

18

THE CLOSE ONES

Curiously enough, when I talked with my bush pilot friends about what were their closest calls in flying, not one could remember them without doing some serious thinking. It could be that they were unpleasant experiences and best forgotten, or, more likely, none of the pilots had ever stopped to figure out which had been his closest calls. Then, too, none of us really ever knows what was our closest call. As Andy Anderson put it, "There were so many close calls in bad-weather flying that you can't sort them all out." Sig Wien summed up the close calls by saying, "I often think that those of us who survived so many years of bush flying did so not because we were better than the rest but because the combination of events that took them never happened to us."

It was a warm spring day at Walker Lake when the deep snow of winter had begun to soften up and shrink. We were ready to move north for our work on the Arctic coast. With full tanks of gasoline I had a fair overload, but I was on skis and could handle it, thus saving an extra trip and eight additional hours of flying. We had a runway a thousand feet long tramped out in the soft snow with snowshoes. The slipperiness of snow and its strength changes greatly with temperature and this time the airplane just wouldn't gain speed. We were right at flying speed as we went off the end of the snowshoed runway and the wing was nearly carrying the load, so we went skimming along on the surface of the soft snow of the lake, but not quite ready to fly. Ahead lay a mile of open snow-covered lake that ran back into the horseshoe-shaped bay formed by the mountain on the left side, a low hill in the back, and a tree-covered peninsula on the right. With everything ready to fly and just a mile or two per hour more speed needed, I used up the mile of snow. I was ready to cut the throttle and settle into the soft snow with a day's work ahead getting the airplane back to the runway when a little breeze from the canyon gave me the added mile or two lift and we were in the air. We were in the back of the small bay by then and I had the choice of trying to outclimb the low tree-covered hill or turning in the small bay. There are times when the air is just "dead." Warm and still the air lay in that snug little bay, and I couldn't gain speed, or, of course, altitude. We were right into the back of the bay and I didn't have a choice any more, for I never could have made it over the hill and trees. There wasn't room to land as I was right up to the trees. Turn I must, and around to the left. A pilot has one direction of turning he favors, and most right-handed pilots can make a left turn better than a right one. We were but ten feet in the air and the turn had to be a fairly steep one to miss the trees and mountainside. With the trees just off the right wing tip and the left wing tip just missing the snow with the little tremors that come just before a stall, buffeting the controls, we came around the shoreline in the back of that little pretty bay. It felt as if I had been flying for hours, but it must have been only thirty seconds. I was furious at myself for getting into such a spot with my whole family aboard. I should have waited until the next morning when the snow would have been hard from the night freeze, or taken less of a load. Martha sat quietly holding little baby Mark and Jim was in the back with gear piled all around him —and I, well I was wet with sweat as I straightened out and came back a little on the power setting as we climbed up into the lovely blue sky.

I was talking with Sig Wien one winter day. He showed me some plans for purchasing two new jet airliners for his company, and we were discussing the pros and cons of jet engines on the wing or the tail for our Arctic operation. I told him of a problem I had had with my aileron.

"I have had problems like that twice," said Sig. "Once I was flying a Cessna Air Master on floats. We had cut an escape hatch door in the roof in case of accidents. It was hinged on the front. I was flying along in quiet air when there was a bang just like an explosion. I lost almost all control on the rudder and elevators and I thought something had blown up. The ship started to fall off, and I was at a loss what to do when I realized the escape hatch had come loose and was standing up at an angle. I tried to control the airplane with one hand and fasten the hatch with the other but couldn't. I finally had to let go all and fasten the escape hatch.

The hatch must have really disrupted the air flow into the tail controls, for all the controls were completely disrupted."

It is surprising how little it takes to affect the control of an airplane. Sig's other problem came near to being his last.

"I was flying a Cessna Air Master near Umiat on a cold, white day. There was a little hill ahead of the take-off and I pulled up steep to clear it. I couldn't maintain the rate of climb, so I pushed forward on the stick, but the controls were stuck and I couldn't get the nose down. I was almost in a stall by then and the control was rock solid; the only way to avoid a stall and crash was to push the stick forward and nose down. It was against all flying instincts, but I thought if I pulled back a little more I might free something, and it worked. That airplane had a long control rod that slid through a bushing and the bushing had seized the rod so that the harder I pushed forward the tighter it held, until a little back pressure let it free. I was then able to get the nose down and gain flying speed easily."

They surely replaced that system of controls in that airplane model as fast as possible.

Sam White's close ones were numerous and when he talks about them they always seem funny. One of the first incidents happened in Sam's old Swallow. Harry Badger hadn't been up in an airplane and Sam promised to take him for a ride. Time passed and Sam decided he might just as well fly out to Harry Badger's place and give him a ride. It was a dead calm, sunny Sunday evening when Sam landed in a field near Harry Badger's house. Harry climbed in and away they went. The field was a little small and there was a pretty birch tree on the far side, and the sun was right in Sam's face. Sam should have taxied across the field and taken off in the opposite direction with the sun behind him since it was dead calm. With Harry in the front cockpit of the open biplane Sam gave her "full bore" and off they went down the field into the sun and hit the top of the birch tree.

There was an awful smack and branches flew, the Swallow faltered, caught its breath, and went right on up with pieces of birch tree dangling from the wings and undercarriage. Sam had his hands full for a moment just handling the plane but when he did look the front cockpit was empty! Harry Badger was gone! Sam just circled the field and landed. When he looked again in the front cockpit he saw Harry Badger rolled up in a ball in the bottom of the cockpit—unhurt, of course, but also unwilling to ever ride with Sam again! Sam pulled the loose birch branches from the airplane and flew on back to Fairbanks.

Sam always had a "thing" about bears, and black ones in particular. When he was a boy in Maine his first bear hunt ended up in his shooting a black hog in the brush. Sam said if you asked about Sam White in his home area years later many of the people wouldn't have recalled him, but if you mentioned about the boy who shot the black hog all would remember him!

The last seven years of Sam's commercial flying career he spent flying out of Hughes and his major trips were to the USAF radar sites at Utopia Creek. This was a one-way strip started by gold placer miner "Mac" McGee along the Indian River, and on a 15 per cent slope so that when you parked your airplane you always turned it across the strip to keep it from rolling downhill into the river. Indian Mountain, where the strip lay, is the roughest air in that part of Alaska. There is a surprisingly long list of hazards to overcome in landing there, and when you go in and out several times a week as Sam did you will eventually meet them all. To start with it is a one-way strip. You land going uphill and take off downhill regardless because you can't outclimb the mountain that rises four thousand feet at its west end! It was bordered by ridges on both sides, which put you in a slot as you approached, and you soon passed the point of no return. Then to make matters worse, winds of every direction and velocity could be blowing in that area at the same time.

Sam learned just how much wind he could handle, and I have often seen him waiting at Hughes for the wind to drop a few knots before going in to Utopia Creek. Sam had also pretty well figured out what directions of the compass the winds would come at him from when he knew the wind aloft. Sam could flare out the Cessna 180 that he usually flew and wheel her in on the upwind wheel, reducing power to come to a stop just right.

Added to these hazards were black bears. The garbage dump was near and all sizes of black bears came to feed and lounge about the airstrip. The folks liked to see them about, of course, and would drive them off the airport when Sam was due, but bears don't drive much better than pigs and back they would come again. The hazard of course was in flying into one. Some of the larger bears learned to bluff too by popping their teeth as if to fight, and this discouraged driving them too closely on foot. After a rough landing and after frayed nerves stopped vibrating, the bears were good for a few laughs. We all liked to see them about. It was a bright summer day and Sam checked out the strip for bears and other hazards before coming in. A 6 × 6 truck with about twenty GI's was heading for the strip, so Sam swung into the pattern and just as he passed the point of no return all the black bears on Indian Mountain converged on the strip! "What the hell, I was committed! I kept on drifting in hoping for an opening. There were sows with cubs, old males, yearlings, just bears of all sizes scattered all over. The opening didn't materialize and I touched the wheels just short of a sow and two cubs and bounced up over her, I came down only to bounce up over a cub, by now my flying speed was gone and bouncing was over. A big male, black as the shade of night, ran in front of me coming from the right and disappeared under the motor, I had the brakes squealing and braced myself for the impact when from the corner of my eye I saw him exit under the left wing. He sure was making time and how he got by the propeller and through the landing gear I will never know. The brakes soon brought me to a stop and I taxied up to the 6 × 6. The GI's all had cameras but had forgotten to take a picture. They asked me to do it again since the black bears were all back on the runway. 'Why not? brother Benjamin, not me. Not again!' "

Sometimes when you think everything is fine, you get your biggest surprise. It was winds that gave Sam his biggest problem on a clear, calm, hot summer day when all seemed secure.

"I was drifting down the slot for a touch-down as safe as if I were in an overstuffed chair in a friend's living room," related Sam, "when a hazard I hadn't dreamed of hit me right between the horns. All three wind socks had hung limp as rags as I checked them before coming in. Incidentally, they changed these wind socks about once a month because the winds whipped them to pieces. Fortunately I was coming in using power from old force of habit and I was about two hundred feet from touch-down when I saw a commotion in the grass beside the runway. Since there was mostly rocks and gravel alongside the runway, I hadn't noticed it until it hit the grass border. It was a dust devil and a violent one and making right across the runway. I hit dead center and it wanted to spin us around into the canyon wall. It then threw us straight up. I came in with full power to hold control and pointed the nose down. I kept walking the rudder and I had a little aileron control and then things let loose and we were falling straight for the ground, nose first! I was looking straight down through the windshield at the spot where we were going to hit and I saw a big black X right there—no fooling, a real big black X. In all my flying I never saw a thing like that before. I shut everything off as we went down and gained just enough flying speed to flare out and made a good landing just stopping short of the mountain. My passenger was an Air Force chaplain, a lieutenant, and he said calmly, 'Well now I will be writing home about that for the next two months.' I felt like an abandoned moose hide on a mountainside. The lieutenant perhaps didn't know how close that one was. Confidentially, when I saw that black X I thought it was all over."

On one of Sam's last trips into Utopia Creek the Air Force boys put on a barbecue for him and brought out the spareribs in a pickup truck. When the cook climbed up in the truck to get the spareribs for the pit the box was empty! A glance across the runway showed three black bears running for the brush each with a bundle in its mouth.

In the summer of 1931 Sam had stored six cases of aviation gasoline with Reginald White, a trader at Lake Minchumina. In the winter he flew in with a Swallow biplane NC-422N to do some patrol work around that area and found a pilot who did not yet know the Alaska code of ethics had used up all of Sam's gasoline and didn't return it. It was a serious breach in the North among pilots. Sam rustled about the place but couldn't find a drop more gasoline. He spent the night there and headed back for Nenana next morning. Soon he was in a gale blowing the wrong way as he flew low above the twisting and writhing spruce treetops. It wasn't a comforting sight and when he reached Nenana he realized there was too much wind to land. He just didn't have the skill to handle that airplane on the ground in that wind and knowing local weather conditions he headed on for Fairbanks, where he soon ran out of the storm but his gas was low. In cutting across a bend in the river the engine quit and he was lucky to miss the trees as he glided in over the riverbank to plunk down in what Archie Ferguson would have called "a controlled crash"; luckily the deep soft snow prevented him from breaking up the ship. It was thirty below, but Sam had plenty of wood and made a comfortable camp with roast moose and rolled oats for dinner. Next morning Joe Barrows flying a Bellanca CH-300 spotted him, waggled his wings, but didn't land for he was too heavily loaded for the soft snow. An hour later Lon Cope appeared in a Fairchild 54. He landed, picked up Sam, and took him to Nenana, where Sam purchased two cases of gasoline; then Lon Cope flew Sam back to the airplane and there was Percy Hubbard with his Eaglerock biplane with a case of gasoline. Percy stayed and helped Sam heat the airplane engine and waited for him to take off. Percy's plane was right on the river in line with Sam's take-off, but there was room enough to get in the air and climb a couple of hundred feet before he got there.

"I went down the river to the proper place, turned into the breeze and booted the gun. Away we went, and when I was just going good I ran into an overflow (water on top of ice under soft snow that is a problem for all and if you slow down you sink in the slush; the colder it gets the worse overflows are), which slowed me down, but I was locked on the gun and kept going. I finally horsed the plane out of the snow and leap-frogged over the Eaglerock. Percy saw me coming and figured there would be a crash for certain. He tried to get out of the cockpit but was too late; when I went over him with less than a half an inch to spare he was draped over the edge of the cockpit like a wet dishrag. I kept right on going and soon we were both in Fairbanks with Percy telling me how close I came to him. He didn't have to—I knew. I had a lot to learn about flying. The thing about it was that we both laughed as though it was a good joke."

Who was master of the close calls? The answer to that one is simple—anyone who survived them to the end.

Whenever flying in the western Arctic is mentioned, one name stands out: that of John Milton Cross. He is sometimes confused with Joe Crosson, another of the all-time great bush pilots. John Cross was born in Goddard, Kansas, on March 1, 1895, and graduated from the University of Kansas in 1919. From there he went right into the Air Service of the Signal Corps. He was active in the Army Air Corps or in the reserves until 1965, when he retired with the rank of lieutenant colonel at the age of seventy. After World War I he worked rebuilding old Army planes, ferried, test-flew planes, and barnstormed. In the late twenties he lived in Wichita, Kansas, where at one time eleven aircraft companies were building at least one type of airplane apiece. John Cross test-flew for Swallow and Straugh (later Wiley Post's plane), taught students, and as a reserve officer flew with the Army Air Corps. John's first pilot's license was an old Aero Club of America International license issued in 1918. In the late twenties the CAA started issuing licenses and John revived license NO-866. John still holds a commercial rating, single- and multi-engine land and sea, instrument, and an A & E license NO-11461. As of November 1, 1966, he had a recorded 21,157 hours in the air. In flight hours John leads all the bush pilots. There are a few airline captains with more hours aloft, but it isn't fair to compare an hour in an airliner with one in a bush plane, where you heat and handle the airplane yourself before you ever get it into the air and even there some of those flight minutes can seem like hours.

John Milton Cross drifted in to Alaska in the fall of 1934, but before coming here he had a couple of close calls that are memorable. The first came when he was working at the Swallow Aircraft Company as a test pilot.

"A pilot came in and complained that the oil ran too hot and the engine vibrated," he recalls. "The shop installed a larger oil cooler and a new propeller. I gave the plane a test flight, flying very low for a half an hour over the hot Kansas wheatfields at high throttle setting. The oil ran cool but the vibration became worse and I landed. We found the left upper fuselage motor mount fitting broken, and the right upper fitting cracked. Another five minutes of flight and the motor would have swung down, slamming the plane into the ground."

In the early 1930's, Jimmy Doolittle resigned from the Army Air Corps, took a reserve commission as a major, and went to work for the Shell Oil Company flying a Travelair "Mystery S" racer. Jimmy had a spectacular approach that never failed to draw all the pilots when he arrived. Diving from two thousand feet he would level off at rooftop and cross the airport downwind at high speed. He then would pull up vertically until he lost speed. He would snap-roll straight up twice before coming in to land and meet the crowd.

"At Richards Field, Kansas City, Missouri," John recalls, "I was landing a PT-3 straight in when I saw a racer flash down the runway toward me. I pulled up, but the PT-3 was too slow and the racer directly in front of me. At a thousand feet he hit me from below, taking the PT-3's tail with him. Doolittle did a wing-over and landed his crippled racer. I parachuted into a field of corn and sand burs."

In the fall of 1934 John brought a Bellanca up to Cordova and made a few trips for M. D. Kirkpatrick (Kirk), who was managing a new stockholders' aviation company. Kirk referred to the stockholders as "sack holders," a name that pretty well described the early aviation backers across Alaska. Many banks had firm rules against loaning money to bush pilots.

From Cordova John went to Anchorage, the seat of aviation in southern Alaska. Here he put on a nail apron and helped Fred Bowman build a hangar at Merrill Field. He overhauled airplane engines and flew a little, but the older pilots felt he was "potentially dangerous competition" and he returned to Cordova to work and fly for Kirk.

It was rough work at Cordova, giving flying lessons, driving a 35 gas caterpillar on the night shift, and hauling freight for the Brenner Mine. Flying a Bird airplane he and Joe Malloy went down in the tall spruce timber when the motor quit after take-off. They snowshoed out to McCarthy, returned with a Robin, repaired the Bird, chopped a clearing, and flew it out. Later in the winter, the Robin sunk in the snow on Brenner Summit on landing, damaging a wing. John snowshoed back to McCarthy. Here he picked up repairs, went back up the mountain, patched the wing in a snow hut, and flew the Robin back.

In the fall of 1936 he joined Noel Wien, flying Noel's first Cessna with a Warner engine. From here he and Noel flew to Nome, where in clear weather Noel instructed John in Arctic flying and left him in charge of the Wien station at Nome. Thanks to Noel's careful instruction, John soon felt at home there and has since that date called and considered northwest Alaska his home.

Later Sig Wien came to Nome and took over the operation of that station for Noel, while John moved farther north to Deering and organized his own outfit, "Northern Cross Inc." John operated the base until 1941 using a Stinson and two Wacos. For a while he worked alone, but most of the time he employed another pilot in addition to a mechanic and radio operator. From his Deering base John ranged across the Arctic to Barrow and south to Cordova but most of his flying was servicing the Kobuk-Kotzebue area.

John not only pioneered in aviation but also in aircraft radio-telephone as well. As a member of the old Aeronautics and Communications Commission he helped establish territorial stations at Fairbanks and Nome. The old home station, KAXQ Deering, reported and relayed weather messages in addition to handling government messages through the ACS. The old Mukluk frequency 5652.5 KC served the bush very well. It often skipped and had blind spots, but someone would usually hear the message and relay it.

In 1941 John Cross was recalled into the Army Air Force and served for the duration of the war. Upon his release from active duty, operation of Northern Cross Inc. was resumed, but the day of the solitary bush pilot was past and the company was given up in 1947. John returned to flying for his old friend Noel Wien and flew out of Candle, Barrow, Fairbanks, and then Kotzebue. He retired from Wien Alaska Airlines in October 1964 to do a little free-lance flying, private flying, and flying with the Civil Air Patrol.

The big new country was always there, a great land to explore, and in the fall of 1960 Mr. and Mrs. J. C. Hammond (Jap and May), my son Jim, and I decided to explore the Alatna River using canoes from its headwaters. The trip was a series of problems from the beginning. Bad weather delayed our start, the freeze-up came early and caught our party, so I had to carry the canoe part of the way and then make the trip alone to pick up our airplane. Jap, May, and Jim returned to the little lake where we had started and waited until it froze solid enough to hold up the floatplane. It is possible to land a floatplane upon ice, but you have to use a great deal of care and handle things gently.

It took a week for the lake to freeze and I spent the time at Walker Lake. I flew over the folks once to let them know I had made the trip out and then waited. The days had been clear and cold and I figured the ice would be thick enough, but when I flew over the ice Jim's willow-stick sign told me the ice was an inch thinner than I felt was safe. There wasn't any real danger from the ice breaking, since I was on floats and water is a floatplane's element. At worst it would hold me until I stopped and then I would settle through and be stuck. The landing was routine, and while the ice cracked and a little water came up on the ice it held and we were careful in loading it.

I took May and a load of gear out on the first trip to Walker Lake and returned as soon as possible. I had a three-hundred-mile round-trip flight and as the day progressed a sullenness in the air developed that signaled the approach of a long-drawn-out storm. Snow began to fall as I neared the lake on my return trip and I knew darkness would come early. Jap and Jim hadn't been sure I would make a second trip and hurried about in the fading light to get me loaded up. The wind had changed and came softly from the Arctic prairie, bringing snowflakes with it. The wind from down the pass worried me, for with my load and the short lake I had no choice but to take off into the wind and up the gently rising pass. It looked flat but I knew it rose at a deceptive rate and I had a maximum load. There wasn't much time to decide and, anyway, I had just taken a heavier load out a few hours before but down the canyon.

Jim had to guide me into take-off position by pushing and pulling the tail around since a floatplane on ice wants to go straight ahead. We backed it up as far as we could and climbed in. I settled myself into the seat, shook the seat of my pants loose, and checked out the airplane, deliberately closing off all thoughts except those of flying. Take-off procedure was to get full power as quickly as possible, let the airplane pick its run and not fight it, but handle it like a spirited horse, giving it its head. At the three-quarter point of our run I gently eased back to see if it was ready to fly— it was not! We should have come up and away but didn't. Frost must have gathered on the wings' surfaces. A glance at the instruments showed full power and all normal, with air speed building fast, but we weren't ready to fly. I would have cut the power had I been in water or on wheels, in which case I could have got on the brakes. There were no brakes on the floats racing across the glare ice on their narrow skatelike bottoms. If I had cut the power, I would have shot on across the glare ice and smashed into the rocky shoreline, wrecking the airplane. Distance was deceptive in the shadowless gathering dusk and falling snow.

The human mind is the most wonderful computer ever imagined with its billions of little memory cells and procedure patterns. "Ask and you shall receive." —And there was the answer: "Straight ahead. Don't worry or hurry the ship. There is a little up current of air where the wind spilling over the bank hits the ice . . . use it. Ride it up. You can't outclimb the rise of land, follow the creek; there is a little lake a mile up, turn there and come back down the creek."

The course was plain. The rest was up to me. Seventy-five feet from the bank I brought the *Arctic Tern* up hard with full flaps. She came up like a spirited horse rising to a jump and we caught the upsurge of wind just right. Up over the bank we rose, clearing the rocks by a few feet, and as the plane began to settle I let off a notch of flaps while lowering the nose. I lost a few feet of altitude but gained a few miles per hour speed as we headed up the creek. My passengers didn't say a word nor move. Rocks and prairie were tearing past inches below us while the airplane controls trembled on the verge of a stall. I would buy a few feet of altitude with my precious mile-or-two-per-hour safety margin and sell it again in a little dip to regain those miles of safety back for the next rise. It seemed many miles to the lake despite the speed the land was flashing past below. It was a tight turn around the lake, but the respite from climbing allowed me to gain the speed I needed for the U turn, and when I came down the valley I was in the clear.

"You know, Bud, it was as if a hand were under the airplane lifting us over the ridges and rocks," Jap said as soon as we were in the clear.

One of my closest calls didn't have to do with flying, poor judgment, or even the mechanical, unless you want to blame it all on the start.

We had gathered up all our gear in early spring to take a little family outing at our Walker Lake home, which was well stocked with provisions. We were coming in across the north end of Walker Lake when the snap on the left side of the cowling came loose, letting it bang about in the wind. It was similar to having the hood of your car come loose. I was afraid it would tear off, and since we were on skis over a good landing area, I let the ship down upon the soft snow, making a feathery landing. The snow was soft, and while it took only a moment to refasten the cowling, we would have to trample down a short runway in order to take off again.

I put on my snowshoes and started around the airplane when I felt the snow settling. It takes time to turn around on snowshoes—time I didn't have. I just raced straight ahead, feeling the snow sink at every step. I went full throttle for fifty or sixty feet before I felt solid footing. I had heard Martha gasp as I started out and when I looked back I knew why. The lake was open between us! The five-foot-deep snow had enough inertia to support me momentarily, but my passing had triggered the action and a hole fifty feet across just opened up. Gas bubbles from below had brought up warm water, melting away the ice under the deep snow, but leaving the snow roof intact until I came along. I sounded all the snow then, and as it was getting late we made camp. It turned warm and snowed hard for a week so we had to tramp a runway twice before we finally made it to the cabin.

Most of the bush pilots' close calls were the result of trying to get through bad weather instead of waiting a few days to clear up, or from starting out in good weather and meeting bad weather past the point of no return and having to go on.

The Reverend Bill Wartes ran into the latter situation in August 1957. He was flying from Barrow to the mission conference at Anchorage. He had his wife, Bonnie, Leona Simmonds, and Elizabeth Ahmaogak along, which gave him a full load as usual. He planned to go by way of Anaktuvuk Pass, but just twenty-five minutes from the pass he ran into a wall of fog. He decided to try Chandler Lake Pass then to the west. Bill made it right up into the mountains this time, but he didn't know the pass and fog came up from the valley floor, hiding the ground, and a thick overcast covered the tops of the mountains, forming a wedge. Bill thought he was following the pass until he realized he had made a mistake. It was a blind canyon and now too narrow to turn around in!

Aerobatics are done in an empty airplane with the rear seats empty and several thousand feet up in the clear blue sky, not with a fully loaded floatplane in a canyon too narrow to turn in with clouds above and fog below and a rock wall ahead. At moments like that life belongs to those who think and act fast. It was the old fighter pilot's chandelle that brought him through. He dipped his nose for speed, hugging the right rock wall until he brushed the fog layer below, and then came up in a loop rolling out to the left to come back out the canyon. From there he scouted around the mountains and made it through to Summit Lake, where he had wanted to go in the first place. He was about out of gasoline but had ten gallons of gasoline cached there, which would see him on to Bettles. Luckily, a stiff breeze was blowing across the small lake, for it is tough to get off with a heavily loaded plane. After coffee with the Eskimos there, Bill continued on his way.

Two autumns ago I had a strange experience. I had left the Arctic coast in a howling dust storm! As I proceeded inland I ran into low visibility and finally heavy snow as I crossed the Brooks Range. I was flying a Super Cub and they were never made for my long frame. I finally ended up with an awful charley horse in my right leg—the kind where if you can stand erect and flat-footed it will go away, so I tried standing in that tight cabin. I managed to get on my feet flat-footed, my back along the roof and my head down, so I looked out the lower part of the left window, with the stick in my right hand right between my knees. In this position I managed to get a cramp in the left leg as well and couldn't move. It was snowing hard and I was down right at treetop level in the narrow John River Canyon following the stream. It was early November and all was frozen solid. Snow was two feet deep there, and sensible bears as well as sensible pilots were at home, but there standing on the frozen river all covered with snow was a grizzly bear and he looked up into my face as I looked into his as I flew by in my literally "cramped" position. It took me half an hour to get the cramps out and sit back in the seat. A little while later I was at Bettles Field and could walk about. It was getting dark and snowing hard so I stayed overnight. About an hour later Paul Hagland came in with the Beaver. He had been going up the John River Canyon as I came down! We must have passed within a few feet of each other in that snow, for both of us had been following that thin line of frozen river to avoid flying into the canyon walls!

Jim Freericks was flying out of Nome. "We received a call in Nome from the teacher at Diomede Island, the only white person there, that one of the women had flipped and was driving everyone else on the island crazy," recalled Jim. "Would the pilot [me] please come and get her? After some discussion I determined that the only ice there was shore ice, since it was early winter and the straits between Big and Little Diomede hadn't frozen over yet. It was pressure ice, ice piled below the cliffs and impossible to land an airplane upon, so of course I refused to go. They then asked how much room I needed, and thinking I would be in a Cessna 170, I told them I needed a strip six hundred feet long and thirty feet wide. The entire village then went to work with shovels, picks, and bars making a runway on the pressure ice. It was an unbelievable task. In three or four weeks they called me again and said they had the runway ready but in the meantime the shop had recalled the Cessna 170 and given me a Norseman on skis. I needed a lot more runway for that big airplane, yet I didn't have the heart to refuse them after all their work. I decided to take a look at the runway, so the people would know their work was appreciated at least. I took two men along to help in case the woman became violent. I didn't think the wind would be good and I could gracefully turn back.

"As luck would have it, the wind was blowing straight down the runway at thirty miles per hour. (Diomede Island has no landing field and the cliffs rise straight up from the sea; the shore ice was piled at the base of the cliffs and it is a wild spot at best.) I backed off, made a low, slow approach, and plunked her in right on the end of the strip. I was the hero of the moment and the entire village turned out to help me turn around. Luckily, they did, too, for it was a big job, but I finally got turned around, taxied back, and turned around again for take-off.

"The crazy woman didn't appear unhappy, and I saw she had only one arm. I was somewhat relieved, for if she became violent my two men shouldn't have much trouble restraining her. She was enjoying it all, doing an Eskimo dance anytime she could find room. I sat one man directly behind me in the back seat, the lady next, and the other fellow on the outside. The co-pilot's seat was empty. I instructed my handlers to keep a close watch on her. It had taken us two hours to get into a take-off position, so I warmed up the Norseman and poured on the coal. I just had full throttle on and was accelerating nicely when that one arm came up, grabbed the throttle, and jerked the power off.

"There being no brakes on a ski ship, as you well know, I sat there horrified, waiting to drive into the pressure ridge. Thank God there was enough wind to slow us down, and, having pulled the mixture control, the prop stopped and we canted up against the first pressure ridge, stopping with no damage. Two hours later we were in position for another try after playing musical chairs and putting the woman on the far-off side. It was a routine flight the rest of the way."

Jim had a second interesting flight under similar conditions at Nome. This time he took the marshal with him and flew to King Island. There was a good spot to land about a mile away on the sea ice, and the village elders brought the problem woman out to the airplane on a dog sled. Jim had the Cessna 170 and the woman was a little thing about five feet tall, weighing about a hundred and ten pounds. She couldn't speak English and they didn't speak Eskimo. Jim gave her a cigarette and she smoked it happily. Jim put his passenger in the back and they had a pleasant flight all the way back across the broken-up ice and open ocean to Nome. Here the lady thanked Jim, shook hands, and departed. It was the next morning when Jim realized what might have happened.

The marshal put her in a cab and started off for the airport with her to send her on to Fairbanks. It must have dawned on her that she was being sent outside. There was an old saying in Alaska that there were three sides to Alaska: Inside, Outside, and Morning side; the latter being the name of the place in Washington where they sent the mentally ill. This little lady didn't want any of it and she whipped the marshal. The taxi driver stopped to help and she whipped him too. By then a crowd had gathered and with more assistance they got the lady back to the jail, where they put her in a strait jacket, took her back, and put her aboard the airliner. This made her really mad and she broke loose from the strait jacket and tore an airline seat loose from the floor, then proceeded to tear up the inside before they could again subdue her, take her back to jail and eventually get her tied up tight enough for the trip into Fairbanks. Every time Jim is reminded of how she tore up that airliner, he shudders to think of the return trip from King Island in the small Cessna 170 with nothing below but open ocean and drifting cakes of ice. Some of the close calls look closer the more time passes.

Spring weather in the Arctic can be so beautiful that, as George Wood put it, "I'm sure glad I didn't die last winter and miss this day," or it can be so white that you pull the curtains shut in the house because there is absolutely nothing to see outside and the glare hurts your eyes. You might start out in the most beautiful weather on earth and return in the worst—as far as seeing where you are going is concerned.

This kind of situation caught my son Jim and me. Jim had been away to college and was anxious to get home when school closed. He flew to Umiat on the airline and I met him there. The snow was melting fast but I managed to find enough for my skis. It was a splendid day and we headed right for home, flying the ever-faithful *Arctic Tern*. About thirty miles from home we began to meet whiteout conditions, but the warm sun had melted bare spots on the prairie and there was a little clod of dirt here and a bunch of grass there to mark the difference between land and fog. I dropped down to inches above the ground to set my altimeter as we met the fog and then climbed up to one hundred feet. At first the dark spots were fairly plentiful, but as we neared the ocean they became fewer and fewer. We were but five or six miles from home and Martha told me on the radio she could still see the dark runway markers a quarter of a mile away. I figured I could hit them by dead reckoning. Everything worked out fine except I seemed awfully low as I landed. We came to a stop in front of the house and Martha, Mark, and Jeffrey came hurrying out to greet Jim. I went about shutting off the switches and valves. Then I looked at the altimeter and it still read one hundred feet! Jim was looking at it too.

We had flown into a pressure change with the whiteout and a hundred-foot reading really meant zero feet!

"We must have been pretty low, Dad. A good many of those mounds and river island banks rise ten feet in the air. There must have been a few close ones."

19

FAMOUS EXPLOITS

The meeting of Carl Ben Eielson and George Hubert Wilkins is one of those fortunate combinations of history. Wilkins had been introduced to the Arctic by the great explorer Dr. Vilhjalmur Stefansson in 1913. Wilkins had come from Australia to be the photographer on Stefansson's Canadian Arctic expedition. When the flag ship, the *Karluk,* was set fast in the ice just north of where our home now stands, they thought she would be there all winter. Stefansson and Wilkins went ashore to hunt caribou and explore; while they were ashore a violent gale broke up the ice and carried the *Karluk* away, to be crushed later near Wrangel Island, Siberia. With the *Karluk* went all Wilkins's gear and, you might say, his reason for being in the Arctic as well. He could easily have headed for home on the first transportation. Instead he followed that master of Arctic teachers, Stefansson, for three years on foot, exploring and living for months upon the moving ice pack. Coming from Australia where even the poorest man had a horse to ride, Wilkins never enjoyed walking.

Alfred Hopson, the young Eskimo boy who had at times traveled with them, told me many years later, "No man could stay up with Stefansson, for he could walk like a caribou, but Wilkins tried."

Perhaps after so many miles of following his leader, Wilkins began to dream of flying, and while they were camped at Collinson Point, to be exact, Wilkins first decided to fly in the Arctic.

"From then on," Stefansson told me later, "Wilkins planned and dreamed of using airplanes and submarines to explore the Arctic."

It was most fitting that when the atomic-powered submarine *Nautilus* surfaced at the North Pole half a century later it carried with it Wilkins's ashes to scatter there in the heart of the land he had loved and explored.

Carl Ben Eielson came from North Dakota. He arrived in Alaska to teach school but had dreams of flying and he found the people of Fairbanks ready to support this new means of travel. Ben Eielson was already a good pilot and he had the courage to pioneer and try to make flying pay. In a way you could call Ben Eielson the first Alaskan bush pilot, but considering the airplanes, the facilities, and routes the term bush pilot is premature. He was an explorer. It remained for Noel Wien to become the first real bush pilot. The Russian newspaper *Chudak* called Eielson, "The Great Arctic Pioneer Pilot." The Russians shared an admiration for Eielson's deeds with his fellow Alaskans. Had Eielson and Earl Borland not met their deaths that white November 9, 1929, in the Hamilton airplane off North Cape, Siberia, Eielson most likely wouldn't have gone on with bush flying but would have gone on into airline organization and aerial exploration around the world.

Wilkins and Eielson met in 1926 when Wilkins hired Eielson as one of the pilots for the Detroit Arctic Expedition. Wilkins's Arctic training with Stefansson had taught him to rely upon a few well-trained men and a little carefully chosen equipment in the Arctic land. Wilkins's backers felt if a little was good, a lot would be better, and proceeded to just swamp him with gear and personnel. There were two airplanes, a large single-engined Fokker called the *Alaskan,* and a trimotored Fokker called the *Detroiter.* There was a ground party of snow tractors that was to set out from Nenana and reach Barrow. It started out as an advertising and testing program for the Snow Motors Company and would take a little equipment such as a radio station and some men to Barrow overland. The snow tractors were Swedish-built and had a young Swedish engineer along with them. They were propelled by two cigar-shaped drums with spiral fins. In heavy drifted snow they would work after a fashion, but in the loose crystallized snow of the interior they did not work well and would haul no load. In two weeks they got as far as Tolovana from Nenana, a distance of roughly sixty to seventy miles, and were left there. They came back to Nenana on the river steamboat the following summer. The old Alaska Road Commission experimented with them, but to no avail, and they disappeared into limbo. When Wilkins learned it was to be a part of his expedition he tried to veto it but was outvoted. The Detroit

Arctic Expedition was the biggest thing in flying that had ever hit Fairbanks. There were even eleven newspaper cameramen along. It is a wonder Wilkins was able to accomplish anything that first year with such an unwieldy crew.

The airplanes were assembled, and amid fanfare and with the whole town present they were readied for flight. Major Lanphier was at the controls and Wilkins was beside him as they started up the *Detroiter* for a test flight. The trimotored Fokker was hard to taxi and one wheel stuck in a snowdrift. The outboard propellers were directly ahead of the wheels and cleaning snow was a dangerous job. In the excitement of the moment the likable photographer Palmer Hutchinson, who was always willing to help, rushed in and cleared the snow from in front of the wheel and gave the signal that all was clear. Lanphier advanced the throttle, and instead of stepping away from the propeller Hutchinson stepped into it and was killed instantly.

A few days later they tried another flight—this time in the single-engined *Alaskan*. Ben Eielson was the pilot on this flight and Wilkins rode along. The take-off was fine and they flew about for nearly an hour with the *Alaskan* doing beautifully under Eielson's skillful hands. As Wilkins put it, "I lost my heart to the *Alaskan*."

Perhaps because the *Alaskan* handled so easily, Eielson felt he could land her without making a pass or two at the field. As they approached the field Eielson throttled back, the ship stalled, and smacked down two hundred feet short of the runway. It slid ahead through the fence, taking off the landing gear and twisting the propeller. No one was hurt. You might think that after this sort of a start that Wilkins's faith in Eielson as a pilot would have been badly shaken, but it wasn't. Wilkins, while he hated to direct men, knew his men and never wavered in his faith in them. He wrote that he would have liked to have had Eielson fly the *Detroiter* the next day since Eielson wasn't likely to make the same mistake twice. With Lanphier, the brilliant commander of the First Pursuit Squadron there and recommended by the Detroit backers, Wilkins knew he had no choice but to have Lanphier fly the *Detroiter*.

The next day Wilkins climbed into the *Detroiter* with Lanphier, and after a hectic take-off Lanphier bounced the big ship into the air, narrowly missing the snowbanks at the sides of the field. Wilkins and Lanphier had thoroughly discussed the necessity of making several passes at the field before landing. Lanphier made several stall landings in the air to feel out the ship and apparently decided he knew the *Detroiter* well enough, for, much to Wilkins's surprise, as they neared the landing field Lanphier cut the two outboard engines and the *Detroiter* stalled. The three-ton Fokker fell to the ground in exactly the same spot as the *Alaskan* had hit. The *Detroiter*, being heavier, broke up much worse and for a while it looked as if the end had come, but when they finally stopped both Lanphier and Wilkins were unhurt. The *Detroiter* was a wreck, though, and would take a long time to repair.

It took the mechanics in Fairbanks three weeks to repair the *Alaskan*, and by that time it was March 31. Wilkins didn't feel that there was time for trial flights, so they loaded three thousand pounds aboard the *Alaskan* and, with Eielson at the controls, they headed for Barrow.

On this first flight Wilkins and Eielson, the unbeatable team, showed what they could do. Wilkins, the master navigator in whom Eielson had implicit faith, and Eielson, the pilot in whom Wilkins placed unquestioning faith, functioned as a unit. The maps of that time were inaccurate and for the most part nonexistent over the course they were flying; therefore, Wilkins had to chart the course by compass and shots of the sun as a sailor would at sea. It was a first for Arctic air navigation. They left Fairbanks in clear weather and headed north. Wilkins soon realized that a terrific tail wind was driving them north. Wilkins was the foremost Arctic meteorologist of that day and he knew that a south wind would mean fog across the Arctic prairie. As they approached the Brooks Range at nine thousand feet, they could see the fog. It boiled up along the north edge and lay a solid blanket of white on beyond. Wilkins described it in his book *Flying the Arctic:* "It was a weird and uncanny sight. We seemed only a speck in a boundless world . . . nothing to judge space or distance . . . I'm sure we could find nothing more weird if we traveled through space to the moon. The monotony and uncertainty of it would drive any man crazy if endured for long."

Endure it and rely upon their instruments they must though, for it was a solid sheet. Two hours later they came to the end of the fog and Wilkins saw unmistakable water sky ahead, like hangs over an open lead in the ice pack, while below lay the ice pack! They had already passed Barrow and were flying north across the ice into an unexplored area. The thrill of heading into unknown land lured them on and they flew an hour and a half straight north into the area never before seen by anyone.

Eielson was apprehensive, for in truth he was not a good navigator and was often lost and had to trust Wilkins implicitly. Wilkins was a superb navigator. When they were an hour and a half out they turned back for land, but as they neared the shore they found the storm had moved on out to sea. The long hours of flying were beginning to tell on the men, and as they again entered the storm they had only the compass to go by, for they could no longer see the sun. Eielson thought he saw houses, but there were none. In the storm they both began to see what looked like houses everywhere in the storm. Wilkins knew what we all who venture into the unknown must know: DO ONE THING AT A TIME AND MAKE SURE IT IS BASED ON SOLID FACTS. The only solid facts were the compass, air speed, and time for Wilkins to navigate by while Eielson flew the *Alaskan*.

For an hour they flew through the white void and Wilkins was beginning to think they had better turn back north and find a smooth place to land when he saw the unmistakable cutbank shoreline southwest of Barrow. They had only to follow it up to get to Barrow. Drifting snow poured over the cut-bank shoreline southwest of Barrow. They had only to sight to Wilkins even from the air, for he had traveled through it on foot many times. It made being in the shelter of the airplane sheer comfort. The first point on the coast Wilkins positively identified was the lagoon where the Wiley Post and Will Rogers monument now are. "Only fifteen miles to go," he told Eielson—what a relief to have positive proof of where you are.

In the whiteout time dragged. Visibility was less than two hundred yards and Wilkins began to wonder if perhaps he had made an error. Had he identified a lagoon and point that existed somewhere else? A sod Eskimo house appeared on the bank and then a church spire with a two-story house near and they went past them in the storm. A half mile of lagoon went by and then there were the houses of Browerville. It was Charlie Brower's Cape Smythe Whaling and Trading Station where Wilkins and Stefansson had walked in when they lost the *Karluk* in 1913. Wilkins drew a hurried sketch of the layout, showing Eielson where to land.

Even in the joy of arrival there was one more unknown to handle. For the first time a landing with wheels had to be made upon the snow of the Arctic. Many said it would end in disaster. Eielson brought the *Alaskan* in low over the sand-spit and touched the snow as light as a feather. They taxied to the bank near the trading post and shut off the engine. It had been ten hours since they had left Fairbanks. When Wilkins opened the plane door he realized what kind of a day it was. A high wind drifted snow and it was 40 below zero. A few Eskimos came out to look at their first airplane while Charlie Brower and Fred Hopson came rushing to greet the explorers. It was a happy reunion.

The next day an Eskimo trapper came in and told them he had been trapping foxes down the coast when he had seen them fly by going north. In about three hours he had again seen them come back. He had thought he was dreaming until he saw the airplane on the lagoon. This gave Wilkins an exact check upon his navigation and he could plot the course exactly to where they had been. He had returned to within two miles of the exact spot from which they had gone out. Twenty-five years later when I made a long exploration flight across the Arctic ice and returned to within twenty miles of the point I had gone out from I felt I had done very well.

It stormed for five days and during this time they set up a portable wireless with a hand-cranked generator and sent the first wireless message ever transmitted from Barrow. On the fifth day the storm let up and they took off for Fairbanks, arriving there without trouble. It was the successful completion of the longest nonstop Arctic flight made to that date. Wilkins wanted to haul more gasoline into Barrow as soon as possible for an exploration flight far out over the Arctic ice. He had planned to do this hauling with the *Detroiter*, but she was a long ways from flyable.

They remained in Fairbanks one day and departed for Barrow, flying on a compass course. It was much the same as the first flight, except Barrow was clear and they landed easily. The Eskimos were much impressed by the second trip and said, "We thought at first your coming here in a flying machine was nice. It was such a thing as medicine men in old times did, but when you left we began to wonder if we had been dreaming, now you are here again, we know the air-planes are a fact."

They landed in Barrow with a cargo of 200 gallons of gaso-line to spare. Ten hours later they were on their way back to Fairbanks. It had been a little too rough taking off across the drifts so they shoveled trenches in the snow for the wheels to roll in. While Wilkins was helping turn the *Alaskan* he caught his mitten in the spoke of a wheel and broke his arm. At first he felt it was only a sprain but as they flew south he found he couldn't use his right arm and he couldn't hold his navigational instruments. After crossing the Brooks Range they came to what Wilkins felt sure was the junction of the Alatna and Koyukuk rivers. They circled and dropped a note asking the people to tramp the name of the village in the snow. The people tramped out the name of Alakaket. The villages are really twins, though, and the other name of Alatna was the one that appeared on Wilkins's map. This puzzled him, for he felt sure it was the junction of the Koyukuk and Alatna rivers even though his broken right arm hadn't allowed him to use his instruments to keep their position by the sun. He was writing with his left hand and he wrote a note asking the people to tramp an arrow pointing to Fairbanks; meanwhile they were circling, burning up needed gasoline. The people didn't wait to tramp an arrow they just formed an arrow of people pointing the way. When they landed at Fairbanks, they had but one gallon of gasoline left. Here Wilkins found the small bone in his right arm was broken in two places. Wilkins bandanged his arm himself so as not to cause any undue concern, and two days later he and Eielson headed for Barrow a third time!

The loads they carried in that Fokker monoplane with its 400 h.p. engine are unbelievable even by today's standards. The first trip they carried 3,500 pounds in a ship built to carry a 2,000-pound load. On the second flight they put in 4,000 pounds, and on this third trip they had 4,750 pounds. This weight compares favorably with the payload a DC-3 airliner hauls on the same flight off modern runways today!

The 4,750-pound load was almost too much to get over the mountains with, though. It was during those days that Wilkins came to realize the solid courage, airmanship, and sound judgment of Eielson, while Eielson likewise came to appreciate the sound judgment, courage, and navigational ability of Wilkins. As they neared the Brooks Range they saw that a storm was blowing, obscuring the passes, and with the heavy load they couldn't climb above the peaks. Eielson decided to squeeze through between two peaks and Wilkins noted the mountain wall was so close on his side that he felt they would hit it, so he motioned to Eielson, but Eielson motioned there was a peak just as close on his side. The noise level in the *Alaskan* was such that you couldn't talk. Wilkins rode in the back with cargo piled all about him, so he couldn't see out the right side. They were going between two mountain peaks just wide enough to get through and without a foot to spare, and as they vaulted through the gap Wilkins noted the wheel on his side spinning as if from take-off, and he realized they had been so low that the wheel dragged as they went between the peaks. It was an easy flight from then on into Barrow.

They were delayed in Barrow two days by bad weather, which gave Charlie Brower a chance to dress Wilkins's broken arm. While they were preparing for take-off, an Eskimo came running to say the airplane was on fire. Sparks from the stove heating the engine had ignited the canvas engine cover. Luckily only the canvas cover burned off, blistering the paint on the cowling and varnish on the propeller. Nothing seemed really damaged, so off for Fairbanks they went, only to run into a big storm near the mountains; upon turning back they found that the storm had moved in behind them and they had a hard time just finding Barrow again. It seemed like four hours of useless flying just to return to where they had started from, but they had proved it was possible to return in a bad storm.

When the storm cleared they started for Fairbanks again, but the engine ran awfully rough and they landed at once. An examination of the propeller showed both trailing edges were frayed and loose from the fire. It looked like the end of the flying for the *Alaskan* until a new propeller could be brought up. They worked on the propeller, though, for two days, binding the loose parts with brass and balancing it. This time the *Alaskan* handled well and they reached Fairbanks easily.

In Fairbanks a new propeller had arrived from the States and they replaced the brass-bound one, but the new propeller wouldn't pull right and on the fourth attempt to take off they overran the runway, coming to a rough stop. Willing hands dragged the airplane back to the field and they put the old propeller back on. They repacked all the gear and gasoline cases in the *Alaskan* and started to take-off for Barrow again. Just as they reached flying speed, there was an awful crash and the right wing and gear let go. They slid to a stop with the tail high, and gasoline cases came forward pinning Wilkins in. Gasoline from broken tanks poured over the hot engine, but luckily it didn't burn. It was the end of the *Alaskan*'s usefulness that season.

In the meantime the *Detroiter* had been repaired and Wilkins decided to carry on with it, so Wilkins, along with

Lanphier and Wisely, set out for Barrow in the trimotored Fokker. The larger, powerful ship handled beautifully and went up to 11,000 feet easily. They crossed the Brooks Range and Wilkins settled down to eat his lunch. He noted that the ship was flying erratically and passed a note up forward, assuring the pilots they were on course, but no one took the note. When he got up and looked in the cabin he found a struggle going on between the pilots. Wisely had "chickened out" and was trying to gain control of the airplane and return to Fairbanks while Lanphier was willing to keep on for Barrow. Lanphier won and they reached Barrow easily and landed safely.

Wilkins was going on to explore the Arctic ice with the larger *Detroiter* and what gasoline they had, but the spring fog set in and they were held up day after day. While they were waiting they heard on the radio that Byrd had flown from Spitsbergen to the North Pole and back.

Then, on May 13, 1926, they watched as the dirigible *Norge,* flown by Roald Amundsen, Ellsworth, and Nobile, passed by on its flight across the Arctic from Spitsbergen to Nome.

Wilkins had wanted to make this same flight in 1919, and although he had the money to finance the trip, no factory would sell him a dirigible because they felt the Arctic was too severe a land for their products.

On that thirteenth day of May as Wilkins watched the dirigible *Norge* pass by, fulfilling his dream, it mattered little to him who was at the controls; the fact that the *Norge* had safely crossed the Arctic was what counted. Wilkins turned to Lanphier and remarked, "This is the greatest thrill of my life."

Just seeing that speck in the distance meant that much to Wilkins, for it was broken low clouds at Barrow that day and they just saw the *Norge* far off through the clouds and the *Norge*'s crew never saw Barrow. Wilkins's joy in the success of someone else was perhaps the key to his fantastic success and ability as an explorer.

They waited in Barrow hoping for good weather until June 4, when the spring breakup started and all hopes of exploring further that year ended. Water was already forming upon the ice as they flew to Fairbanks and stored the airplane for the season.

In February 1927 Wilkins was back in Fairbanks with two new Stinson biplanes to use in exploring the ice. One was called the *Detroiter No. 1* and the other the *Detroiter No. 2.*

His plans were to use the Fokkers to haul supplies to Barrow, and if he were able to complete his exploration of the unknown Arctic regions north of Alaska, he would then use the *Alaskan* to fly from Barrow to Spitsbergen.

The skis on the *Alaskan* were damaged on the first take-off at Fairbanks and it had to stay behind. The two Stinson *Detroiters* then flew on direct to Barrow, and Joe Crosson brought Mr. Smith up in a Swallow biplane, making a most remarkable flight considering he had never flown that route before. Crosson then returned to Fairbanks via Kotzebue.

It was early March by the time Wilkins had things all in order for his exploration. Wilkins was not trying to fly over the North Pole at this time, but he was searching for land in the Arctic Ocean to the north with an eye to establishing a weather station there. Wilkins, like Stefansson, was first of all a scientist interested in study and research. After exploring the unknown Arctic Ocean north of Alaska, he would fly on across the Arctic finishing up his work.

On the flights across the ocean they carried sonic equipment for recording the depth of the Arctic Ocean wherever they landed upon the ice. In addition, they carried the following emergency camping gear; it is almost identical to the gear I still carry. It consisted of a pocketknife, snow knife, a saw, snowshoes, shovel, back pack, first-aid kit, light double tent, gasoline stove, nesting aluminum cooking utensils, rope, sunglasses, an ax, sleeping bags, tool kit, matches, Bausch and Lomb binoculars, skin needles, extra fur clothing, fishnet, a rifle and ammunition, a kerosene lantern, hard candy and enough dried foods to last a month. Stove fuel was carried in small cans designed for a single filling each. All was designed to fit together and serve crosspurposes whenever possible. On flights across the ice they carried gear for retrieving seals shot in the open leads.

On the first exploration flight across the ice that year Wilkins and Eielson had a chance to put all their emergency gear to a test. It was −42 degrees at 6:00 A.M. on March 12, 1927, when Wilkins and Eielson in *Detroiter No. 1* left Barrow heading north into the unknown. At 6:50 they passed a big open lead, then came older ice, and at 8:15 they crossed a lead a mile wide, but by 9:15 they were over solid ice and hadn't seen a crack in fifteen minutes even. At 11:15 the engine was running badly and Eielson decided they had better land and fix it. It was −30 degrees on the ice and they were roughly 550 miles north of Barrow, just halfway to the North

Pole. While Eielson worked upon the engine, Wilkins cut two holes in the three-foot-thick ice and detonated a sounding device that gave an ocean depth of five thousand meters. Clouds covered the sky, so Wilkins couldn't get an exact fix on their position.

For nearly two hours they worked on the engine. They took off the cowling and carburetor and finally it ran smoothly, but only turned up 1400 RPM. It was hardly enough power for take-off, but after five attempts they were in the air and heading for Barrow; however, in ten minutes the engine was missing fire so badly that they had to land again. It was only because of Wilkins's many months on foot on the ice that he was able to guide Eielson in to a safe landing spot.

The wind was blowing harder, blowing snow, and visibility was fading as they worked dismantling the ignition system. Eielson froze four fingers so badly that the little finger of his right hand had to be amputated later; however, he never mentioned this to Wilkins at the time. After an hour's work they tried the engine and it ran beautifully.

It took two runs to get off, and at 2:20 P.M. they were in the air again but bucking an increasing headwind. By 7:00 P.M. it was impossible to see the sky or ice below clearly and Wilkins directed Eielson by touching him on the right or left arm. There were but two hours of fuel left in the tanks. At Wilkins's last accurate observation they had over a forty-knot sidedrift to the west. They were flying at five thousand feet and only a dull glow on the northwestern horizon showed where the sun had departed. Wilkins passed a note to Eielson: "What do you think; let her go straight ahead as long as she can, then glide straight ahead?"

Eielson slowly nodded his head. No word was spoken. The time was 9:02 when the engine quit suddenly. The fuel was gone. Eielson, calm and cool, steadied the gliding ship with his eyes glued to the turn-and-bank indicator. Near the ice the airplane began to pitch and roll in the rough air, but Eielson held it steady dead ahead. You could dimly see the broken ice. The left wing and ski struck simultaneously. The *Detroiter No. 1* bounced and landed smoothly. All about them in the night loomed the broken ice. The wind shook the plane. They rested on an even keel but both skis had broken and turned on their sides. After a brief look about they climbed back into the plane where Eielson stretched out on top of the empty gas tank in his sleeping bag while Wilkins wrapped up in his and slept sitting up.

They awoke in a howling storm that made moving about inadvisable, but even in the storm they could see their landing had been a real miracle. They had landed on a smooth spot forty-five feet wide and ninety feet long! A west storm was now blowing. Wilkins cut a hole through the six-foot-thick ice and took a sounding. He found they were drifting north of east at six miles per hour. There was a possibility that a wireless message might get through and the *Detroiter No. 2* fly out after them. Wilkins figured they were then one hundred miles northeast of Barrow. The storm blew, changed directions, and blew some more with winds up to forty-five knots. The *Detroiter No. 1* shook in the storm and snowdrifts formed around her. They saved precious gasoline by burning the cylinder oil, using a little wood from the plane for a wick. They made sleds from the cowling, the tail ski, and bits of the cabin walls. The *Detroiter No. 1* would have to be abandoned. Her skis were broken and her gasoline tanks empty.

It was Sunday, April 3, before they were able to start for land. Their walk to land is one of the greatest feats of ingenuity, faith, courage, and stamina I know of. Wilkins was the leader, his knowledge gained from years spent on the ice with Stefansson, while Eielson with unwavering faith followed. They dragged the sleds for five hours and then made a snowhouse camp. It was the first Eielson had ever seen and it had been twelve years since Wilkins had made one. The Alaskan Eskimos had never seen a round snowhouse until Stefansson built some for them. The round snowhouse is from Greenland, but is most useful anywhere good snow is found. It was at this first camp that Wilkins realized how seriously Eielson had frozen his right hand, for it was nearly useless and pained him steadily. There was so little fuel for the gasoline stove that they used it only to melt drinking water and ate their food cold, with no heat in camp, of course.

They traveled day after day over ice so rough you had to crawl over it part of the time. On the third day they threw away all their European clothing and dressed completely in native skin clothing. With this big reduction in bulk they could discard one sled. That afternoon they came to an open lead running east and west. It is in this area that I do much of my polar-bear hunting today. They paused here to test their drift and found they were moving east at two miles per hour to the east. There was an ice bridge fifty yards across the lead and they hurried to cross the clear bluish water on it. The edges of the bridge were crushing and a sounding from the other side showed a drift of one mile an hour to the west for that ice field.

Wilkins would have liked to have camped on the lead, shot some seals for food and fuel, and then moved on but he feared the delay on account of Eielson's hand. He knew that part of it would have to be amputated, and while he had done this sort of work before, he wanted to get Eielson to a hospital and save as much of the hand as possible.

Camping upon sea ice in cold weather is exacting work, and when living in unheated camps hoarfrost must be beaten from clothing regularly. All clothing must be turned, beaten, and scraped free of all traces of frost or it will become a mat of ice and be useless. Socks or mittens that were damp had to be worn under the parka against your chest to dry them. Both men were soft, but the days on the trail hardened them up.

Day followed day of making a snowhouse camp, cleaning frost from clothing, sleeping, breaking camp, and moving on again. The ice became very rough as they neared the land-fast pack, forcing them to abandon the sled and backpack all their gear. At times the ice was broken so badly and covered with soft snow that it was as easy to crawl across it on all fours as to try to walk. Finally they came to the old broken land-fast ice that was stationary. On April 10, just a week after they had started, they came to a wide stretch of new ice too thin to walk upon and in places the ice hadn't formed yet. Seals popped up in the open places, but Wilkins knew they were nearing shore and there was no need to add more weight to their packs by killing a seal.

They had to cross the young ice, though. In one spot it was about fifty yards across and looked strong enough. They could cross here or walk many miles trying to find a better place. There was also the chance that the tide or current might open the lead wider if they waited. Eielson stepped upon the new ice and broke through to his knees, but his long water boots saved him from getting wet. They scouted about and found a little safer place to cross. Wilkins went first and by walking spread out he made it almost across, but just as he turned to tell Eielson to come on he went right through! I can understand how he felt. I have been in the Arctic Ocean myself. It is so cold it burns and you are rendered numb. By using his ice pick and throwing himself forward Wilkins was able to pull himself up onto the ice and roll toward the old ice. Just before he reached the old ice he again broke through but he could reach the old ice with his ice pick and pulled himself up onto it. Eielson had luckily been up on solid ice but he was transfixed with horror at seeing Wilkins in the water. It was a scary sight and Eielson had to cross that way yet! Wilkins slipped from his eighty-pound pack and threw Eielson a line that he tied to his pack and then Wilkins pulled it across the thin ice. Relieved of the pack, Eielson spread-eagled himself and crossed safely.

Wilkins and Eielson hurried to some rough ice and took off Wilkins's clothes at once. Luckily, Wilkins's pack hadn't become wet and he had dry socks and boots in the pack and he put these on at once. They squeezed and scraped as much water and ice from the pants and parka as they could and Wilkins dressed fast, for it was 10 below. The wet clothes would only dry upon the wearer and they had no extras. They had discarded everything except half a sleeping bag. They slept in their clothes with their feet both in the same sleeping bag. Sleeping in one's clothing is a poor practice, but on this trip it saved much weight and bulk. It took Wilkins two days to dry out his wet parka and pants and he didn't sleep much the first night in the damp clothes.

In two days Wilkins's clothing was dry. So falling into cracks, pinching and skinning their feet and shins, falling getting up and going on again, one step—ten steps, on they moved until on April 14 they came to a high-pressure ridge. It tired Eielson just to think of climbing over it, but Wilkins, the old ice traveler, was overjoyed, for he recognized it as the big ridge that marked the end of the broken ice. If all went well they would sleep on shore the next night, and if Wilkins's navigation was right they would sleep at the Beachy Point trading post.

It was clear the next morning, and from the top of the ice ridge they could see an unbroken line of white to the south that spoke of the shore ice and prairie beyond. No more stumbling in ice cracks, the danger of thin ice and rough pressure ridges. They walked half an hour, rested, and walked on again. When they left the airplane they had thirty-eight pounds of condensed food and half a gallon of gasoline. There was still five pounds of food and a quart of gasoline left. By 10:00 A.M. they could see the roof of the Beachy Point house and they came to a dog-team trail heading toward it. They proceeded leisurely toward the house, talking away. During the hard days they hadn't talked much beyond giving instructions or discussing procedure. Now they began to talk about all that the future held.

As they neared the trading post they saw figures moving about and a dog team came their way. It was Alfred Hopson, who had been one of Wilkins's traveling companions when Wilkins first came to the Arctic in 1913. He quickly took them to Beachy Point, where Anton Edwardson made them comfortable. In two hours, Takpuk, the old whale hunter, was on his way with his dog team across the two hundred miles of snow to Barrow with the news and a week later Graham came for them in the *Detroiter No. 2*.

While they waited they decided to amputate Eielson's little finger from his right hand, but they were able to save the rest of the hand. The men in Barrow hadn't been idle. They had searched everyday with dog teams along the coast and Graham had searched from the air with the *Detroiter No. 2*. Since they hadn't received any of the wireless messages, it made the search worse than looking for a needle in a haystack. They couldn't even be sure of what continent to look on, for the men could have been in North Asia as easily as North America.

Wilkins and Eielson had proven pretty conclusively that there was no land north of Alaska and that landings were practical on the sea ice far out. They set a standard for us all in that long walk back across the ice, demonstrating that man on foot could survive in the ice and even make a long journey.

The passing years have proved them right—there is no land north of Alaska. Dick McIntire, during World War II, did locate a large island near the North Pole that wasn't the usual sea ice. A closer examination proved it was heavy glacier ice drifting. There are no icebergs in this part of the Arctic Ocean generally, but this one must have come from the eastern Arctic. The Russians had a scientific drifting station in 1935 at the North Pole for nearly a year and after World War II the U.S. put a scientific drifting station on the ice island Dick McIntyre had discovered, calling it T-3. This island drifted all about the Arctic Ocean and eventually broke up in the North Atlantic some twenty years later. Today several drifting ice islands have been located and are used as year-round observatories. Dick McIntyre is now one of our leading Arctic pilots and operates the Frontier Flying Service in Fairbanks.

For Wilkins the spring season was progressing rapidly. Wilkins and Graham made several long flights across the prairie, mapping, and one flight across the pack ice. Graham had not wanted to fly the pack ice and had made this clear to Wilkins before he was hired. Eielson's hand was still useless and he was unable to fly. Wilkins even thought of making a flight across to Greenland alone in the *Detroiter No. 2*. The new propellers sent up for the Fokker ship were not right; in fact were useless. All in all, things just weren't right to finish the final stage of the work—the trip across the top of the world —so Wilkins decided it was best to take all his men home and close up the expedition, thus keeping his promise with all and with his backers at the Detroit *News*. On June 18, 1927, Wilkins paid off his men in Seattle and returned them to their homes.

Wilkins went on toward Los Angeles. He was sitting in a hotel room in San Francisco feeling let down, thinking over plans for selling the two Fokker airplanes, and wondering how he would ever get across the Arctic. He had decided he would have to fly alone when he saw a vision flash by. Wilkins had planned, used, and visualized airplanes for eighteen years (Wilkins himself was a superb pilot). The vision appeared and then was gone! Wilkins thought he must be dreaming but he knew it was real. He telephoned all the airfields in San Francisco but could find no trace of the airplane. He had seen the word Los Angeles on the tail and headed on south. He didn't have far to go, for he located his dream plane at the Oakland Airport. It was the first Lockheed Vega ever built.

In Los Angeles he met Mr. Loughead and Mr. Jack Northrup, "men of great charm and vision and time has only magnified their good qualities." They were the builders and chief designers of the Lockheed Vega. On each of his Arctic trips Wilkins had purchased the latest available aircraft for his work and the many years since have proved his judgment right both in men and machines. Right then he purchased Lockheed Vega No. 2. How he would pay for it he didn't know, but his faith in the airplane, its builders, himself, and his fellow men was implicit. He and Eielson would fly that machine across the Arctic. Once again Wilkins's vision was right, for the Lockheed Vega, its designers, and builders went on to write aviation history.

The expedition was of the size Wilkins liked now, and he stayed right with the Lockheed Vega as it was built while all concerned learned from one another. When the airplane was finished, Eielson came down and learned to handle it at the factory. The name *Detroit News—Wilkins Arctic Expedition* was painted in deep blue letters on each side of the orange-colored fuselage. Wilkins, with his own money and help of a few loyal supporters, provided the money for the meager expedition. It was just an airplane, the two men, and four hundred pounds of gear that went north this time. It was a small fraction of what the former expedition had been, but it was the size Wilkins had always wanted. On Sunday, February 26, 1928, they arrived in Fairbanks and the plane, X3903 (X for experimental, not licensed yet), came up on the freight train the next day.

In Fairbanks they tested out the airplane thoroughly and on the morning of March 19 all was in order. It was –24 degrees as they took off and headed for Barrow. The Lockheed Vega lifted its big load and handled it beautifully as they headed on the now familiar course for Barrow. It was –40 degrees, calm and clear at Barrow, while a warm welcome awaited them there with old friends. They stayed with Charlie Brower in the big trading post and Tom Brower got busy working on the landing field for their take-off for the long flight across the Arctic. Wilkins and Eielson felt that Barrow was their second home.

The equipment they carried was similar to that carried on all previous flights but was updated a little. The Eskimo women set to work at once making the special fur clothing for each man, while Wilkins worked out his navigation charts on the trading-post table and Eielson prepared for the long flight.

The navigation for this part of the world is unique in that the time zones all come together at the top of the world and in addition they would pass through a 165-degree swing of the compass in order to travel in a straight line. As they passed north of the magnetic North Pole the compass would point south in order to keep on a north course.

On the seventh of April conditions were right and they climbed aboard, but the wind had swung across the runway, and although they tried a take-off, the heavily loaded plane couldn't rise and they went off the end of the runway, breaking a ski. These were the beautifully streamlined metal skis used before but not nearly strong enough for this hard use. Wilkins had tried to get the manufacturer to redesign and strengthen them, but to no avail. The skis were riveted together and it was not possible to strengthen them after they were made. In case of just such a mishap Wilkins had brought along a second pair of strongly built wooden skis that cut speed a couple of miles per hour but were strong enough. While they changed skis, the Eskimos worked with hand shovels making the runway as long as possible on the Barrow Lagoon.

Four days later they tried to get off again and failed. They went up over the bank but luckily nothing was broken. The Barrow Lagoon was just too short for the load they had to take off. I have felt the same way many times on that lagoon. I could always double trip, though, for I didn't have to cross the whole Arctic Ocean. Tom Brower figured the Elson Lagoon would be the best place to take off from. It lay a few miles out toward the point and it was longer. Tom hitched up his big dog team and dragged the Lockheed Vega to the Elson Lagoon. Here he assembled all the Eskimos with shovels and for days they worked clearing a runway just wide enough for the airplane down to the ice. It took a week to make a runway a mile long by shoveling, picking, and sawing away the snowdrifts. It is work you have to participate in a few times to appreciate. When finished there was a narrow strip just as wide as the airplane skis with snow backed up on each side and a mile long. It would take skillful handling to keep from hitting the sides and going out of control on take-off, wrecking the airplane.

It was a six-mile trip from the trading post to the Elson Lagoon by dog team. The problems Wilkins had to surmount just to get the airplane in the air were staggering, but on April 15, 1928, early in the morning, Eielson arrived with the hot oil wrapped in a sleeping bag, they gave the airplane a final check, poured in the hot oil, and Eielson climbed in. Wilkins pulled the propeller through and the Wright J-5 Whirlwind engine started. Wilkins climbed in the navigator's seat in the back and shouted, "Let's go!"

The Eskimos pushed on the plane and under "full bore" the skis slipped from the wood blocks that kept them from freezing in the ice and they raced down that narrow runway. Wilkins could see the tail just missing the blocks of snow and ice as Eielson skillfully handled the ship. The air speed built steadily 50—60—70, and there was the end of the runway, but Eielson lifted the ship, she cleared the drifts, the skis kissed the snow just once more, and they climbed up and away.

They swung out past the sandspit at Point Barrow and on

north. This flight was like all the others they had made together, with Wilkins doing the navigating and Eielson doing the flying. For the first hour they flew at five hundred feet, working slowly up to eight hundred feet, and as the gasoline burned up lightening the plane they climbed up to three thousand feet in two hours. Wilkins thought of the many days spent driving dogs in this ice and walking over it as the miles passed. From on high they could see and read the patterns of the ice like an open book.

From the looks of the sky far ahead, Wilkins knew they were approaching a storm, and he navigated to use its winds to an advantage as long as possible. They had hoped to find an island where a meteorological station could be established, but they saw none. As the hours passed they wrote notes back and forth. They were meeting the edge of the storm area while clouds towered here and there above them. They were up to nine thousand feet and soon plunging in and out of the clouds. About this time Eielson gave a shout and showing through the clouds were the peaks of Grantland. After hours of flying across the pack ice it was good to know they were right on course. When they reached the peaks of Grantland, the last gap in exploration of the Arctic was pretty well closed as far as sighting new land was concerned. The job was really over. Should they try to land upon Grantland and take the safe way home from there? Should they go on and land upon Greenland? Wilkins knew there was a massive storm between them and Spitsbergen. Should they chance it on across? In reality there was only one answer. Landing on Grantland or Greenland would likely mean losing their airplane, and an airman won't give up his ship; he will stay with it to the last. Neither would Wilkins or Eielson give up the trip on to Spitsbergen, storm or no storm, and on across the top of the world they went.

North of Greenland they ran into −48-degree temperatures, and after they passed north of Greenland it was across broken ice and the North Atlantic all the way. It was as if the two men were flying alone, for Wilkins rode in the back and could only see a part of Eielson's shoulder up front, while Eielson couldn't see Wilkins at all. They were into and out of the clouds, and with the compass quite unreliable, it was hard to keep a straight course; then the storm was all about them.

Hour after hour they flew on through the wild storm. Luckily it was daylight all the time this far north. The storm flipped them about like a leaf. Wilkins figured they were nearing Spitsbergen. They had been in the air twenty hours and gasoline reserves were nearly gone. They were up at eight thousand feet when down through a break in the storm they saw two sharp mountain peaks. It was Spitsbergen!

Down through the wild storm Eielson brought the airplane, holding well out to sea so as not to fly into a mountain; they dropped right down to just above the wild waves. Oil had spattered the windshield so badly that Eielson could only see out either side window. Blowing snow impaired visibility but they saw a smooth patch of snow-covered land go past, and then there was mountain dead ahead and they had to swing out to sea to miss it. They decided to return to the smooth spot and land. Wilkins could see better than Eielson and he passed notes as fast as he could write them.

"Turn right."

"Now to the left."

"A bit more."

"There it is right ahead."

I don't see how Eielson read the notes and kept his direction. He swung the ship around in the storm and brought the Lockheed Vega in for a smooth landing. Once down in the blinding snow you could see only a few yards.

Wilkins jumped out to drain oil and shouted at Eielson to open the tap. Eielson just sat there. He couldn't hear a thing. After twenty hours and twenty minutes of sitting behind that faithful Wright J-5 Whirlwind engine listening to its steady thunder, Eielson was momentarily stone deaf! It was several hours before he could hear normally again.

They hurriedly shoveled snow around and over the main skis and tail ski, then tramped it hard to keep the airplane from being blown away. They then climbed inside to munch dry biscuits, pemican, and chocolate. They were too tired to sleep for a while, and as Eielson's hearing began to come back, they talked of the flight and of how happy their many friends, who had so helped to make this flight possible, would be. Wilkins had kept up a regular schedule on the wireless with Leon S. Vincent, the schoolteacher in Barrow, but as Wilkins only sent and Vincent had only a receiver, it was not possible to tell if any of it had been received. Later Wilkins did learn that his messages had been received until he passed Greenland. The last messages Mr. Vincent received was: "KDZ 1:20 A.M. Wilkins Arctic Expedition . . . Greenland . . . storm . . ." and then the signals faded away.

Barrow had no contact with the outside world and no one

knew Wilkins and Eielson were even on their way, except for the folks at Barrow, and of course no one knew they had landed at Spitsbergen. These things mattered little to them as they sat talking of their trip, thanking the Lord for their safety and for the many people who had made it all possible. They were sure they were on Spitsbergen, but where?

Finally they slept for a few hours and awakened to find the storm still blowing. They walked around the airplane and slept some more. The storm blew for five days and then quit. In the meantime they had drained all their fuel and put it in one top tank. To their delight they found there was twenty-two gallons, or enough to take them anywhere on Spitsbergen.

They had landed at 6:35 P.M. on Monday, April 19, and on Saturday they tried to take off again, but with no one to push the airplane and break it free to start it sliding they were stuck. They had a specially built light block and tackle rigged for just such an emergency, but someone had stolen it in Fairbanks and it couldn't be replaced.

Wilkins tried to push and then get in as the ship started, but the propeller blast and speed of the ship were too much for him and Eielson took off without him! When Eielson circled he saw Wilkins still there on the ice so he landed again. Wilkins rigged a rope ladder back from the cabin, and holding to this with one hand he pushed the ship free again. This time he hung onto the rope and started working his way forward. Eielson feeling the weight in the tail felt all was well and took off. In the blast of sub-zero air Wilkins's bare hands began to freeze, he was slipping off and he grabbed the rope with his teeth but as the ship left the ground he realized he would never make it to the cabin and let go. The tail hit him a whack as it went by knocking him end over end. Luckily, the deep snow and heavy clothing saved him from serious injury. Once again Eielson had to land. They had used up nearly half of their gasoline supply in these efforts.

Once again they tried and Wilkins kept one leg in the cabin and pushed with the other. For a while it seemed as if they were stuck and then the ship moved and they were on their way. Eielson was most happy to have Wilkins aboard! They hadn't been in the air five minutes when Eielson shouted, "What is that over in the bay to the left?"

Wilkins knew from the location it could only be Green Harbour. They flew past the big surface coal mine and landed smoothly beside the radio towers. The long flight was ended. Steamships called here regularly and they could ship the

Lockheed Vega home from here. It had brought them twenty-two hundred miles nonstop across the top of the world.

Three men on skis came hurrying toward them, and as Wilkins was draining the oil they arrived. It was T. H. Bowitzihlem, manager of the government radio, and he introduced the others. They all spoke English, but Eielson, who was just getting out of the airplane, called to them in Norwegian and gave them a real brotherly greeting. No explorers anywhere were ever accorded a warmer welcome than the few winter residents of Spitsbergen gave Wilkins and Eielson. The wireless soon carried to the world the news of the completion of the flight and congratulations poured in from every corner of the world.

One piece of information that bore mute evidence to the violence of the storm they had landed in was that the radio operator at Kings Bay had lost his way going home from the radio station to his nearby house and frozen to death. Wilkins and Eielson realized how lucky they had been to have found the island and landed an airplane there in such a storm.

The steamship *Holby* was at that moment on its way from Kings Bay and they loaded the Lockheed Vega aboard by taxiing it alongside and lifting the airplane right on deck.

The king of Norway received them when they landed, and there were parades. George Hubert Wilkins was knighted by the king of England and became Sir Hubert Wilkins. President Hoover presented Carl Ben Eielson with the Distinguished Flying Cross and the Harmon Trophy. There were congratulations and medals from almost every country.

They had blazed the trail that the airlines of the future would follow, and as I flashed across that same trail a few days ago riding the stratosphere at the speed of sound, it seemed as if I could see the little single-engined Lockheed Vega, and the wild storm, as my old colleagues opened the trail for us to follow. I'm sure the many honors gladdened their hearts, but the knowledge that they had done the job they had set out to do step by step and had been worthy of the trust so many had placed in them was the greatest satisfaction of all.

The praise and acclaim of the public is nice but often neither realistic nor lasting; the remarks of our fellow colleagues are more accurate and enduring. In this regard the greatest tribute to the flight Wilkins and Eielson made came from Admiral Byrd, Dr. Stefansson, Nansen, and Amundsen. These men made the history of Arctic exploration and flying.

Amundsen summed up Wilkins's and Eielson's flight thusly: "No flight has been made anywhere at any time which could compare with it."

The passing years have proved the great explorers right. No flight made before or since can compare with it from its concept to its completion.

20

KISIK, THE PILOT'S FRIEND

Thinly scattered all across the Arctic were the native people who had called that land home for longer than anyone knew and who possessed a love born of living close to the land they understood. We usually think of the explorers as going into an uncharted wilderness alone, but this isn't exactly true. The land was uncharted only by our European standards and the explorers were guided by the people who lived in those lands.

One beautiful summer day I landed at a little tent camp on the back of Shoalwater Bay in northern Canada. The people were hunting beluga whale there and they spoke some English. I drank a cup of tea and we talked in halting Eskimo or English with many signs and smiles. In an hour I was ready to depart, heading on east. We walked to the beach where my floatplane sat amid the skin whaleboats. An old man took my arm and pointed east across the bright blue water at a thin blue line. "You stay, one sleep," he said, and he put his head on his arm and held up one finger.

I smiled and thanked him. The thin blue line on the horizon meant nothing to me. A half hour later it did—solid fog. Those people had known a solid wall of fog that I couldn't get through was coming. I had burned up an hour's gasoline that I needed badly to find that out. They were all waiting for my return, certain I would be back.

"It good," the old man said, "you come back, stay one sleep." And he held up one finger and laid his head on his arm to show how long the fog would last. I stayed "one sleep" and the fog was gone. All the people were happy now, as if they had provided the clear air for me to travel in; and, I suppose, in a way they had.

Many, many an Indian or Eskimo has helped me understand the land and taught me, and it was always in a spirit of kindness and with dignity. Never once did they make me feel like the impatient fool I must at times appeared to have been. Their attitude toward me reflected the security they felt in thmselves, the dignity of their way of living, and their sense of belonging to the land. I grew to know many of these people and, in fact, you might say literally all of them, for there weren't many scattered across the top of our continent and I, in time, visited them all. I never did get to know any of them better than I did Kisik and his family. I will set down his story here as we came to know it.

The first memory George K. (Kisik) Wood could recall was that of breaking loose from his mother to run back and lie down again beside his father. Several men were laid out there in a row upon the pea-gravel beach near Kotzebue. His mother came back and took him gently away again, for, as he put it, "You see, the men were all dead."

An epidemic had wiped out most of the people at the little camp in the mouth of the Kobuk River. The remaining few were fleeing upriver. George couldn't remember how many escaped, perhaps ten, but his mother and baby brother were all of his family that survived. There were a few people living here and there along the Kobuk River and they helped all they could but, "People don't have much to help with in them days."

One trading boat came up the river, and when it put in at the village of Kobuk, George was lined up with the other children. A deckhand saw him standing there stark naked and gave him an orange, a fifty-cent piece, and a man's shirt. George didn't know what the orange or the fifty-cent piece were, so he gave them away, but he wore the large shirt, for it kept the mosquitoes away.

"People were always kind. Some of the old people in the houses were fierce, though, if a boy played too much inside. I learned to watch the woman's hand. They distributed the food and if their hand turned your way, my, you were in luck!"

His grandparents lived at a big round lake called Nayutak Lake ("lake with a round island with gull's nest") that lay some two hundred and fifty miles upstream in the timbered interior. It was for his mother's parents' home on this lake that they headed. For those on foot the trail was a long one and winter caught them. George recalls that they finally had to leave his little brother, for they just couldn't make it with him. A few evenings later his mother went out to find food and never returned. In looking back across the years George could once again see the silent spruce forests, willow thickets, dark of winter, and soft snow of the Kobuk River Valley and the handful of starving, ill-clad people. His mother he remembered well, and her loving care as she tried to save her two boys and finally abandoned one so that the other might live. Then she must have realized that even her own presence was more of a burden than the party could carry. George remembered how tightly she held him and hugged and kissed him before she left, and he knew she wouldn't come back. They all must have known.

"It was the way in the hardest times. One member of each family was saved if possible so that the family wouldn't be wiped out. Everyone tried to keep that one alive."

All this took place at the turn of the century. George never knew when he was born or where. The rest of the party made it through to his grandfather's home at Nayutak Lake. George's memories of Nayutak Lake were happy ones. In describing the fish in that lake he recalls, "Talk about fat!" No higher praise could be bestowed upon a fish by a starving boy. He also remembered hunting grouse with a new .22 single-shot rifle and then losing it in the lake when he tipped over his kayak while hunting pike. His grandfather had told him not to take his .22 out in the kayak, and it took a lot of diving to find the .22 so Grandfather wouldn't know he had disobeyed him.

George wandered in the big mountains with his uncle, hunting the white sheep, whistling marmot, and caribou. He loved the joy of the climb, to smell the warm sheep meadows on high, and the vast view from above: the world of peaks, sky, sun, wind, and adventure. In winter he went trapping and saw his first kerosene lantern. It was the most wonderful thing to him and he felt he could go on trapping forever right through the night. They caught sable, ermine, mink, and lynx. The animals were often frozen solid in the trap and the trapper would place them in his sleeping bag to thaw them with his own body heat while he slept. A lynx was a problem, though, for lynx often have fleas.

George never lost his love for kerosene lanterns and carried one with him all his days. They meant security in the dark and adventure to him. In this I agree with George; a kerosene lantern has always meant adventure to me since I was first allowed to carry one on our Illinois farm to explore the mystery of the night; from the African plains of old Tanganyika to the high plateaus of northern India, and across the vast Arctic I, too, have used a kerosene lantern. On safari, with camel or elephant caravans, dog team, canoe, and airplane trails, the kerosene lantern is the old standby.

George's wanderings finally took him into Alatna, where he was enrolled in the Episcopal Mission School there. Here the teacher asked his name.

"Kisik."

"Isn't there more? That isn't enough name for a young man."

"No. I'm only Kisik, and so she put the name George Wood on me. George K. Wood, and I'm George K. Wood ever since."

The Koyukuk River area was booming since the Gold Rush was on, and George worked in the mines or hunted game to sell to the miners. Until George was around twenty years old he traveled the Koyukuk area. He was especially fond of chocolate candy. One time he and his partner, an Indian of the same age called Big Charlie, found an old cache and there was some chocolate candy in it which they ate.

"You talk about trouble! They call that chocolate candy Ex-Lax."

It was only natural that George would team up with some prospector. He and John Segars had traveled together and finally, as the gold seemed all located in the Koyukuk area, they made their way up the John River and through Anaktuvuk Pass. From there they followed the Anaktuvuk River on out across the Arctic plains to the Colville River and on to the Arctic Ocean.

Neither George nor John knew how to live on the timberless prairie and they made many mistakes. They were cold all the time in the prairie winds until they learned how to dress and obtained Eskimo clothing. They didn't know how to travel, pitch camp, or trap in that land, but the friendly people they met showed them the ways of the Arctic. With a timberland man's dependence upon wood when the winter set in, they moved out on Jones Island, where there was a plentiful supply of driftwood for fuel. They pitched a tent camp there and built a snow blockhouse around it. This arrangement makes as snug and warm a camp as there is. They had managed to pick up two dogs and made a small sled from the driftwood.

"There were plenty fox [white Arctic fox] about and you can hear them bark or holler here and there right close to the camp even, but we don't know nothing about trapping them, and we got very few. One night we heard the dogs bark, I took the kerosene lantern and John took his rifle. He had the Lee straight-pull rifle, and we went outside; I held up the lantern as we walk around the house. John was ahead and I coming along behind holding the lantern so he could see. On the last corner John turned around and pointed the rifle at me. 'John,' I said, 'John! Don't you know me?' Well, the bear was right behind me standing up on its hind egs. It had been following me and when it stood up for a better look John saw it. Then it run and John run around me and shot twice, but he don't hit the bear. We followed the track awhile but the bear isn't hit. Then we go inside, make the cup of tea and laugh. 'George, that bear stand right up behind you!'

" 'John, I think you thought I am the bear!' Oh, we have a lot of fun them days."

At Christmastime they traveled to Cross Island where the Takpuk and Oekpiek families were living. They had killed two whales there that fall, for Takpuk was a great whale hunter and there was penty of food. The people from around the area for fifty miles or more gathered there to celebrate Christmas that year. It must have been a gathering of one hundred peope or more. Here George met the person who was to change and shape his life from then on; here he saw Nannie. "Saw" is the right word, for although they both saw each other they didn't speak on that first meeting.

I often wondered how the early Eskimo romances proceeded, so I asked George how he and Nannie ever got to know one another if they didn't speak.

"The old people saw it all and they had decided."

It was Christmastime nearly fifty years later when I flew across to the Neglik, picked up George and Nannie, and brought them to our home for Christmas. All the other Eskimos lived in towns now and we were the only people left living on the open prairie. Martha and I had a Christmas tree. It was the first George and Nannie had ever seen and we all had a wonderful Christmas Day. There were presents for all with many good things to eat, while our two little boys played until they fell asleep. George and Nannie sat holding hands, looking at the lights of the Christmas tree, and talking softly in Eskimo. George had then asked Martha if she would read a little from the Bible; after this as we sat drinking a cup of tea they were telling us about their early life. Over the more than twenty years of close association with the Woods family we had come to know them well, but this Christmas night George and Nannie were going back into the past to tell us of the days long gone.

"When did you next meet after that Christmas at Cross Isand?" I asked.

"It was summer and we were at the Foggy Island when I saw Nannie again." And they both smiled at each other.

"What happened then?"

"Well you know how a young man and a woman are," George said, rather at a loss for words. "There was a missionary who traveled to Foggy Island and we got married."

"We hurry to the tent to make the baby," Nannie broke in, and we all laughed.

George was thinking of how the long trail from where he left his father unburied on the beach until he met Nannie had changed him from an inland man of trees, rivers, and mountains to a man of the open grassy prairie and the sea-ice life.

"I met Nannie and I'm stuck here ever since."

"Stuck, eh?" Nannie teased.

Their home was a tent on the prairie in the summer and a snow-walled tent or sod-baked driftwood house in winter. Old John Segars went on prospecting alone in the summer and trapping alone in the winter.

Through the years thirteen children were born and only three survived. Nannie had told Martha how each had died, wanting to know what had happened. From what we could gather common diseases had killed most of them, with the common cold being the leader. Two of the children were nearly twenty when they died of a cold brought in by a trapper traveling back from Barrow by dog team. Barrow was the source of most diseases and travelers spread the diseases from there. The last child died from an injured spine that was hardly detectable at first but grew worse over the years. She was a pretty girl named Martha and was about seventeen when she died. Martha was buried just across the river from where our new home stands. George and Nannie had visited the grave that day while riding around on my new Ski-Doo. George had reported that the little cross that marked the grave had been knocked down by caribou perhaps. I'm sure one of the reasons George and Nannie always felt so close to my wife, Martha, was because she so reminded them of the lovely girl they had lost. When we first met the family Lydia was a small child. She had been the last of their children and now she is married with two little girls and a little boy of her own.

We realized that George and Nannie had shared more of life and living than anyone else we had ever known.

"Where were you born, Nannie?" Martha asked.

George and Nannie exchanged glances and began to laugh for apparently the spot where Nannie was born had been a lifetime joke.

"Nannie was born on the garbage pile at Barrow."

"No . . . ," Nannie put in. Nannie never had mastered English like George had.

"Yes, Nannie. It is true. You were born right where they dumped the trash."

Nannie then went on explaining to Martha in halting English, with pauses while George translated some word for her, how when she was due the family had made a little snow house on top of the garbage pile because it was a good spot. It was full winter and all the land was drifted over with snow and frozen hard. There was no heat in the little snow house and there were no midwives; Nannie's mother had delivered Nannie herself. Food and water had been passed in and out through a little opening but no one entered until the baby was a few days old. It was their way of protecting the mother and baby from diseases.

I have discussed this system with doctors and they all tell me it was a good one, and that the loss of mothers and children was probably less than in the best hospitals of that era.

The early way of living on the prairie was for two families to travel together. In summer they would move back up the rivers almost to the mountains, where they lived on fish, parka squirrels, ptarmigan, and caribou. The diet of the early people was 99 per cent meat. In the early winter they moved to the Arctic coast to trap white foxes and trade with the few traders for cloth, tobacco, needles, ammunition, cooking pots, and other essentials of life. Fox skins were the medium of exchange and money was unknown.

One of the famiies they traveled with had an old medicine man along. By "family" was meant all the people that made up a family unit from the youngest child to the oldest great-grandparent, just all those closely related or in need of a home. There was, of course, no such thing as an orphan, for with or without parents a child fit into one of these family units. There were many things the old medicine man could and couldn't do. There were so many taboos to his eating that he usually cooked his food separately. One night the medicine man fell ill and he sat up all night beating the drum and hollering to keep the evil spirits away.

"You better put your faith in the Lord and get some sleep," George advised him, but he went right on beating the drum and hollering all night long.

"How did he make out?" I asked when George had not said anything for a while, silently recalling those long-past days.

"Well he died. We buried him there on the Kuparuk River. You know, where that little stream comes in above the small overflow glacier? Right on the high bank above there. We put his medicine drum and things in with him."

It was while the Wood family was living at Foggy Island in 1931 that they saw their first airplane. It came from the east following the coast in the summer. George took a picture of the floatplane, its pilot and woman passenger. I had seen the picture, developed and then printed by the light of a Coleman lantern, and yellow with age. From the picture smiled the faces of a young Charles and Anne Lindbergh on their flight north to the Orient.

Our airplane was the next one they saw and I gave them their first ride. They accepted as quite natural the airplane and the things I brought and the better way of traveling and living. The tragedy of losing their two oldest children was still fresh in their minds, and they had moved away from Foggy Island, never to return. The family had moved west along the coast to Oliktook Point, which would become the Radar Site POW 2 many years later.

One by one the families were moving away. Jack Smith, the last of the free-lance traders, had died and was buried at Beachy Point a few hundred yards behind the trading post that now stood empty. The snow buntings nested about it in summer and snow drifted about it all winter. There were no supplies in the land any more and the people used to the new ways wouldn't go back to the old life. The press of civilization was turning Barrow from a small trading village into a big city of the Arctic, with its siren call of movie house, coffee shop, government dole, and high society. None could resist it except George. Perhaps because he had grown up around mining camps George wasn't so smitten by the new activities at Barrow.

"I can live way better here. I tell you the job won't last in Barrow and the people will be up against it. I don't need the movie house and that coffee shop." George would look at his sealskin hunting boots, his tent, and the prairie while talking more to convince himself than anyone else.

"There is too much sickness and too little to eat in Barrow for me."

The problem of too little to eat in Barrow was to be the key to the future for George's and Nannie's lives and to a great extent to Martha's and mine, although at that early date none of us recognized it.

On various exploration trips I would end up in Barrow for supplies. I shipped my gasoline and equipment to here by boat. I knew everyone in the village and they would want to know how things were at their old homes along the coast. They missed the fresh fish they had been used to, for there are no fish near Barrow, and they asked me to bring in some of those good Colville River fish. There were no fishnets available and it took me a long time to finally locate some netting at the Adams Net and Twine Company in St. Louis, Missouri. George knew how to hang a fishnet, having seen willow root fishnets made when he was a boy. As he and I worked hanging those first nets, he showed me all he knew. Much I know about the Arctic and of quiet living I learned from George, and he even taught me a great deal about Arctic flying.

There was a lot of excitement as we set the new nets and they worked beautifully, holding the big five- to ten-pound fish tangled by the gills. I was soon hauling a full airplane load of fish into Barrow every time I went there. I would circle the town to let the people know the fish had arrived and I would see the people heading for my landing site on the Barrow Lagoon and often there wouldn't be enough fish to go around. As I was going into town anyway and the fish were a backhaul, I was able to sell them at a low price for that area and they sold quickly. George and Nannie couldn't believe the amount of cash I brought them back for their fish. It was the first money they had ever had there.

Soon the people in Barrow asked for dried fish. "Could George Wood make pipsic [the old style of sundried fish]?" This launched George and Nannie on a career of drying and smoking fish each July. They made the best smoked fish I have ever tasted, with, of course, the most loving care possible.

The back-haul system of selling fish didn't last long since the demand for fresh fish was much greater than my occasional flight to Barrow could fill. George and Nannie had given up their nomadic life of following the seasons on the prairie and when George had a chance to get some lumbers from an abandoned Coast and Geodetic Survey camp at Atiagaru Point, some thirty miles to the west, he hauled in the planks with a dog team. From these one-by-twelve planks and two-by-four studs he built a comfortable one-room home with a large enclosed storm porch. He later added a second room and built a little powerhouse for his electric generator. I hauled in the airplane all the rest of the building materials back to complete the house. Martha, Jimmy, and I lived in a snow-walled tent that winter season, and I flew fish into Barrow. Every day it was flyable I was on my way to Barrow with a load of fish. Some days I made two trips, leaving in the dark and returning from my last trip in the dark.

If the day were clear I had no difficulties, but on a foggy day I was stuck. The problem was trying to tell what the day would be like long before daylight, when I had to start heating the airplane engine. George and I would go through a little ritual each morning. We would go outside in the dark and look at the sky, smell the wind, listen to the sound of the snow underfoot, feel for precipitation upon our faces, look for stars if the morning were overcast—and it nearly always was—to see if there were holes in it; then I would listen to what George had to say. In this way we would decide what the day would be like. In looking back over it now, I realize our weather-predicting system was the oldest known to man. It was primitive and simple but fairly reliable, and I delivered tens of thousands of pounds of fish using it.

Martha knew there wouldn't be enough fish to keep me flying steadily from the Woods' nets alone, so she set out a few nets of her own and soon was catching as many fish as the rest.

Life had changed for George and Nannie. They had a very good income and could purchase what they wanted.

Nannie taught Martha how to live comfortably in a tent. Living in a tent is one of the ancient arts of homemaking and Nannie was a master at it. There is a security and freedom to tent life that is found in no other way of living and there is no more versatile home than a tent. Martha learned her lessons well, too, and we have spent many happy times in tents around the world. Martha taught Nannie how to cook European style and they put in many hours cooking. Nannie proved a surprisingly good pupil and became a good cook, turning out some superb baked things. In later years when

Martha had a modern home and every convenience possible, George and Nannie loved to visit us and enjoy Martha's cooking.

Shortly after the last Eskimos, aside from the Wood family, had moved into Barrow, and I had established a fish market there, flying along the Arctic coast became commonplace. The Distant Early Warning (DEW) sites were put in every seventy-five miles along the coast and the sight of even several airplanes in a day was not uncommon. There wasn't enough fish at the west channel where George and Nannie lived to supply the Barrow market steadily and we decided to build our permanent home on the prairie over on the island between the east and the main channel, about twenty miles away. Here there would be fish enough for a permanent operation for us. After selling the first few loads of fish to the people at the airplane, I had decided that system wouldn't work and sold all the rest of them to Tom Brower for resale. The processes of modern business completely escaped George and he never could understand why it was if fish retailed for fifty cents a pound it didn't go to the fisherman and pilot? Since whale muktuk (whale skin and a thin strip of blubber) sold for one dollar and twenty-five cents a pound, why not sell fish for the same price? "Just put the price on it and the people will take it."

In preparation for the cold winter, George and Nannie would stack up little tepee-shaped stacks of drift willow along the riverbanks. This enabled the willows to dry out, and they stuck above the snow of midwinter and could be hauled home on the little hand sled. He who didn't stack up driftwood in the summer hunted for it under the snow with a shovel in midwinter. George and Nannie worked as a unit all the time and when our little son Jeffrey learned to talk he always spoke of them as one. It was always George-and-Nannie, and he used the name to mean either of them.

One day Martha and I left Mark and Jeffrey with George and Nannie while we flew inland. A heavy snowstorm blew in and darkness fell so we didn't get back as planned. Jeffrey was just learning to talk, and as Nannie tucked him in bed he told her, "George-and-Nannie, Jeffrey Todd needs water." The little boys loved the old folks and were playing happily next morning when we flew in.

One day Reverend Wartes flew by on his way to Barter Island and spent the night. In the hurry of getting us launched the next morning Nannie had all sorts of problems including a "stuck stove." Her faithful chunks of dry cottonwood soaked in diesel fuel wouldn't even burn. I solved the problem for her when I found Apiak had put her wood in water instead of diesel fuel, and we soon had ·the fire going. The real blow fell when we had departed in the airplanes. Nannie and Martha sat down for a quiet cup of tea when Nannie jumped up and exclaimed, "Look, Martha . . . no butts."

Martha looked and realized there were no buttons showing on Nannie's dress because it was on wrong-side out! Nannie just hoped that the minister hadn't noticed her special party dress was on wrong-side out!

One Sunday we flew across to visit the Woods and found them busy working away. This surprised us, for George and Nannie were solid Christians and wouldn't consider working, hunting, or fishing on Sunday. Since we also observed Sunday they knew something was a little out of order and finally George asked, "What day is this?" Then they burst out laughing. "I'm all mixed up. We thought Sunday was yesterday."

New foods always interested Nannie and with good Arctic appetites we all enjoyed eating. Nannie made an art of eating, and anything Nannie liked was good. She enjoyed food because of its flavor, not because it was highly advertised, nor because of its color. New foods—like bananas, lettuce, or cucumbers and so on—that we brought in were a never-ending delight, and how Nannie used them was a source of delight to us. She tried eating the first banana as one would an apple, without peeling it. The head lettuce somehow ended up boiled like cabbage. The first bunch of grapes Nannie examined she held up and said, "I'm like a rich man."

Martha and I couldn't quite get the connection between a rich man and a bunch of grapes. Nannie saw our puzzled looks and brought out a child's picture viewer, then snapped it to the right picture—of a rich man reclining on a couch eating grapes.

Nannie's curiosity was boundless. She dearly loved to see what new things Martha had, and when we graduated to having doors on all the cupboards Nannie stood it as long as she could and finally exclaimed, "I look Martha." She got up, opened the doors, and looked in every shelf!

After a cold winter the Arctic spring bursts upon us in beauty and glory that has to be experienced to be understood. George had been quite ill during the winter. He had spent a few hours walking in the glory of the spring. Martha and I were going over the airplane and George came by. He stood in his old sealskin water boots and shirt sleeves, looking across the thousands of miles of awakening prairie. "I'm so glad I didn't die last winter," he said, in compliment to the miracle of spring.

The day of the dog team had passed and George bought a snow machine. It was one of the early models—and compares to the modern snow machines like the first Model T Ford compares with a new Lincoln Continental—but it was still way better than the dog team. Off George and Nannie would go across the limitless prairie to gather drift willow or just take a ride. When George took off on the snow machine Nannie had better be on the sled, for it took all of George's skill and time to handle the machine, and with a parka on, it is next to impossible to look behind you. One day while coming across the twenty miles to our place George went over a bump and Nannie bounced off! This he didn't discover until several miles later. In the meantime Nannie saw her transportation go off leaving her and she had no alternative but to start walking. George was surprised when he stopped and Nannie was nowhere in sight. He retraced his trail and found Nannie walking. They made some really remarkable trips with the old snow machine and even went to Barrow a few times. Nannie always missed the dog team and George often spoke of the happy days when he trapped with one of the little boys wrapped up in furs on the sled. Yet they wouldn't go back to the year-round jog of feeding and handling a team of dogs again, any more than we would go back to the horse and buggy.

I made some root beer while Nannie watched with disapproval. A few days later when I offered her a bottle she turned me down flat and left. That evening she and George came over and we had a good laugh. Nannie thought it was whiskey I was making and she disapproved of alcoholic drinks every bit as much as my Grandmother (a direct line descendant of Captain Bradford of the *Mayflower*) did. This was true of nearly all the older generation of Eskimos I knew. The thing that hurt most was when their children left for Barrow one by one and, as Nannie told Martha, "They go on that whiskey . . . there too much wildness in Barrow."

There were just the old folks there on the prairie now and they were getting well up in years. We worried about them there alone, especially in midwinter when the days are dark and cold. They had to work hard then getting in enough drift willow just to keep warm. We often suggested they should stay with us during those days when the sun was away at least, but with a pride and independence of those born and living free they kept to their own home. A warm and friendly home it was too, for Nannie is a wonderful homemaker and one of the world's most gracious hostesses.

With the new ease of airplane travel, they would go into Barrow to visit for a while in the winter and here they would pick up some Barrow-nurtured malady. Barrow had developed to the point of needing a policeman and a jail. Sergeant Sinn was the first officer sent up and he described the disease germs in Barrow as being about the size of a double-O buckshot and just as deadly. On one trip to Barrow George and Nannie both picked up measles. It was on this trip that some welfare worker discovered George and realized he could classify for relief aid to the dependent! They had it all figured out just how much he should draw monthly. George wasn't sure what it was all about until they got to the dependent part. This George did know for he was as independent a man as ever lived and he resented the suggestion keenly. I don't know what he told the welfare man, probably very little, for he had too much self-respect to tell anyone off, but he was still indignant when he told me about it two months later.

"If I'm really down and helpless I would take it . . . but to offer such a thing to a man who isn't is the worst thing I know of."

George knew an insult when he saw it, even if it came wrapped in money. It is a pity more people don't have his insight. He was really wealthy. George had lived a rough life from childhood, but a free and happy one. He now had a comfortable home with electric lights from his own Onan generator. He had boats, motors, a snow machine, and a good business; Nannie had a modern home with even an electric rotisserie and vacuum sweeper; and their family was grown up and had a good income from their fishing and trapping. There was plenty of fuel each year from drift willow and plenty of game about.

Each fall, when the Indian summer days arrived, the urge to wander would return to George and Nannie. They would close up their home and with their camp gear in a boat they headed up the Colville River. They were going squirreling to trap the parka squirrels used in making fancy parkas, and, of course, the squirrels were good eating, too. There were really many of the prairie-dog-sized ground squirrels right around their house and so tame you could feed them from your hand when they came in the kitchen. The real reason for going was the adventure of being together and traveling once more through the land they loved. They would be gone for two or three weeks and, as Nannie put it, "Make the camp . . . break the camp . . . . George and I make tea on the river bar . . . hunt the berry, trap the squirrel," and every moment was an adventure.

Mark and Jeffrey were like the Woods' grandchildren, and as soon as Mark turned five he went squirreling with them. I would fly by and see the little white tent on the riverbank, with the boat pulled up in front, and the three tiny parka-clad figures so like dolls on that wild expanse of prairie. On one flight I realized the boat was up on the mud a little too far so I landed. High water had put it there while they slept, so we laid drift willow to make a slide and slid the boat back into the water and they were ready to travel on.

George was always the pilot's friend and was ever-ready to help; explorer, bush pilot, government pilot, airline pilot, or renegade, he treated them all alike, and in the end all were pretty much alike. They were all warmed by the long days of summer and chilled by the dark cold days of winter, while all too frequently dying in the same kinds of accidents. This last, George was painfully aware of, and so he said one day when I brought him the news of the crash and death of a pilot we knew.

"I don't like to make friend of the pilot because it hurts too much to lose him."

I remarked that I had been his friend a long time and that I also flew a lot. He thought that over for a while.

"It is true . . . but you are one of the people. You are of the country. You won't ever be stuck."

I prized all of George's and Nannie's compliments and heeded their reprimands as I did those of Les and Patty James or the older pilots, for I knew they were meant to help and did help. If I made a landing that they didn't approve of or left on some flight without every last item of emergency gear including extra fur clothing and sewing needles to repair it, Nannie or George saw it and told me about it.

Trapping has become a sport more than a business in all Alaska even in the Arctic, and we all look forward to the opening of the white fox season, December first. The white fox pelts are quite blue until that date but pure white after then. None of us despise the twenty to thirty dolars each pelt brings, but the fun is in being out and in catching them.

Nannie was good at trapping squirrels, but George was the "Foxman," and that winter when the white fox season opened he and Nannie took a half dozen traps apiece to set among the net sites where the foxes came to look for scraps of fish.

"I feel a pity for Nannie. She don't know about how to set the trap to catch the fox. I show her, though, and we each set the traps."

Nannie then proceeded to catch fox after fox and George, in telling us about it said, "I'm really happy when Nannie get the first fox. The second fox she catch I lose my pity for her, the third fox she catch I catch one too, but the fourth fox she catch I pity myself! Well none of us catch any more fox after that. Nannie get four fox and I only get one."

It was the old trapper's last fox. Later in the winter they went to Barrow where George picked up a skin disease. They kept him in the Barrow hospital for quite awhile and finally sent him to the Anchorage Hospital, where he stayed all winter and spring. Nannie stayed in Barrow, but as the days grew longer and the rivers began to break out Nannie returned to her old home on the prairie. The Arctic Research Laboratory plane brought her back along with her year-old granddaughter and a little fifteen-year-old girl. Luckily our son Jim arrived there at the same time and was able to help Nannie get things started. George wasn't there for the summer fishing season for the first time and no dried fish were made. In late July George returned from the hospital.

"He will get better at home. The hospital can't cure him," the Reverend Samuel Simmonds said of his lifelong friend. "He is a free man of the open prairie."

George did recover fast at home and when I flew by he wanted a few things from Barrow: milk for the granddaughter and some Camel cigarettes for himself. It was pouring rain when I returned. I was flying our Super Cub and walked from the river flat up to the house carrying the milk and cigarettes. George didn't come to the table when Nannie served tea but lay on his bed. We talked of the fall, flying, fishing, and how he felt. He told me of how in the old days when some "old fellar" was about dead he would ask for some porcupine meat and after eating it he would be good for a couple of more weeks. I was taking Mr. and Mrs. Seeligson and Lew and Tom Moorman after sheep and George considered wild sheep the finest meat of all. He wondered if I could bring him a little piece. I said I sure could, and he said he felt it would perk him up a little, which he needed to do because he wanted to take Nannie squirreling.

The rest I learned from Reverend Simmonds in Barrow a few days later when I flew back from the hunt. He had just returned from the Negilik, where he had conducted George K. Wood's funeral.

George had been feeling steadily better and as the beautiful Indian summer days were here again he took a walk one evening in preparation for the squirreling trip upriver. When he returned, he began coughing and a few minutes later he was dead. They dug his grave into the permanently frozen soil that lies just below the prairie sod, and buried him there beside the little lake where so often he had helped me heat the airplane and we had tried to forecast the weather together.

The trail of Kisik's free nomadic life ended here and with his passing a big chapter in America's history closed too, for Kisik was the last of the race of free nomadic men who once populated all America. The rest are all in towns earning wages or on government dole. George never knew how old he was, but from what dates and people he could remember we figured he was about seventy.

George left us with a record of quiet courage and faith in ourselves. When things were strange he would say, "Don't be afraid of it." When the problem seemed impossible he would say, "Stick with it my boy. You will win."

21

BUSH PILOTS AS INDUSTRIAL GUIDES

When industry or any other project ventured into the uncharted areas it was just assumed that the local bush pilots would guide them, set up their bases, and supply the new camps. This was true whether the venture was a lone prospector, a new military base, an oil-exploration project, or charting a new shipping lane across the top of the world. Progress made on all fronts in Alaska would have lagged many years behind had it not been for the bush pilots. Yet the work was routine for the pilots since it was taking new men into an area the pilots already knew well, and then teaching them to live and operate there.

One day, in our monthly mail, there was a letter from Captain W. S. Hall of the Northern Transportation Company, The Route of the Midnight Sun, asking what I thought of a water route from Canada's Mackenzie River across the Arctic Ocean and into the Colville River. Was such a route possible? When could ships operate? How far up the Colville River could ocean-going ships operate?

Big decisions must rest upon the answers to small questions. An oil company wanted to ship in a complete oil drilling camp for drilling test wells in the most remote part of our Arctic. The plan was to ship by railroad and truck the heavy equipment from Texas and the other areas to waterways in central Alberta just north of Edmonton. This is the head of the vast Mackenzie River system that serves the northern part of our land and the Arctic coast in the same way the Mississippi River system serves the Midwest and Gulf Coast. At the waterways the equipment would be loaded on barges to begin the trip down the Mackenzie River to the Arctic Ocean, then across the Arctic Ocean following the north coast of

Canada and Alaska to our home in the Colville River Delta, where it would proceed as far up the Colville River as was practical.

I answered the letter as best I could, outlining the things I knew and the dates we could operate. There were a lot of questions I couldn't give exact answers to. The vast Colville River Delta was uncharted, and yet in that maze of waterways only one channel was likely deep enough to permit passage of the ocean-going equipment from the sea into the main river. It was early winter and the river was frozen and I couldn't make any test surveys, so the answers had to be based upon my past observations. A letter from Captain W. S. Hall thanked me and said I had helped a great deal; they were now able to reach a decision. Would I be able to guide the operation through the pack ice and up the river if they decided to go ahead? I answered that we would do our best.

We had put in a busy year in the Arctic, and during the dark days of midwinter we decided to take a trip to Fairbanks. Here we would leave our airplane with Jess Bachner, to have it all gone over while we took the commercial airline to the deep south for a few weeks' vacation, returning to our Arctic home when the long dark winter days had passed. As Sig Wien put it, "It isn't the cold that bothers so much in Alaska as it is the length of time it stays cold."

I had just parked the *Arctic Tern* at Fairbanks airfield and was going in to close my flight plan when the mechanic on duty said Jim Freericks wanted to see me in the office. Fresh from the Arctic and all dressed in furs from head to toe, we headed up the stairs in the Wien hangar to the offices above, Martha was dressed in her Eskimo woman's parka, Mark and Jeffrey just little bundles of fur and clutching their little toys, and me in my heavy fur parka. In the office Bud Hagburg and Jim Freericks introduced us to Lloyd Logan. Lloyd was a tall, solidly built man in his late forties with the confident look of those who handle men and machines in the remote areas.

"You will hate me for this," Jim said, "but can you go right back into the Arctic?"

Western Geophysical wanted to set up a complete oil-exploration camp to travel across the Arctic prairie making seismographic maps of that area. A complete camp, tractors, drilling units, and a hundred cargo airliner flights of gear and supplies would be needed to haul in the camp.

Martha and I looked at one another.

"When do they want to start?"

"Tomorrow!"

I thought of the fifty-below temperature and darkness of late winter that we had just left on that vast white prairie.

"What experience have they had in the Arctic, Jim?" I asked.

"They haven't had any experience at all, Bud. That is why I want you to help us set this thing up. Martha can handle the radio, we can use your place as a base to set up the camp. You can direct the operation, train the crew, and besides I need you to even find the sites. That's the whole ball of wax . . . There isn't anyone else to help."

Martha and I looked at each other and smiled.

Yes, we would help.

The vacation could wait for another season. We outlined plans for the operation with Lloyd Logan while looking at a big map of the area to be covered. The first project was to fly in a D-6 caterpillar. It was too heavy for a single load, so it would have to be taken apart and assembled there. With it we could clear a runway upon the ice, put out a portable string of runway lights, and the operation could go on twenty-four hours a day. We would put up a plywood shed, so equipment could be assembled inside, out of the extreme cold. Our Onan light plant would furnish light and we could work with our little caterpillar until the heavy equipment could be put together. While the camp equipment was being hauled in by the C-82 flying boxcars the C-46's would be hauling fuel and high explosives to the little frozen lakes at strategic points along the exploration route. Was it possibe to land a C-46 upon these lakes as they were, for there was no way we could make runways on them? Was the ice thick enough to support C-46's?

The next morning it was 55 below zero as Jim and I prepared to take off in the Cessna 180 to fly across the Arctic prairie to locate and check those lakes. Ice fog blanketed Fairbanks and as we waited for an instrument take-off clearance our oil cooler froze up. Back to the hangar we went to thaw the oil cooler, and again it froze up as we waited for clearance. On the third try Jim asked for clearance as we taxied out and we were on our way. That was a long, cold, dark day of flying on the white prairie, for it was mostly overcast, but by good luck we managed to locate every lake, check it, and make it home to Colville by moonlight. Jim had the gasoline figured mighty close too—the motor quit right beside my gasoline cache as we landed. A few minutes later we had the furnace going in the house and the airplane all wrapped up with a heater under it for the night.

Luckily, it hadn't been a year of heavy snowdrifts as yet. Even with this, though, it was marginal, as are all such operations into an unknown area. Flying a light ski-equipped airplane into unknown areas is one thing, landing a big airliner on an unmarked drifted lake is another. Back in Fairbanks the next day I asked Jim what the next step was.

"We take in a fully loaded C-46 to try a landing. It is loaded up right now. Will you be ready in the morning?"

"Yes, I will be as ready as I ever will."

It is one thing to talk about theories and quite another to put them into practice, especially when lives and equipment are at stake. I'm no heavy aircraft pilot. I have used them and know what they will do in my own small operation, but this operation was different in scope; nothing like it had ever been tried. It wasn't backed by unlimited government money and equipment; it was a private enterprise and it had to pay its own way.

The familiar form of the C-46 old 58 Victor, veteran of many Arctic trips and the breakup at Lake Peters, was waiting for us in the ice fog and dark of a 42-below-zero morning. Jim Freericks, Bill Lavery, and I were the crew. The destination: the Arctic prairie, to land upon the ice of an unmarked lake, to leave a load of diesel oil and high explosives. There would be no radio contact for this might trigger the electric primers of the explosives. Jim was pilot, Bill was co-pilot, and I was the navigator and runway "picker-outer." I love to watch Jim and Bill fly a C-46, for they know the old birds like a horseman knows his horse.

As three pilots will on a long and uncertain flight, we began discussing flying and the early days we had all known. Neither Jim nor I had flown the coast from Anchorage to Seattle in the early days before radio navigation, but Bill had and he told of one of his worst flights when the weather just let down on him. He was flying a twin-engine Lockheed Electra over the water and at last he was forced to use the marker buoys that the fishing boats steer by to make his way up the narrow channel to Juneau. To follow those markers up that twisting channel in near-zero weather with an airplane is one of the most terrifying experiences any pilot can endure. I know. I did it once with a light seaplane. The very thought of flying a fast twin under those conditions scares me yet.

It also scared Bill's passengers. Sitting directly behind the pilot's door were three that Bill recognized as an Anchorage pimp and two prostitutes. Through the open door Bill could hear parts of their conversation. It was apparent that they didn't expect to get out alive and the pimp was bemoaning and whining about his fate until both prostitutes had enough and told him off.

"Why, you miserable excuse for a man . . . You got me into this business . . ." One of the prostitutes must have said the pimp should pray, for Bill heard the other say, "It won't do him any good to pray . . . it is too late . . . it's way too late . . ." and there were some cuss words to punctuate it. Bill couldn't hear it all, but that was the gist of it, and so with his scared passengers Bill fought it out from marker buoy to marker buoy, never daring to lose one or he would pile head on into the mountain. Luckily, he knew those channel markers from clearer flights, for he was but a few feet above the waves and those markers were put in for the use of boats traveling six or eight knots and able to stand still, not for airplanes at one hundred fifty knots and no stopping.

Lavery is one of the old names in Alaskan bush flying and I never tire of hearing Bill tell of his early flying experiences. The stories are invariably funny, but the line between humor and tragedy is often a very thin one.

We had a happy surprise that day for the sky was clear and the Arctic prairie lay a study in white and pink as a low sun shone from the direct south at high noon. In the slanting rays of the sun the snowdrifts cast long shadows and looked a lot bigger than when we had seen them the day before under whiteout conditions.

"Is it all right, Bud?" Jim asked, as we flew by the intended landing area and our shadow paced us up and down over the drifts.

"It is okay, Jim. Just come in right across that point, line up on the little round island, and touch down just beyond the point."

When it is your turn to make the decision make it! Don't try and spread out your problem and blame among those present. Indecision has likely killed more pilots and caused more people trouble than any other form of self-torture. I wasn't afraid the ice wouldn't hold us, but I was worried about the snowdrifts that looked so much larger in the light of the low sun. If we nosed over our cargo of oil drums and high explosives would break loose and fly forward like the Charge of the Light Brigade.

You don't handle a C-46 like a Piper Cub. They are heavy and swing in a big turn. They come in fast, you can't see too much through the windshield and you sit quite a ways up above the ground. The pilots fly as a unit, with one handling the controls while the other handles the flaps, gear, and calls off instrument readings, especially the air speed. I watched the drifts come toward us. I didn't have anything else to do but watch at this point. Jim handled the airliner as if it were locked to an invisible glide path. It was well above stalling speed but held there by power, and as we crossed the point the throttles came back and the wheels touched. The airliner moved majestically straight ahead with sheets of snow flying as the big wheels burst through the drifts. You could feel the ship hesitate a moment as it met each drift but you could have sat upon a box of high exposives without a seat belt and drunk a cup of coffee without spilling a drop.

In this way each lake was tried out. Some of them did throw the C-46 about a bit but all proved useable, and the big move was on. It sounds easy writing about it now, but we were always aware that lives, machines and equipment hung in the balance at EACH landing. Once again Wien Airlines broke the trail.

As soon as the landings were proven safe I flew the *Arctic Tern* back home, while Jim Freericks brought Martha, Mark, Jeffrey plus our pet cats, turtles, parakeets, groceries, lumber for the shed, and the first of the Western Geophysical crew —Smiley Marlette, Henry Swazie, and Mac Towns. It was up to us then to get things started.

A C-46 will handle larger snowdrifts than any airliner I know of but we had to have a much better field for the C-82's. With their small nose wheel they can't buck big snowdrifts at all. Yet we had to have two flights with the C-82 to bring in the D-6 caterpillar before we could plow the drifts off the runway. Our little caterpillar just couldn't handle the big drifts: Jim and I walked up and down the runway looking for the best spot while Smiley Marlette dragged the strip as best he could with our little caterpillar and then we marked out the new runway with empty 55-gallon oil drums. In the cold frost formed on the drums so that they had to be swept clean before each landing so they would show up black against the white snow.

We all worked eighteen hours a day getting things in order.

The men took one look at Martha's lovely furniture and carpets in our upstairs living area and refused to enter there in dirty greasy workclothes. For luckily we have full living and working accommodations downstairs but the radio was upstairs so that Martha made dozens of trips up and down stairs to answer the radio each day in sending weather reports or guiding aircraft through.

It was clear and cold when Jim and Bill went north from Fairbanks heading for Colville with the C-82, O-6 Bravo, and the first part of the D-6 caterpillar aboard. As they neared Colville ice fog rolled in, hiding all. Visibility was down to a hundred yards when we heard the C-82 overhead. With Martha operating the radio, I went outside to listen and point to where the airplane was, then Martha relayed his position to Jim. It was our instrument-approach system! Jim made two runs before I felt he was lined up right for the runway. I signaled he was right on course and the distance. Martha relayed the information to Jim and a moment later I heard the engines throttle back followed a little later by the sound of taxiing. I couldn't see the C-82 until it came within a few yards. From above Jim had had better visibility than I, so once he was exactly lined up with the runway he had been able to see the barrel markers that led to the runway. We had laid barrels in a line on their sides a hundred yards apart for half a mile with two barrels end to end to mark the start of the center of the runway. The runway then had barrels upright along its edges.

All the big equipment was taken apart or designed to just fit inside a flying boxcar. Our fastest unloading time was eleven minutes and our longest time two and a half hours when the first 16,000# drilling rig got stuck on us. We had to work fast or the airplane engines froze up in the −30- to −50-degree air. If we weren't through unloading, every half hour work was stopped while the engines were started up and run a few minutes to keep them warm. The weather stayed cold calm and mostly clear so that not a single flight had to return because of weather.

We put the plywood garage up and soon had a Coleman spaceheater going. This heat helped a lot in thawing out equipment before we could assemble it and start it up. We put the D-6 caterpillar together first and started it right up so we could keep the runway in good shape. We strung out the runway lights and airliners came and went steadily. At one time we had three unloading at once. The camp kitchen and bunkhouse trailers came in first along with the big Nodwells —enormous track vehicles and track trailer carriages.

Lloyd Logan had stayed in Fairbanks to supervise the loading-out operation, but now that the bulk of the equipment was in he came on up to help assemble it. They put up the bunkhouse trailers and kitchen, started up the electric generator, and Milo, the cook, came in and the camp became self-sustaining. Martha now had only the radio to manage and I was busy training the crew to handle the Arctic prairie.

Two weeks later they were bringing in the whole crew. I remember that one airliner landed and many of the men were dressed in street clothes and low shoes. They clustered around the door, looking out, while we put up the ladder. Mark, then five, had been out every day riding the caterpillar with Smiley or "helping" with the unloading. He was standing there all dressed in furs. "Is that a child out there I see?" one of the men exclaimed.

Some of the men wouldn't even get off the airliner but went right back to Fairbanks. It was a good riddance, for men of that kind have no business in the Arctic. It was true of some of the equipment too. The special diesel engines "made for the Arctic" wouldn't keep running even when started in the warm garage. We sent radio messages to the factory and got back such helpful advice as, "take off the fan belts." Any high-school boy knew that! For a moment we felt we had been insulted. Then we realized that it was all they knew of the Arctic and once again we were on our own. Mac Towns and I talked it over and realized the answer was almost as simple as "take off the fan belts." We would just have to cowl down the engines like the bush pilots had done, until they would stay warm, and we could regulate the temperature around the engines. It is a simple answer to operating in the Arctic. We don't STAND THE COLD, WE PROTECT OURSELVES FROM IT. The Alaskan won't STAND THE COLD—that is, suffer from it—that the Roman, New Yorker, or Montanan will, and neither will our machines, nor the explosives. We were to learn this as the drilling got under way.

Wien Airlines wasn't able to handle the volume of freight and Interior Airlines began hauling and eventually all available aircraft were hauling freight into the Arctic. In just three weeks' time all was ready. An entire seismographic exploration camp was assembled on the river in front of our house. All the camp was mounted upon track-equipped trailers and pulled by the enormous Nodwell tractors. The camp looked like a short freight train as it strung out across the prairie. A helicopter had joined the party to guide the crews and carry men or supplies between units; there was a survey team to mark the sites, and the exploration party was ready to depart.

We had made up a wind, temperature, and weather chart with the important dates—like when rivers would break up—on it for Lloyd. We had tried to prepare them in all ways for life on the Arctic prairie. Martha would keep constant radio contact and give advice through the days ahead. When the sun returns it comes back fast and it was well up in the sky on a clear day when the camp moved away. Lloyd Logan lead the procession in a Nodwell, the big cookhouse fell in behind, with the bunkhouses, drilling rigs, and the caterpillar tractor following. The units had looked so big as we assembled them, but now as they swung out across the prairie they looked like toys.

Mr. and Mrs. Clever La Fleur—Cleve and Bercy—of Sulphur, Louisiana, had arrived a few days before to hunt polar bear with us and we all stood in the window of our snug home and watched them go. We had seen the operation though from the first and trained them to look after themselves in our land. As they crossed the frozen river now they were moving out on their own and it was like seeing part of your family off.

Two hours later I was outside and noted that a line of "fish belly" clouds had spread across the eastern sky. We were about due for a wind according to our records. I felt rather foolish sending out a storm warning on a calm, clear evening but I had Martha call Lloyd Logan on the radio and tell him he had better make camp in formation for a big storm from the east. Lloyd thanked me and a few hours later he reported all was in order as the first puff of an east wind rattled our shutters. As darkness closed down we listened to the wind rise to sixty or seventy knots in a few hours and then calm. A few minutes later it struck from the west just as violently. It is the only time I have seen such a quick rise of wind and a complete reversal of a storm in the Arctic. Some tropical storm must have gone astray.

It was calm and clear next morning with the snowdrifts all hard and polished. Lloyd Logan reported that the camp had come through perfectly, and due to the proper alignment of buildings nothing was drifted under. Lloyd had learned his

Arctic lessons well. I couldn't say the same for myself. I had shipped up some aluminum roofing for a new building and I stacked it carefully with heavy planks on top. I knew at the time I should have tied all the roofing together. Now in the bright sunlight I could see there wasn't a sheet of roofing left. The two-by-sixteen sheets of aluminum had literally gone with the wind!

The main object in seismographic work is to drill a line of holes around a hundred feet deep and place a charge of high explosives in each hole, detonate them in a pattern, and record the echoes and tremors of the earth on seismographs. This is highly exacting work, requiring a precise pattern and exact timing. One day Lloyd flew in with the helicopter; he had a problem. What could be making the explosives ignite erratically? Or not ignite at all? Could it be the couplings? I went over the hook-up and felt it was the explosives. At first Lloyd was sure it couldn't be the explosives since they had shot the same kind of explosives in colder temperatures to the south. Lloyd felt it was the hook-up with the couplings changing and acting like thermo-couplers. By now Lloyd was convinced that Arctic temperatures were different from those same temperatures farther south and had to be treated in a different light.

"I should have warned you about that make of explosives," I told him, "for I found it wouldn't go off in my ice cellar work. The other brand did shoot well though. I just never thought about it."

Lloyd left, half convinced it was the explosives, and a few days later he called on the radio to see if I would be free for a moment. A little later the helicopter came in with Lloyd and an explosives engineer from the factory. We talked a bit, and I told them what little I knew about the use of explosives in the Arctic.

The engineer listened carefully. "I'm afraid you are right and it is embarrassing too since our competitor's powder does shoot."

The explosives would fire at −100 degrees in their laboratory tests but they woudn't fire in our temperatures and a million dollars' worth of time, freight, and materials were lost. The defunct powder had to all be gathered together and destroyed later in the summer.

Martha put in a busy season on the radio helping with information and guiding in lost pilots. Radio waves often skip about and since most all of the radios were tuned to the same frequency—2945.5—it was like a party line and what one station missed would be relayed on by another. Closeness of an aircraft to a station doesn't always mean it can work that station.

We were just sitting down to dinner one evening when we heard a clear voice on the radio almost as if he were talking to himself. "I wonder if that faithful Colville Radio is listening? . . . Colville Radio . . ." and then followed the message.

It was Merrill Wien, son of the famous pilot Noel Wien. He was heading for Alaska from an ice island near the North Pole, where he had delivered a load of supplies using a DC-4. He had lost contact with the other stations in Alaska and had called to us to relay his position. It is lucky for us all that our radio has the best range of any, due to its location I suppose, and due to Martha's expert and faithful handling of it. Never underestimate the value of the operator of any equipment!

While we were busy getting the seismic crew in operation we heard from Captain W. S. Hall. They wanted to proceed with the route across the top of Alaska. What did we recommend? I felt we needed a special boat to explore, sound, and mark the river and the channel through the Delta into the ocean and we ordered one from the Grumman Boat Company of Marathon, New York. The boat had to fit into a flying boxcar. The boat we needed was on display at the Boat Show in New York City. Fred Brendt, of the Grumman Boat Company, took their display boat off the floor, fitted it up with a special fathometer that would record accurately in shallow water, and sent it on its way by fast freight to Seattle. The Reverend Bill Wartes checked it in Seattle for me and found it hadn't been properly tied down. The boat had slid back in the car damaging its propeller system. Bill hurriedly repaired it en route from the railroad yards to the steamship. It again went by rail from Seward to Fairbanks where Jim Freericks loaded it on board the Wien C-82 flying boxcar and flew it up to Umiat for us. By now it was mid-July, with continuous daylight, and the prairie was a world of waving grass, flowers, and birds.

To mark the channel I ordered a hundred ten-pound fishing anchors and bright day-glow inflatable buoys that the crab fishermen use to mark their crab pots on the ocean. For anchor line I ordered ½-inch nylon rope to use in buoying the channel. Mel Anderson of Seattle Marine and Supply Company had seen to it that each item was there, knowing full well how important every one was. Ed Parsons had converted an aircraft radio for use in the boat and we installed it. Our son Jim and the Warteses' oldest son, Mark, were to handle the work with the *Explorer*—as we called the new boat— I would guide the ships through the ice with the *Arctic Tern*, and Martha would coordinate all our efforts with the radio.

I had a theory that a map of the deep-water channels in Arctic rivers could be made easily and accurately by photography in the early spring when the breakup was taking place. During the winter the shallow water all freezes solidly to the permanently frozen soil below, while the deep water didn't freeze to the bottom. When the breakup comes and the water rises, the ice that was frozen to the bottom would be flooded while the ice over the deep water would float up. An aerial photograph taken from several thousand feet up would show the white ice lanes as the deep-water channels. We had some ideal clear days during the breakup so I was able to make several aerial photos of the Delta area that turned out beautifully. I had them blown up to map size and instead of having to spend weeks looking for channels we had an accurate chart of the area and needed only to check out the deep channel with the *Explorer*.

The Wien crew at Umiat had unloaded the *Explorer* and put her on the Colville River for us, and hauled all the gear to the boat as well. It was a warm July day when I flew Martha, Jim, Mark, and baby Jeffrey up to Umiat, and we set to loading the boat. Mel Anderson hadn't been able to get all ten-pound anchors on such short notice and some weighed thirty pounds, giving us a ton of anchors alone. Once loaded, I started the *Explorer* and ran it up and down a quiet stretch of the river to check it out. It ran beautifully, so Martha, Jim, and the two little boys set sail down the river for home. I waited at Umiat an hour for them to get a good start, and then I followed in the airplane to check their progress.

I found them ten miles down stream in a stretch of open river making good time. I landed the *Arctic Tern,* taxied up beside them, Jim threw me a line, and we made fast. Martha broke out the basket of fried chicken and thus we traveled downriver eating a picnic lunch. It was warm and beautiful drifting down that wild river with the high cliffs on the west and the great flower-strewn prairie sweeping away to the east. The water was clear, the gravel bars clean with clumps of flowers here and there, while on the banks you could see wild geese feeding and there were caribou on the distant skyline. It would have been wonderful to have traveled on forever in such a beautiful land, but the river swung into the cliffs speeding up where it would be hard to handle our boat-airplane flotilla. With lunch finished I cast off, took to the air, and headed for home.

The heat of the day gave way to fog at midnight so thick you couldn't see the riverbanks. Time was short and Jim traveled on. In the fog he took a wrong turn that lead him away from the mainstream through a twisting channel that wandered across the prairie for twenty miles before it returned to the mainstream again. The winding and distance didn't matter. What did matter was the stream was shallow in places and in the fog it was impossible to read the water accurately. Time after time they went around. Martha worked steady throwing a lead line ahead to find the deepest water. It was hard to handle the big boat in shallow water and the current would put it up on gravel bars and then the water piling up behind would drive it in tight. In some places there just wasn't water enough to get the boat across. Jim would have to go over the side, shift cargo, tug, and work the boat across. I don't see how he ever managed it. Hours later as the fog began to clear they again joined the mainstream. Jim suddenly brought the boat around to avoid some brush and snags in the main channel, when he realized the obstacle was the velvet-covered antlers of a swimming moose! Martha and the little boys had gone to bed. She heard Jim shut off the engine and throw out the anchor.

"When I can't tell a moose from a mud bar it is time I got some sleep."

At ten A.M. they were tying up in front of our house. As soon as Jim had unloaded his boat he went right to work putting out the marker buoys. Captain Hall, Captain Garvey, and a river pilot named Albert Lafferty flew to Umiat in N.W.T.'s DC-3, the *El Dorado*, and I flew them over the routes we had picked out using our *Arctic Tern* on floats and then Jim ran them about the river so they would be familiar with the new area, and we picked out an unloading site about thirty miles upriver. We called it Pingo Beach from two pingos (small conical hills about thirty feet high pushed up on the prairie) nearby. Here the enormous 750-ton barges could be unloaded.

The worst spot we found on the river was a point after the channel entered the ocean. We needed five feet of water to clear, and here in this vast ocean shelf there was just five feet of water for about three hundred yards through a narrow channel. With an east wind and a drop of water on the shelf the boats couldn't cross. Jim and I searched the vast expanse of shoal water with him using the *Explorer* and I guiding him from the air, but we had found the one and only good channel in the river on the first try by using our aerial photography at breakup. In reality it was an excellent route and in populated areas a dredge would have deepened the channel through that bar in a few hours' time. There in the Arctic we had to do with things as they were.

By early August the *Radium Dew* and its barges were waiting in the Mackenzie Delta. I made a long reconnaissance flight across the route, giving Captain Alex Reed a report on the ice. He felt it was safe to try, and the operation went into gear. There were 5,000 tons of supplies to move on eleven barges. It would take two shuttles. When the sea was free of ice the *Radium Dew* put its barges out on long towlines, and when the ice closed in she gathered the barges about her like a mother duck and pushed on ahead. I flew back and forth to radio the best path to take through the ice, while the boat and barges moved ahead through the open lanes. I had to be careful not to steer them into a closing lane, thereby getting them caught or crushed. In just two days the *Radium Dew* anchored the barges behind the safety of Thetus Island in the Colville River Delta and began relaying the 750-ton barges one at a time through the narrow channel across the bar. Fortunately, the water held and a day later all the barges were across the bar anchored in the deep river channel.

In the continuous daylight the operation continued on a twenty-four-hour-a-day schedule. It looked as though a small village were going upriver as the *Radium Dew* and its barges pushed on to Pingo Beach to unload. To us who had for so long brought in our few supplies first by dog teams and then small airplane, it seemed like a miracle to see so much brought in so easily! Even the big airlift that had set up the seismographic party had taken all the air freighters in the north over a month to haul 500 tons of unassembled gear. Their total effort was eclipsed by the load of a SINGLE 750-ton barge, and the *Radium Dew* could handle ten barges at once under ideal conditions. The barges were so large you had to look to find a D-8 Caterpillar or a Kenworth diesel tractor-trailer truck on one, and we didn't have to assemble them; they just dropped a ramp and drove them ashore. When a barge's deck was cleared I could take off and land our Super Cub on it!

While they were unloading the first barges, the *Radium Dew* went back to the Mackenzie River and returned with the last of the barges. All of the supplies were in for British Petroleum (B.P.)—Sinclair's drilling operation. The housing, fuel, well casing, tractors, trucks, oil-well rigs—in fact, everything necessary for a year's operation—was in.

When I was in Fairbanks during the summer I found, to my surprise, that the local experts, who had never seen the Arctic, gave the *Radium Dew* but one chance in a hundred to succeed. Hadn't men tried for centuries to use the Northwest Passage and failed? Didn't the ice pack often block the big Navy operation at Barrow? From these well-known facts they were right in their predictions. What they didn't know was that, while shipping from the west coast around Point Barrow is most dangerous and often impossible as well as fantastically slow and expensive because of distance involved and the way the heavy ice packs hem in Point Barrow, these problems are lacking in shipping from the east. Along the north coast of Alaska there is lighter ice and few currents. Northern Transportation has for years operated a fleet of modern vessels in the Arctic Ocean bringing supplies down the great Mackenzie River system, which compares with the Mississippi River traffic system, to support commerce of the entire Canadian Arctic as well as the DEW Line sites in that sector. The Canadian government maintains an aerial ice patrol that collects daily reports on ice conditions in the Canadian Arctic. From July through September ships operate from the Mackenzie River into the Arctic Ocean. The problems encountered in our operation in extending the shipping lanes west across the top of Alaska were only those that could be expected in pioneering any new route. Once the first risks are taken the operation becomes routine.

There were no customs agents in the entire Arctic, so a new system had to be established and some old laws revised. Arrangements had been made through the Anchorage customs to clear the cargo of the *Radium Dew;* therefore, when the last barges had reached Pingo Beach, Martha sent a radio message to Lee Adcock in Anchorage. He arranged for a chartered airpane from Ward Gay's Sea Airmotive. On this special flight from Anchorage to Pingo Beach were Lee Adcock, who took care of the customs brokerage; Kiefer Gray, of the Immigration Department; and Fred Biery, of the U.S.

Cusoms Bureau. They went over the cargo and flew back to Anchorage the next day.

The season's work was coming to a close. The *Radium Dew* headed downriver with its cluster of empty barges riding high. Jim followed in the *Explorer*, picking up the marker buoys and deflating them behind her, but all wasn't to end so easily, for as the *Radium Dew* neared the bar a wind came up from the east and the water dropped to three feet over the bar. There is no perceptible lunar tide in our part of the Arctic Ocean, and in the fall as long as the east wind blew the water would stay low on the shelf.

For three weeks the wind blew steadily and the *Radium Dew* lay tied to the riverbank at the edge of the open sea. All that lay between her and the freedom of the open sea was that three hundred yards of low water over the bar held there by the steady wind. In late September ice began forming out from shore and snow fell. I went over all my weather records and noted we had a rise of water about freeze-up each year. Captain Reed and I went over the best procedure for wintering the ship, if worst came to worst, and we waited. Then in heavy snow the wind ceased while a hush fell upon the land and the water flowed back upon the bar. It was pitch dark before there was five feet of water in the channel and it was snowing hard. Captain Reed was ready to try, though, and with the *Explorer* leading she pushed out. The snow was so heavy that the lights were of little help and the *Radium Dew* could follow the *Explorer* only on the radar screen, while the *Explorer* groped her way in the snowy night using her fathometer to follow the narrow channel.

At midnight Captain Reed radioed he was across the bar with the last barge and making up his tow to head for home. We followed his progress on the radio, and ice blocked him at Camden Bay. It was still snowing, but I was able to fly the *Arctic Tern* through the storm, keeping just above the waves, and scout an open lane through the ice pack for him. He picked up the rest of his empty barges at Kangigivik Point and headed on for the Mackenzie River. Two days after the *Radium Dew* left Colville, we were just sitting down to dinner. The wind was rising; it was a black stormy night of the kind that makes you thankful for a snug home. We were just ready to say the evening blessing when a voice from the radio called: "Colville Radio . . . The *Radium Dew*."

Martha answered: "The *Radium Dew*, Colville Radio. Good evening, Captain Reed."

"Colville Radio, the *Radium Dew*. Good evening to you. We are safe in the Mackenzie River and pushing twenty-eight barges on upriver now. We all thank you folks for your wonderful help. Have a good winter. We will see you again next year. A Merry Christmas to you all."

"A Merry Christmas to you all. It has been a lot of fun working with you folks. We will look forward to seeing you next year."

There were many things we had to be thankful for that night as we ate our dinner on the very top of our continent.

With the exploration and pioneering work for the new shipping line, the last link in America's coastal shipping was complete. There will always be room for advancement in methods, but we now had safe and economical shipping to all parts of America, even into the most remote Arctic.

The following years proved conclusively that the commerce of the Arctic depended upon water transportation from the Mackenzie River system, which links our Alaskan Arctic with the South Forty-eight by safe economical rail and water transportation. Anything that can be loaded on a railroad car at any point in America can now be delivered easily and economically to any point on the Arctic coast of Alaska. The old trade routes followed by the first Eskimos were once more in use, for the soapstone lamps used by the early Alaskan Eskimos came from the eastern Canadian Arctic, while the jade, flint, pitch, and hardwood came from the south via the mountain passes and down the Mackenzie and Colville rivers.

The oil companies learned slowly to live *with* the Arctic. This was something the Russians have always known and used to defeat both Napoleon and Hitler—the simple lesson of staying put or shipping by water in summer when all the Arctic prairie is soft and traveling and working with heavy equipment over land in winter when the prairie is frozen hard. The Arctic is one of the easiest areas of all to operate heavy machinery in during the winter. Only a patrol grader is needed to smooth off the snowdrifts on the prairie or frozen rivers and the massive Kenworth diesel trucks roll easily along those highways, hauling the heaviest of loads, while oil derricks rise on the open skyline.

It was the end of an era, and none but a few of us knew it had closed. America was all settled. The explorers, voyageurs, and mountain men had led the era westward from the Atlantic Ocean while the wagon trains followed to the Pacific Ocean. The gold seekers had taken it north into Canada and Alaska, where the bush pilots had picked up and carried it to the trail's end—into the pack ice of the Arctic Ocean.

22

"IT LOOKED LIKE A CLOVER FIELD TO ME"

The ability to read from the air what you see on the ground and interpret it correctly can only be acquired with experience. It is an all-important skill to those who fly beyond the airports. An error in reading or interpreting can be disastrous, but it usually just gives you a good scare, or at worst a "washed out" airplane—which means a plane that has been rendered unflyable until it is taken back to the hangar for major repairs.

With the completion of the Alaskan Highway and its string of airports, it became easy for any enterprising pilot to follow the highway to Alaska—and many did. It was a peasant flight, and after the war construction of airports all over Alaska made it possible for a pilot with courage to venture on beyond the road's end. At Fairbanks you had to be careful, though, or you could easily get lost and end up out of gas, for the gas stations are few and far between. Every pilot who has flown much in interior Alaska has become badly confused or downright lost at some time or other.

Into that "badly confused" category falls the commercial pilot whom I hired to take Cliff Collins and Leo Beard of Mt. Pleasant, Michigan, from Fairbanks to Hughes. We were going on a hunting trip and I planned to meet them with a floatplane at Hughes. The pilot flew confidently from Fairbanks to "Hughes" and landed his passengers, only Cliff Collins, himself an old pilot, said, "The sign there says Bettles." The pilot had flown at right angles to his course and ended up at Bettles, almost as far from Hughes as when they had started. He was on the Koyukuk River, though, and he followed it easily on to Hughes.

I was in Hughes in 1950 when Mr. and Mrs. Bob Kittenger of Chicago, Illinois, flew in with a new Navion. They had flown up the Alaskan Highway and were taking a vacation flying about Alaska. They wanted to find a little gold, so Les told them where they could pan gold a few miles from Hughes. Mr. Kittenger wanted to know about landing his airplane near there. Johnny James was flying his Stinson Station Wagon regularly over that run and knew the landing areas well. He and I both showed Mr. Kittenger a river bar a few miles from where the gold was that we felt would be safe for his tricycle-geared Navion. Then I headed off on a flight into the Arctic, Johnny left to fly downriver, and the Kittengers went out to pan gold. They flew around and easily located the spot where they could pan for gold. They also found that it was quite a walk from the gravel bar we had marked for a landing to where the gold panning would be done, but there was an open grassy area right beside where they would be panning and it looked like a clover field to Mr. Kittenger. He had flown his Navion off fields that looked exactly like it in Illinois.

He knew his mistake the moment the wheels touched. That grassy runway was niggerheads and the small wheels of the retractable-geared Navion plowed in clear to the belly. The ship didn't nose over, but it did stop fast, springing the landing gear and bending the propeller. When Johnny James returned from his downriver flight and found the Kittengers not back yet, he went looking for them; he found them waiting for him. Mr. Kittenger borrowed some jacks from Les, and with some Indians to help him he walked back to his airplane, jacked it up above the wet niggerheads, and blocked up under the wheels so that it wouldn't freeze down in the fall. There was no way to get the airplane out until after freeze-up. Mr. and Mrs. Kittenger spent a few days visiting about Hughes and flew home on an airliner.

That fall Bill Strandberg took his caterpillar, after the ground had frozen solid, and hauled the Navion back to the Hughes field on a Go-Devil (a big, heavy sled). An airplane mechanic came out from Fairbanks and made the Navion flyable and then ferried it back to Fairbanks for repairs. The Kittengers have returned to Alaska several times since, but Mr. Kittenger has never landed on an unmarked strip since simply because it "looked like clover field to me."

There are literally hundreds of similar cases involving misjudging a landing area. Most of the serious accidents are those of "Sunday pilots" who do not use their airplanes enough to be familiar with them. The fact that they have their own airplanes and are licensed pilots doesn't necessarily mean they have the needed skills to fly safely. And every year there are serious accidents involving this class of pilots. The aircraft companies are also at fault, for in their desire to sell more airplanes they stress too much how easy the machines are to operate and all they can do. What airplanes and their inept pilots can't do often makes the headlines. Airplanes aren't infallible machines; they are affected by every change in the weather. Neither are pilots infallible; their abilities change, and so do landing areas—what was safe to land on in the morning might not be after lunch.

Of all the variables in aviation and Arctic flying, no one ever put them to the test more than Jules Thibedeau. In so doing he left a trail of wrecked aircraft across the north and a list of accidents that no one has equaled or is ever likely to approach. Some said he was a good pilot; many said he didn't know a darned thing about aircraft and survived on luck alone—and you can find evidence to support either side.

He soon acquired the nickname of "The Walking Pilot." How he earned this name is a subject of disagreement; some said it was because he walked away from so many wrecks, while many others said it was because he spent more time walking back from attempted flights than he spent flying. Some people said he had so many wrecks because of the junky equipment he flew, while others said he made junk out of anything he flew. At any rate, when he "bought the farm" on December 23, 1965, on the white Arctic plains in the dark 50-below weather, it was in a brand-new blue-and-white Piper Comanche, carrying a load of Pepsi-Cola and one passenger, Ronnie Edwardson. Even on his last flight the opinions were divided, with some saying he had thirty cases of Pepsi-Cola aboard and others saying he had fifty. Some people thought he was headed for Barrow and some said he was headed for Barter Island. In any case, the Pepsi-Cola was consigned to Herman Rexford at Barter Island and anyone could have counted the cans of pop at the wreckage site, for although they were scattered over a couple of acres of hillside, about eighty miles southeast of the junction of the Anaktuvuk and Colville rivers, they were all countable. The previous evening, Jules had indicated to me he was flying to Barrow, and from the location of the wreckage he could have been going either to Barrow or Barter Island, and very likely Jules didn't know to which place he was going himself but would have gone the easiest route open. Unfortunately, he plowed head-on into that white prairie just before Christmas on next to the darkest day of the year when ice fog and a 50-below-zero temperature ruled. No one walked away from that impact. It was a total disaster and the wreckage was not found until six months later.

The first time I met Jules was in Barrow in late November 1953. The snowdrifts were getting big, hard, and rough. I had been on skis for six weeks. I was out on the Barrow Lagoon, preparing for take-off at the same spot where the Wien Norseman was to ram the *Arctic Messenger* a few years later when a beat-up old Piper Cub flew in on little wheels and landed, going every which way on those hard drifts before it came to a stop. The ship taxied up to where I was and out stepped a happy young man. He introduced himself as Jules Thibedeau, and I was struck at once by his open, honest manner and pleasing personality. The first part I was to learn later bore no resemblance to the truth, but his pleasing personality was real. He said he had come up to Barrow to fly and had a "contract" to haul all the fish into town. Since hauling fish was a good part of my business at that season, I welcomed this news as anyone else would have when told they had a new competitor in their back yard. Bush flying always was a bit of a dog fight, though, but the mutual hazards we found held us together, and a bush pilot would help his biggest competitor if flying safety were involved. Thus I asked Jules about his landing gear, saying the time had passed for safe operation upon wheels.

"I have a good set of skis," he told me, "only the Wiens are jealous of me and have them in their hangar at Fairbanks and won't ship them to me."

I advised him to get his skis soon, and also some heavy winter clothing, for he was lightly dressed. I figured he didn't have the money to pay for the air freight on his skis and the Wiens had asked for cash. In this I was wrong; he didn't even own the skis!

Jules flew the rest of that winter hauling whatever he could using wheels. He learned to find the smoothest spots amid the drifts, and he kept going. He also located every gasoline cache in the Arctic and one day told me that he hadn't purchased a gallon of gasoline all season. Most of the gasoline caches had been left by various government agencies for whatever reasons and were more or less abandoned, while others had been left by the Arctic contractors many years before. It was all kinds of gasoline in the various stages of decomposition, for gasoline deteriorates with age.

Repairs didn't make much worry for Jules. He didn't have an airplane long enough for you to get familiar with it, so I don't recall which one it was. He had trouble with a piston and I saw him fixing it up. He had found a piston in an old automotive engine that fit the cylinder. That it wasn't the same weight, design, metal, or for an air-cooled engine didn't matter—it fit the hole and the engine ran.

As Bob Cooper, the pilot who rescued Jules the most often, has said, "Jules didn't waste much money on such frills as airplane instruments and maintenance."

Every other time when I flew into Barrow someone would ask me if I had seen Jules or if I knew where he was. He had left for such-and-such place and hadn't returned. After several futile searches I began to realize that where Jules said he was going and where he actually went were often different places. Reverend Wartes and I both spent many hours searching for Jules and even found him a few times. From 1954 until the final search there were eleven massive organized aerial searches for Jules by the Search and Rescue and many, many times that number of searches by private pilots. Every make of aircraft was used in these aerial searches from the smallest Cub to the massive Army C-130's. Bobby Fisher,* the veteran ice pilot of the Arctic Research Laboratories, himself spent 150 hours looking for Jules on the last search in a Cessna 180. It costs from fifty dollars an hour to operate the Cessna 180's to perhaps five hundred dollars an hour for the C-130's, and several thousands of hours of aircraft time were used in these searches. The cost in worry to loved ones and friends, and the hazards encountered in these searches is staggering, but it also shows the human compassion and love for one of their own. In money spent, the figures would have passed the million-dollar mark, and this prompted Jess Bachner to remark, "It would be cheaper if the people would just set Jules up in a mansion and give him a million dollars not to fly."

In between crashes and walking back, Jules was flying. He flew anything anywhere at anytime. No one can say Jules lacked nerve, or that he didn't try. He got into the polar-bear-hunting game and did everything including flying into a

---

* Bobby Fisher died in a crash at Barrow November 21, 1968. He was flying an Aero Commander when he lost an engine and crashed shortly after take-off.

bear. He brought back stories of a polar bear "three feet wide between the ears," which, if this bear were built like other bears, would have made it as big as an elephant and rivaled the twelve-legged polar bear of Eskimo legend.

One day I found Jules at Barter Island and expressed my surprise at not seeing him at Barrow for a while.

"The marshal has been a little stuffy about a business deal there," he said. "I came over here for a few days."

A little later he moved into Fairbanks.

Just what kind of a pilot you would class Jules as I don't know. Sam White, in his straightforward way, said, "I wouldn't call him a pilot at all. He wrecked too many airplanes."

That he was ingenious all will agree. Jess Bachner saw just how ingenious he was one evening. Jules had flown Cliff Fairchild's Super Cub up to the North Slope to pick up a hunter on the Hula Hula River where Jules had left him on a rather rough crooked gravel bar. The hunter had tried to straighten out the strip and had piled the rocks in the old curve while Jules was away. Jules didn't know this and hit the rockpile in the dusk. The tough little Super Cub wasn't hurt, but both tires blew. They were the large over-sized ones and with them flat Jules was stuck. Most of us would have waited for someone to come in after us, but not Jules. He took off the wheels and took out the valve stem. Then he poured the tires full of fine sand. The tires looked fine— only they weighed about one hundred and fifty pounds apiece! The Cub easily packed this extra load out and Jules headed for Fairbanks, but on the flight in, the vibration shook out all the sand except for that in the bottom of the tires. Jess Bachner saw him coming in to land and all looked normal until he touched down. Instead of rolling, the Super Cub just stopped! The ship wouldn't taxi at all, and Jess said it was all his jeep could do to drag it to the side of the runway out of the way of traffic.

So Jules flew, landing on mountain tops, in creek bottoms, on the prairie, in the pack ice, in daylight, or dark, in good weather, or in bad. Jules discovered George Wood early in his flying career and George sang Jules's praises loudly for a while.

"I just depends upon that Jules," George told me by way of reprimand when I was a little late delivering his mail—for free of course since I never charged George a dime in all the years of flying. As the years passed, George didn't have too much to say about Jules and his silence spoke louder than words.

No one could help but like Jules. He had a personality that knew no rebuff from man or circumstance. He had the enthusiasm of a small boy and the nerve of a man. Each of us in our own way admired him and all we pilots marveled at the way he could keep his pilot's license after a series of accidents and how he always had an airplane to fly. The answer to the last may be that he usually flew someone else's plane.

I didn't see much of Jules after he moved to Fairbanks. I would run into him at the hangar or on the street to exchange a moment's news. Then in the winter of 1965 we spent a few months in Fairbanks, so Mark could go to school and I could talk with my old bush pilot friends to get all the facts as straight as possible for this book. Our son Jim had crashed right in front of me a few days before but luckily had escaped without harm. I had a cold, dark flight across the Arctic into Fairbanks. The Christmas season was joyous for us there together and we went shopping at Fairbanks' lovely supermarket, Foodland. In the press of busy shoppers I saw a friendly face across the crowd as I stood with my loaded cart in line at the check-out counter. Jules came up with his nineteen-year-old stepson, Ronnie. We hadn't seen each other in quite a while and the Christmas spirit was in the air.

"I've just bought up a new Piper Comanche, Bud," he told me, bubbling over with enthusiasm as usual. "I'm getting a new Cessna 185 next summer too and I'm moved back to Barrow."

"That's fine, Jules," I told him, and really meant it too, for he had surely earned the right to succeed in flying.

"I'm getting a lot of things for the kids," he said, indicating presents and produce piled high in the shopping cart. "I will just make it to Barrow for Christmas."

The clerk had tallied up my groceries and Jules had more shopping to do, so we drifted apart.

That was on December 22, and on Christmas Eve I was out at the hangar wishing all a merry Christmas when someone said, "I heard Jules Thibedeau is missing." None of us knew when he had left, nor where he was going, but we all knew he was flying the wrong type of aircraft to be going into the Arctic in the dark of winter. Still no one was greatly concerned, for we had all lived with Jules being lost for some twelve years and we figured the tough, resourceful little pilot

could take care of himself. The general consensus was that
he had likely landed at some gasoline cache in the dark and
had bent the propeller on a snowdrift. Right after Christmas
the search began. Thibedeau had stopped for gas at Bettles
and here all trace of him ended. The Eskimos in Anaktuvuk
Pass saw an airplane that fitted the description of his blue-
and-white Comanche circle the village twice at twelve thirty
and fly on north on December 23. Bob Cooper found an Eskimo who was hunting caribou thirty miles northeast of there
and he had seen an airplane flying toward Barter Island at a
little after that time. This would indicate Jules was headed
for Barter Island. Every kind of aircraft available was put
into the search with the Civil Air Patrol, Air National Guard,
U.S. Air Force and private pilots joining in. The airplane pilots
on all runs kept a lookout. The small airplanes combed the
area along Jules's path and checked out isolated cabins, while
the massive C-130's ranged far afield in the dark, hoping to
see a flare or light. The temperature ranged in the minus
fifties and the Arctic prairie was blanketed in ice fog, so that
even in the three-hour flush of twilight that marked high
noon you could see very little.

The midwinter cold is very hard on small aircraft and
miserable to try and work in. It takes more time to heat airplanes and care for them than you get to put in flying. Even
in flight frost forms on the windows and windshield so you
have a hard time seeing out. You work in the dark, with big
mittens on, frost forms in your eyelashes and sticks your
eyes shut even, if you touch metal bare-handed it burns you
like hot metal, the skis won't slide on the sand like snow, and
things break easily. Had Jules been flying a ski ship none of
us would have worried. Yet we all still expected him to walk
out to somewhere. In all the many searches for him before
he had rarely been found but had walked in.

The sun came back to the Arctic and the winds drifted
across the endless expanse of prairie. Jules's brother, "Shorty,"
and Bob Cooper kept up the search, but even for them the
hope of finding anyone alive was gone. They searched just
to find the wreckage. The Fairbanks *Daily News Miner* on
January 26 ran a full-page story and picture captioned "Jules
Thibedeau—Walking Pilot Down for Good?" The question
mark wasn't needed for those of us who had known Jules.
The tough, resourceful pilot would have once more walked
out in that length of time if he had been alive.

It was a hot summer day on the Arctic prairie with the

land a world of green grass, flowers, and twenty-four-hour-a-day sunshine when an oil exploration party flying in the area spotted the wreckage of the blue-and-white Comanche scattered over the gentle hillside. The conditions couldn't have been further from what they were on that midwinter day when Jules Thibedeau and Ronnie Edwardson crashed. Fate had terminated the logbook of one of the most colorful pilots of the north; death had closed the flight plan.

In looking back over the years and Jules Thibedeau's flying career I wonder whether if things had been a little different just how far Jules might have gone with his pleasant winning ways, his will to take chances, to work hard, and friendly smile if the Arctic hadn't claimed him for its own.

Jim Freericks has the dubious honor of being at the controls of the largest plane to ever land in the Arctic on what "looked like a clover field" and wasn't. Jim's contribution to it was simply that he was the pilot chosen, and the error wasn't that the field hadn't been checked out. It was a combination of little things that delayed the flight to the deadline.

It was late in the spring of 1958—the year we started our new home in the delta, the year our son Mark was born, and the year Stan Fredricksen and Clarence Rhodes were lost. Wiens had finished hauling in our home using the famous old C-46—853. The U.S. Coast and Geodetic Survey wanted some freight hauled into the beautiful hourglass-shaped twins, Peters Lake and Schrader Lake, which lie in the mountains south of Barter Island. It was already breakup time across the Arctic, but the lakes being in that mountain fastness where it can and does snow even in July were still frozen.

All was ready when fog off the prairie came in and obscured things for two weeks. When the weather cleared there was mechanical trouble with the aircraft and another delay. By this time Jim was worried about the safety of the ice on Peters Lake, where the best spot to land had been selected. The Coast and Geodetic men had the Air Force charts showing the thickness and safety of ice. Jim sent Keith Harrington up in the Cessna 180 to give him the weather, wind, and general runway landing information. The Coast and Geodetic men believed that according to the charts the ice was safe, for it was fifty-four inches thick. As Jim later told me, "None of us involved in the operation could have been considered Arctic experts—then or now—but we all furthered our education."

The strength and character of ice is affected by many factors, such as the composition of the water it froze from, the temperature, the light, and its age. The men didn't realize that the high sun of summer goes through the surface ice like a lens and "candles" the ice turning it into long vertical crystals, and in its later stages fifty-four inches of ice won't even hold a man safely, let alone a fifty-thousand-pound C-46. It was just in its first stages of "candling" with the surface still hard.

Jim and his co-pilot, George Stinton, lined up old 853 and brought that fifty thousand pounds in as light as a feather on the well-marked runway and all went beautifully. The C-46 had almost come to a stop when the main gear just settled right through the ice. The airliner came to rest flat on the ice with the wing holding it up nicely, and the propellers were bent back because they were still turning when they hit the ice.

Jim just sat there completely disgusted with it all, and suddenly he realized someone was on the ice shouting at him. It was George Stinton. He had turned off all the switches, opened the door, and was already out on the ice shouting for Jim to get out before it all went through! Jim knew there was no need to hurry, for while the "candled" ice would not support the weight of the plane on the two small areas contacted by the wheels, when its weight was spread out over the whole surface it would hold the airplane until the ice melted. It would melt faster now too because the presence of a dark object would absorb the heat from the steady sunshine of early summer.

Salvage operations began at once. At first there was hope of jacking up the airliner and laying planks for support, with it empty perhaps it could be moved ahead to more solid ice. If it would hold up long enough for the airliner to start moving, then the ship could easily take off again. There had not been any damage to the airplane except for the curled propellers and new propellers, along with jacks and planks, were flown right in. But it was all to no avail. The ice "candled" faster with the presence of the plane to help and the jacks punched holes in the ice instead of raising the airplane. A crew of mechanics took out radio gear and parts of the engines that water would damage. Its sister C-46 flew over the lake and the crew threw out a load of empty oil drums. These were lashed inside and under the wings and tail, as were inflated rubber rafts.

The ice melted quickly and all speculated on what would happen. What did happen was that 853 floated so nicely that water never entered the cabin. A small boat and outboard motor towed it to the best beach as soon as the ice melted, and they winched it up onto the beach.

The mechanics put back in the parts that had been taken off and installed the new propellers. Jim started up the ship and checked it all out. The lake shore was flat and with the right wind Jim felt he might be able to take off and to this end he taxied a few feet only to have the ship settle right through the prairie sod to the permafrost a foot below. After that they jacked up the ship and left it until freeze-up.

When the land was frozen up hard once more Al Moseley took Jim Freericks and Dick King back up to Peters Lake in the Wien Cessna 180 to start up the C-46 and when the wind and weather were right fly it back to Fairbanks. The Cessna 180 landed nicely and the new, hard ice held up well, but instead of unloading the airplane, walking over, and checking the ice near shore, they taxied right over to shore. Here shale ice and soft snow had slowed up the freezing and the 180 broke right through. Luckily the water was shallow and the wheels hit bottom and so no damage was done. The winch was already there and after much breaking of ice they pulled the 180 up on shore, dried it out, and Al Moseley flew on back to Fairbanks. Jim and Dick were left to await a strong east wing that was needed to help lift the airliner off that rough short field.

It was two weeks before the right wind came along; in the meantime Jim and Dick had some good fishing and made several false starts when it looked as if the wind were rising. Finally the wind came and they busied themselves heating the engines, but by the time they were ready to go the wind had died down quite a bit. Jim walked around the airplane, deciding what to do. Should he try it? The mountains were all white with the snow of another winter. Tall, imposing, and beautiful, they stood rising right from the lake in places, steep, majestic, light pink and blue in the rays of the southern sun, for the sun was leaving for another year. How pure and peaceful it was. The lake boomed as a crack raced across its surface while ice froze deeper. The pilots had been away from their families two weeks already and were anxious to get home. You can talk something over but in the end a decision must be made. Just simple waiting wasn't the answer either, for it was getting colder and darker every day and a deep snow could drift the area so they couldn't get the plane out at all that year. The airliner was needed in Fairbanks. What was there to lose? Only the airliner, all the work of saving it from the lake, and perhaps the lives of two pilots. The Air Force teaches the new cadet that they are "a different breed of cats." The pilot is really a different breed of cat. Perhaps it is because he deals with power, space, time, and irrevocable decisions that once made must be followed, and as Jim and Dick walked around 853 sitting there in the mountain fastness beside the frozen lake they checked her over, felt the wind, and decided. They would go.

There was no indecision from here on. There was a definite procedure to follow. The ship was ready with doors locked, Herman-Nelson heater and spare cargo lashed down tight. From up in the cabin the pilots looked over the runway and at each other as they ran slowly through the checklist for take-off. You build up power slowly for a normal take-off, using full power only briefly or you might ruin the engine. The pilot calls the plays and handles the yoke (wheel) rudder and throttle.

"Okay, throw everything up in the kitchen [build up full power as fast as possible]."

The pilots' seats on a C-46 are placed so the noise from both engines and propellers focuses on them with an intensity great enough to almost lift you from the seat. It was the sweetest music this side of heaven that day—in fact, it is the only music that can keep you this side of heaven at times! The 853 rolled away over the uneven ground with power and determination. She took the rough bumps solidly upon her landing gear as she used up precious runway fast. Then the tail became operative and lifted its weight off the ground as Jim nudged the yoke forward. The wing was tightening up and carrying part of the load, the rough runway struck the gear thundering blows as speed increased, but they didn't rock the ship as before, for the wing was carrying much of the weight as speed built up. Three-fourths of the runway was gone. A C-46 can be pulled off in seven hundred feet under ideal runway conditions with good wind at sea level but this runway was hardly ideal, and at three thousand feet altitude! Fortunately there weren't any bad snowdrifts to drain off speed, and the 853 rolled ahead blowing loose snow into a blizzard behind her while she bounded from bump to bump as the end of the runway came and Jim brought the yoke back, the tail levered the load from the gear to the wing, and it accepted it, lifting the gear free of the land. They were airborne and air speed built up quickly as they climbed into the sky. The pilots smiled briefly at each other and went back to the task of flying the airliner. An hour and fifty minutes later they shut off the engines beside the Wien hangar from where they had taxied away just six months before. The cargo had been delivered and the airplane was back safe again, but it surely hadn't been a routine trip!

23

BALANCE SHEET, OR, NO WAY TO GET RICH

Now that the bush flying era has come to an end, we can look back at it and say that none of the pilots ever got rich, most of them went broke eventually, a very few made it all the way through and were able to retire modestly, some drifted into other fields—but most of them died trying. It is sobering indeed to glance at that long list who will fly no more.

The bush planes were extremely expensive to buy and operate. In reality they were frail pieces of equipment used in a mighty tough land. It was no wonder that as soon as a pilot had a little money saved up he would lose it all or more too in some minor or major mishap or have to purchase a new engine.

Bush flying had a built-in self-eliminating element, for as soon as the area a bush pilot pioneered became a well-developed, solid-paying system a scheduled airline developed and the pilot could either become an airline operator or move on. Eventually there wasn't any place to move on to and the airline network covered all Alaska. It was then that the FAA changed all the small operators to air-taxi certificates and officially terminated the bush pilot era. The term "bush pilot" will live on, of course, if for no other reason than that it sounds better and is more romantic than "air-taxi operator." The air-taxi operator of today compares with the first bush pilots about as much as the modern-day rancher compares with the old cowboy who handled the first longhorn cattle and trail herds. There is one big difference, thought—the air-taxi operator still faces the same weather, rough landings, high cost of maintenance, and hazards that his predecessor did. The vast, tough, and at times dangerous land is still there, and he still gets the rough work the airlines pass up. But the pioneering and trail-breaking is gone. His machines are very reliable, he has radio and even radar and often is in continuous contact with his home base, so his wife doesn't live with the awful silence day after day, and yet he has bills that must be paid, the local people don't help at all like the old customers did, and he still has but one life to lose.

Individualist that every bush pilot was, he faced the problem of making a success of his operation in his own way.

Bob Reeves flew the old Pan-American–Grace planes up and down the Andes of South America in the early days of the now-well-known Pan-American Airlines. From there he drifted to Alaska in the early 1930's, to find all the good-paying bush runs taken up. Oscar Winchel loaned Bob twenty-five dollars so he could go on to Valdez. Here Bob, with his experience of mountain flying gained in the rugged Andes, soon was engaged in servicing the mines in that land of mountains that rise right from the sea. His first "stake" he made servicing the Chisna Mines with a Fairchild 51. So it was that Bob Reeves made his way in bush flying by taking the roughest mountain country no one else wanted.

Bob was undoubtedly one of the best pilots ever to hit Alaska. He pioneered many of the roughest and toughest routes. By the time the Civil Aeronautics Board (CAB) got around to dividing up the air routes in 1938 Bob had hauled over a million pounds of supplies and made over two thousand landings on the remote glaciers around Valdez alone. In the States the routes had all been settled but Alaska still remained open. The CAB used the "Grandfather Rights" clause to determine who got what routes when it divided up Alaska. Carriers operating between May 14 and August 22 of 1938 could file on that route. This period caught Bob without airplanes, as his old Fairchild had been damaged by a windstorm, and while it was being repaired he did some aerial mapping around Fairbanks.

The Grandfather Rights rule was as fair as any, but it did turn up some strange routings. Ray Peterson was awarded the route from Bethel to Anchorage; since he was based at Bethel and courting a girl in Anchorage he had flown quite a few miles over that route during the summer. Bob Reeves didn't come off well at all and was awarded a little piece of territory on the Copper River that was already effectively serviced by his competitors. He was starved out. Packing up all his worldly goods and his family, he flew into Fairbanks. The World War II years lay just ahead and it was only natural that as the Army moved in Bob would lead them into many fields. With the attack upon Dutch Harbour, Bob found himself flying the Aleutian chain—again a route no one else wanted. It was the beginning of Reeves Aleutian Airways and, of course, the end of Bob Reeves's bush flying career, yet Bob handled the airline like a bush run and he made it pay! Many Alaskans say Bob's airline is the most successful airline ever operated in Alaska and point to it as a symbol of private enterprise.

Harold Gillam belonged to that elite handful of the first bush pilots. It was Gillam who in company with Joe Crosson found the wreckage of Alaska's first pilot, Ben Eielson, off North Cape, Siberia. Gillam was undisputed king of the bad-weather pilots. He flew when birds were literally afraid to fly. Gillam carried on scheduled mail service when all other pilots were grounded. "He has cat's eyes," some said. He also had a dream of a scheduled airline linking Alaska with Seattle, and to this end he studied instrument flying like no other pilot of that time. At the start of World War II he was flying a twin-engine Lockheed Electra between Anchorage and Seattle.

Gillam left Seattle's Boeing Field on January 5, 1943, with five passengers and freight en route for Anchorage. A little over four hours out of Seattle he was nearing Ketchikan in bad icing conditions and heavy snow, fighting to save his plane and passengers. The last message received was, ". . . I'm in trouble . . . One engine out . . ." You don't have time for long speeches when you are fighting to keep up an iced-over airplane with one engine dead. They struck the mountainside seven miles back from the seashore high up on those rugged peaks. It is one of the greatest tributes to Gillam's flying ability that no one died in the crash, but twenty-five-year-old Susan Baxter, the only woman aboard, had her arm crushed in the wreckage and died two days later.

The search for Gillam is one most old bush pilots don't like to recall. Gillam had searched for so many and had never given up. After two weeks of looking the search was called off. It may have been because of the wartime rush or because most felt he had gone down in the ocean; at any rate, they quit looking. Two weeks later a Coast Guard boat saw a bonfire in the back of Boca de Quadra Inlet and upon investigating they found Tippets and Cutting, two of Gillam's passengers. The news electrified all Alaska and the search was resumed for the rest of the party. When the rescuers reached the crash site, Gebo and Metzdorf were still there and very near dead, but Gillam was gone.

After the crash Gillam worked doggedly, although badly hurt, making his passengers as comfortable as possible. The rescue team couldn't imagine how he ever crawled out of that crushed pilot's cabin at all. For six days Gillam worked, and then he took a parachute for shelter and to signal with and left to try to find help or better accommodations for his party. It took the rescuers a week to find his body on the beach about a mile from where they had found Tippets and Cutting. He had taken off his flying boots, put them up on stakes to dry, and hung up his red underwear to dry and act as a flag if anyone came by while he took a little rest. Thus the searchers found him. Death came as he slept and most likely was caused by overexertion and injuries sustained in the crash.

The pilot's job is to protect his airplane and its cargo. This Gillam did against the worst the elements had to offer for so many years, and he would have succeeded again if one engine hadn't quit on him. He made it to the beach and he would have led rescuers back to his passengers if the searchers hadn't stopped looking for him. His dreams of instrument flying and a scheduled airline linking Alaska are so much reality today that no other form of transportation can compete with the airplanes for passenger service to and from Alaska. All those who ride the velvet-smooth jet airliners in comfort and safety over those runs today owe an unpayable debt to Harold Gillam. "Thrill-em, chill-em, no-kill-em Gillam" (as an Indian boy once wrote of his hero in a poem), the greatest bad-weather bush pilot of them all, died trying.

Not all the bush pilots' efforts to reach financial security ended as disastrously as did Harold Gillam's. There was always the chance to make a "stake" and perhaps pay up. Jim Freericks and Al Moseley decided the time was right to make a little extra money when the oil companies started moving north. Jim and Al borrowed thirty thousand dollars to buy and fix up an old military C-82, the *Flying Box Car*. The airplane had cost near the half-million-dollar mark to build, and if it could be used enough it would soon pay back the amount they had borrowed. In reality, to replace a single engine new would cost thirty thousand dollars and any parts needed had to be scrounged from scrap or purchased new at fantastic prices. The responsibility of handling and maintaining such an airplane is more than any two men should have to carry. The bush pilots were always masters of the "calculated risk," while their calculations and the risks they took made bankers and insurancemen shudder.

In looking back, Jim tells the story of that venture with an accuracy that lets you feel the tiredness of men working way beyond human endurance, the cussedness of a landing gear that won't retract, and the pressure of owing a bank thirty thousand dollars on short-term 8 per cent interest.

"There were mitigating circumstances," Jim explained. "The thirty thousand dollars we had borrowed sat a pretty heavy load on us, and of course we were trying to bail ourselves out of debt as fast as we could. We were flying night and day, so we were weary, tired all the time, and needed rest when we received a call from a contractor in Anchorage. He wanted us to haul two dump trucks from Anchorage to Bethel and a caterpillar tractor from Cape Neuingham to Bethel. We agreed but we hadn't been able to get the right landing gear to retract. We had fought it for two days already, but to no avail. No one could make it retract. The tower would call us saying our right gear hadn't retracted, and a couple of airplanes called us in flight to tell us what we were painfully aware of already.

"We decided to go ahead with the trip anyway; we had committed ourselves, the contractor was losing money every day we delayed, and so we went. We hauled the dump trucks to Bethel and went after the cat. The cat was supposed to be dismantled and a crew there to load it, but there wasn't. We were dead tired but we managed to get the caterpillar started and drove it on board. It should have been two trips, we felt. We didn't know how much it really did weigh and, as I said, we were dead tired, with our nerves shot from long hours and the worry that the right gear wouldn't retract. To make matters worse, the runway sloped at a 15-degree grade in places and ended in the ocean.

"Al and I have both been bugging one another about the way the cat is sitting in the airplane, the way it is tied down, and its position weight and balance-wise. It's my leg to fly, so I taxi out. . . . Al doesn't like the way I'm lining up on the runway and I'm tired of listening to him, so I pour on the coal—everything goes up in the kitchen—and I get the thing in the air. We are just hanging on the props and of course the right gear doesn't come up.

"I decide to fly direct to Bethel, getting there as fast as possible, for if a motor cuts out, down we go, and no matter where we hit, with that big cat right behind us we have 'bought the farm.' This puts us over about twenty miles of ocean and Al doesn't like the looks of that much water. . . . He thinks I should follow the coast. I figure the less time in the air the less time for something to happen. Over land or over water if an engine falters we are dead anyway. He yells at me, 'Swing right and follow the coast.'

"I yell at him to go to hell! I'm driving and when I'm driving I'll do it my way—when he's driving he can do it his way. He comes back with, 'I'm older than you and have more experience and besides I'm not tired of living.'

"We are both shouting at the top of our voices while the airplane is really flying itself at one hundred feet above the open sea. I heard him say, 'I'll sell!'

"'Like hell you will—I'll sell.' We are half out of our seats. If that cabin hadn't been so big that we couldn't reach one another across it or if the auto-pilot had been working we would have come to blows. As it turned out, I compromised and sort of dog-legged the inlet and we finished the trip safely. Ed Parsons even got the gear to working for us a few days later when we were back in Fairbanks, but our parnership gradually deteriorated until we folded it up a couple of months later."

Jim bought himself a Cessna 180 just to have his own airplane. He made a wise compromise and stayed with his airline captain's job for the security and steady paycheck. Jim and I often flew together and still do. We have had our share of tight spots to get out of and I'm sure there are more ahead.

This question was always asked among the pilots: "How does he stay in business—how does he manage to pay for his planes?" It was a good question and of course has no answer. The government in setting up the airline system in Alaska realized it would be impossible for an airline to meet all the requirements and operate at a profit, so it subsidized some of them by making up the losses.

I really can't say for sure how the rest of the pilots managed to stay in airplanes and pay the bills, but I do know how I did it—by my family and I working harder and longer than anyone else in this modern-day world ever dreams of working. This is the way the Jameses at Hughes, Tom Brower at Barrow, and the rest of our friends in the land out beyond have succeeded, and likely is true of all the bush pilots who stayed in business. I have seen a lot of people go north to make a new start and nearly all turn tail and run because they were afraid of the hard work that lay between them and success. The life out beyond is a family life and success can only be obtained as a unit.

I, or rather we, went into the bush flying field because of a love of exploration—fascination with a vast new land, its people who needed help and service, and the wonderful wildlife in the area. It was such an engrossing occupation that once started we kept on. The most remote parts of the Arctic were to become home simply because this was the last unexplored land and in exploring it we came to feel at home there. We came to understand it. With love and understanding came a feeling of responsibility and of protection. As Sam White would put it, we wanted to slow down and maybe stop the "killin' and the burnin' " that follow the exploration of any new land.

By the mid-1950's the bush pilot era had ended in the Arctic, for regular airline service linked even Barter Island and Barrow. There was a little bush work left in between, but very little.

The human population explosion was a threat to the human race itself and every wild animal on earth. People with their new means of travel were spreading into every piece of land on earth, killing off the native animals as they moved in. It seemed that everything that lived must die to make way for more people or their domestic animals. The trend has only increased with passing years. A close look at our Arctic lands happily shows that our game and fish are the only renewable natural resources we have. Fortunately, over 99 per cent of Alaska is not suitable for any kind of agriculture or for domestic animals. It is a land for recreation and the enjoyment of living in open places. This is Alaska's most precious gift to a crowded world. The idea that geographic isolation exists in the world today is an outdated one. The Jet Age closed the last traces of geographic isolation. Those who visualize geographic isolation are out of step with the times. The only isolation left in our world is mental.

We decided to build a modern home in the most spacious part of our great land and we chose as the location the Colville River delta. The construction of our house was necessarily slow, for we had to make a living from our fishing operation and guiding. I had held a guide's license for many years and I had taken out a few hunters each year. We were fortunate in that the top sportsmen of the world came to hunt this remote land with us. With the building of our new home we decided to keep the hunting just the same and take out our two parties of one or two hunters each spring and fall. In this way we could practice ideal conservation, enjoy each hunt, and show hunters the best trip possible into that vast land, while the hunters' chances of success were 100 per cent.

Martha decided right from the start that there would be a closed area to all hunting around our house. It is interesting to note that our home is the only place not in a National Park where you can see the original game of the land from the windows at any season of the year living as it always has lived.

It is remarkable how quickly the animals learn that you are a reliable person, and at times not only trust you but come to depend upon you. One summer at Walker Lake a cow moose swam from the mainland to our island with her new calf and spent the summer with us. She paid us no mind at all but went on feeding while Martha hung up the wash or I pounded away building a new warehouse. On the mainland a mother black bear had three tiny cubs. Each time we met, the cubs would put on a wrestling match for us.

At our delta home the ptarmigan nest right around our door and often sleep right on the doorstep. There are also gerfalcons and snowy owls that live upon the ptarmigan. When one of these shows up, the ptarmigan all head for the house, knowing full well they will be safe there. On one such dash a ptarmigan struck a piece of plywood in the woodpile and injured its left wing. I pulled the big flight feather from its wing so the wing would heal, and when the flock would leave to feed the injured bird would take off running across the prairie after the flock. When the flock would fly back to the house, we would see the injured bird coming running from across the prairie. All season we watched the comings and goings of the crippled ptarmigan. When fall came the ptarmigan all put on new feathers and we often wondered if our bird's wing healed. We only know that one evening when the birds came in they were all flying.

The ptarmigan is a large grouse that turns white in winter. There was a flock of about a thousand that lived about our house one fall, and one day Martha was walking out on the prairie when a gerfalcon came past. The ptarmigan were closer to Martha than they were to the house, and instead of heading for the house, as had been their custom, they flew up and landed around her. I was working up on the house and for a moment I couldn't see Martha as the cloud of nearly white birds landed about her. Some were but a foot or two from her. They knew she wouldn't let the gerfalcon harm them and the gerfalcon knew it, too, for after a couple of disgusted whistles he flew away and the ptarmigan went back to feeding.

The wolverine is one of our rarest and most beautiful animals as well as being highly valuable in the plan of conservaton of our wilderness. Martha has always had a soft spot in her heart for this little wanderer. Wolverines are as plentiful about our place as they are in any area. It always makes our day happier when one of them pays us a visit.

It was near −50 degrees one evening when Martha saw a wolverine coming across the prairie. We all gathered to watch it come, for we are always curious to see how each animal will react to things like our Onan diesel light plant's noise, the smell of people, the airplane, or children's toys left out. What will the new visitor think of each? What he actually thinks we can never know, but we can observe what he does.

This wolverine never paid the slightest attention to the sound of the light plant. He must have grown used to it as he came near. Had it speeded up or quit he would have been suspicious. The human smell he paid no mind to at all, for he had no reason to fear or mistrust it. He checked out the toy fire engine Jeffrey had left out in the snow and he looked all about the house, not molesting a thing. There was a box of scrap meat near the window that I kept there to feed the foxes. He climbed into the box and disappeared, to reappear in a few minutes with a piece of frozen meat in his mouth. This he buried in the snow down near the ground. His job done to his satisfaction, he climbed back in the scrap box but didn't find another piece of meat to his liking, so off across the prairie he went.

About the same time the next afternoon Martha saw the wolverine coming back. We all gathered at the window to see what he would do. This time he didn't spend much time looking about, but went straight to the spot where he had buried the meat. Yesterday the meat had been at −50 degrees and hard like rock; after being buried near the warmer ground all night it was up perhaps 10 degrees and was quite chewable. The wolverine dug up the meat and then sat down upon the snow to eat his meal right below our window. There were still plenty of pieces of meat in the box but he never took any more. He finished his meal and headed on across the prairie.

The many years of flying the bush in the most remote part of our Arctic have given me an insight into the lives of the animals in the wilderness that none before me has ever had. I have taken the time to learn at every turn. It didn't take long to realize that the meat-eating animals are just as important in the pattern of conservation as are the grass-eating animals.

Our home in the delta grew and the wild animals paid us no mind. We were all a part of the land sharing and living together. Our little fishing business grew and we needed help in it. Simon Ned, our Athabaska Indian friend from Alatna, came up to help us, bringing two or three of his friends, and we would put up a season's catch. Alatna is nearly four hundred miles south of us in the timbered region and the men enjoyed seeing the Arctic prairie. We built a better runway and used a C-46 to haul in the supplies and haul out our fish each year. Jim went away to the university and Martha taught Mark and Jeffrey their ABC's, using the Calvert system as she had done with Jim in our tent and log cabins.

We spent two seasons traveling around the world to study conservation in Asia, Africa, and Europe. It wasn't any surprise to learn that the people of these lands felt our Alaskan Fish and Game Commission ranked with the best in the world. The game departments of most countries and states are political plums. Even our Alaskan Fish and Game Commission has its political problems—for example, the bounty system. The enlightened men of the commission want to see the bounty system abolished because of the damage it does to our game, but the politicians who control the bounty system are afraid of losing votes and hang on. The bounty system is doomed. It has been a burden upon all wildlife too long already. It has given many the wrong impression of the value of certain species, leading to such situations as we now have with the wolverine, where we have a very sensible closed season and permit limit on the wolverine set by the Fish and Game Department and a bounty paid on them by the politicians! It is very hard to have a bounty repealed, but we are making progress in Alaska. We have managed to have the bounty removed from trout and eagles.

In building our home we remember each step and advancement in living conditions, like the time we started up the Onan diesel light plant, threw the master switch, and the lights came on. It meant many things to us, such as the end of darkness in the winter days, power for a two-way radio with its instant communication, power for electric tools, power for household appliances, and it meant more too. When all the lights came on, it meant I had hooked up the electric system right!

We dug a one-hundred-ton deep freeze into the frozen soil, making the nicest deep-freeze system imaginable where we can store meat, fish, and fresh produce indefinitely. All the things necessary to operate a small village are there; we have one of the most pleasant and gracious systems of living ever devised by man.

About us lies the space and freedom of a vast land and modern inventions have given us the things to enjoy it with. The airplanes have given us a new concept of time and our lives as bush pilots have taught us how to use it. Our C-46 charters haul the heavy freight now, but our *Arctic Tern* and Jim's *Golden Plover*—in short, our bush ships—make our lives possible and pleasant.

Last season we had a good year of hunting and fishing. Jim had his new airplane—the *Golden Plover*—and we were building a long-needed hangar to house our airplanes. Martha had all the modern conveniences in our home, with her family close about. Simon Ned and his crew were fishing with us again and it was late October on the prairie. The fishermen love their radio and keep in touch with their families through it.

It was near 10 P.M. and we had all gone to bed when we heard a knock upon the door. We don't often hear a knock upon the door there. Simon was standing there, crying and chanting the little prayer for the death of a loved one.

"It's my son, Bud. He's dead."

"Simon, are you sure?" I knew how radio messages get mixed up and hoped there was a mistake.

"It is true, old friend. I heard my wife request for a priest to come bury him."

This was all the message they had heard on "Tundra Topics." I went back with Simon to the fishermen's house about fifty yards from ours to talk with the men and all had heard the request plainly.

What do you say to a man who in the midst of a radio newscast learns his oldest son is dead? No one knew what had happened, only the short message. Simon's worries now were for his wife, Pauline. She was the postmistress at Alatna and kept things going while Simon was away fishing.

Our two-way radio was out with a burned-out tube and I was unable to raise any station with my aircraft radio. At daylight I had the airplane heated and we were heading south. It was real tough flying near the coast, and I should have turned back. Simon, who had shared so many adventures of the Arctic, sat quietly as we plowed through icing fog and then burst out of the overcast into a world of eternal beauty. Far to the south lay the Brooks Range, clear and white in the bright sunshine. The sun was warm inside the airplane with the world of trouble and fog far below.

"My son is with the Lord," Simon said. "Pauline needs me now."

I picked up the radio to call Alatna. I was on skis and the river wasn't frozen there yet, but a small lake nearby might have ice thick enough to hold me. I wanted someone to check it if at all possible. Fortunately, Andy Anderson was flying toward Anaktuvuk Pass and he answered my call. Andy was on wheels and could take Simon from Anaktuvuk Pass directly to Alatna.

We landed our ski plane upon the little frozen Summit and I gathered up his scant gear and walked across to the field. While Simon climbed aboard Andy's plane, Andy told me what had happened. Simon's son had come home from working in the gold mines where he had been employed all season. He then hitched up his dog team and drove up the Alatna River to hunt caribou. A few miles upstream he drove out on thin ice and all went under. The current carried them back below thicker ice.

Andy headed on down the John River toward Alatna. I poured the ten gallons of gasoline I had brought along into the tanks and headed back north. The day stayed bright until I neared home where I met the coastal fog I had flown away from that morning. The fog had dissipated quite a little, so I could see dark objects down through it when I was right over them. When I reached home I could see the house below, but when I tried to line up the runway I would lose contact each time I let down into the fog. Back up I would climb, go around, and try again. The sun was setting and the gasoline was getting low. The fog had spread far inland and looked thicker too. Then I saw a little spark of light below and I turned to try for it. Once in the fog I lost the light, but I kept on letting down. I couldn't see anything, but I knew where the light should be, and suddenly there was the fire and Martha's smiling face just a few feet from my left ski. I knew she would have her fire in the center of the runway on the downwind end, and I let the plane touch down. I sat waiting in the fog for Martha to come direct me to the tie-down, a few moments later she came walking up, carrying an oil can, and with one boot on and a heavy stocking on the other foot. She had lost one boot hurrying out to get a fire started.

"That is the way to get rid of the dirty laundry," Martha said. "I couldn't find anything to light, so I grabbed a pile of dirty clothes, poured diesel fuel on them, and lit it."

I thought of how Archie Ferguson's mother had burned up his dad's pants long ago to show young Archie the wind direction. The old system still worked.

Martha walked ahead guiding me, and I taxied the airplane to the tie-downs in front of the house. Jeffrey and Mark were waiting in the doorway to escort me upstairs. Martha had baked fresh bread and it smelled wonderful in the house.

There was a whole nestful of tiny tropical fish born since I left that morning; Dusty, the kitten, was testing his claws on the rug in front of the fireplace. Cessna, our black and white cat, lay curled up asleep in my favorite chair.

"Daddy, why did you almost fly into the house? I could see your skis right by the window."

"I didn't almost fly into the house, Jeffrey. I knew it was here and I was trying to line up with the runway."

Mark had picked up his old cat Cessna and was standing in front of the fireplace, enjoying the heat with his ear against the sleepy cat's side.

"Daddy?"

"Yes, Mark."

"What makes cats purr?"

A NOTE ABOUT THE AUTHOR

Harmon Helmericks, who was born on an Illinois farm, studied engineering at the University of Arizona before taking off in 1940 for Alaska, where he has lived ever since. Since 1946, Mr. Helmericks has become one of Alaska's most famous bush pilots, and holds the Award of Merit, Territory of Alaska, for "Special Service in the Arctic Regions." Since 1952, Mr. Helmericks has divided his time between running a fishing business, serving as Arctic consultant for British Petroleum and Eastman Kodak, and guiding hunters and fishermen in the Alaska wilderness. Mr. Helmericks holds a rating as Master Guide from the Alaska Game Commission and has been a member of the Explorers Club since 1947. He and his wife, Martha, divide their time with their three sons between their house on the Arctic coast and two lodges in the Brooks Range.